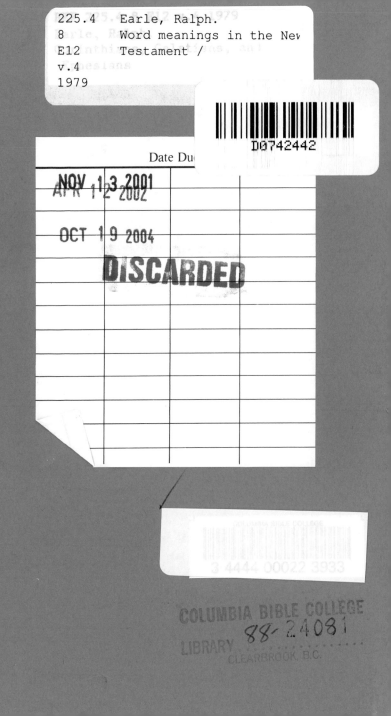

# WORD
# MEANINGS
*in the*
*New Testament*

4

# WORD MEANINGS
# *in the*
# *New Testament*

volume 4

## CORINTHIANS, GALATIANS, and EPHESIANS

by
Ralph Earle, Th.D.

**BEACON HILL PRESS OF KANSAS CITY**
Kansas City, Missouri

Copyright, 1979
Beacon Hill Press of Kansas City

ISBN: 0-8341-0567-5

Printed in the United States of America

# Contents

# Preface

This is the third volume to be published of the six which are projected in this series entitled *Word Meanings in the New Testament*. It covers the books of First and Second Corinthians, Galatians, and Ephesians and along with the already published volumes (3 and 5) completes the coverage of the Pauline Epistles.

It should be reiterated that this work is written primarily for preachers and studious laymen, not scholars. For this reason, all Greek words are transliterated and the discussion is on a practical rather than technical level. The purpose of the series is twofold: (1) to help the preacher understand more clearly what the Scriptures say and thus expound their message more accurately and effectively, and (2) to help all students of the Word to discover the rich mine of truth to be found in a study of the original language of the biblical text.

The material is handled under convenient headings usually including the word or phrase of the King James Version and a recommended alternative that more accurately expresses the meaning of the original Greek. The scriptures are discussed in consecutive order throughout.

Several good English versions of the New Testament have appeared in recent years. But no translation can possibly bring out the varied nuances of the Greek. That is why word studies are important for anyone who would adequately understand and expound the Word of God. May the present work contribute toward that end.

—RALPH EARLE

# Abbreviations and Sources

*(For additional listings, see Vols. 3 and 5)*

| | |
|---|---|
| A-S | G. Abbott-Smith, *Manual Greek Lexicon of the New Testament* (2nd ed.; Edinburgh: T. & T. Clark, 1923). |
| AG | W. F. Arndt and F. W. Gingrich, *A Greek-English Lexicon of the New Testament and Other Early Christian Literature* (Chicago: University of Chicago Press, 1957). |
| Alford | Henry Alford, *The Greek Testament* (Chicago: Moody Press, 1958 [reprint]). 4 vols. |
| Beare | F. W. Beare, "The Epistle to the Ephesians" (Exegesis), *The Interpreter's Bible,* 10 (New York: Abingdon-Cokesbury Press, 1953). |
| Bengel | John Albert Bengel, *Gnomon of the New Testament* (Edinburgh: T. & T. Clark, 1860). 5 vols. |
| Blass and Debrunner | F. Blass and A. Debrunner, trans. and rev. by Robert W. Funk (Chicago: University of Chicago Press, 1961). |
| BS | Adolf Deissmann, *Bible Studies* (Edinburgh: T. & T. Clark, 1901). |
| CGT | Cambridge Greek Testament |
| Cremer | Hermann Cremer, *Biblio-Theological Lexicon of New Testament Greek* (Edinburgh: T. & T. Clark, 1878). |
| DNTT | *The New International Dictionary of New Testament Theology,* Colin Brown, ed. (Grand Rapids: Zondervan Publishing House, 1978). 3 vols. |
| Eadie | John Eadie, *Commentary on the Epistle to the Ephesians* (Grand Rapids: Zondervan Publishing House, n.d.). |
| EGT | *Expositor's Greek Testament* (5 vols.; Grand Rapids: Eerdmans, n.d.). |

Godet

F. Godet, *Commentary on the First Epistle to the Corinthians* (Grand Rapids: Zondervan Publishing House, 1956 [reprint]).

IB

*Interpreter's Bible*

ICC

*International Critical Commentary*

LAE

Adolf Deissmann, *Light from the Ancient East* (New York: George H. Doran Co., 1927).

Lightfoot

J. B. Lightfoot, *Notes on the Epistles of St. Paul* (Grand Rapids: Zondervan Publishing House, 1957 [reprint]).

Meyer

H. A. W. Meyer, *Critical and Exegetical Hand-Book to the Epistles to the Galatians and the Ephesians* (New York: Funk & Wagnalls, 1884).

Olshausen

Hermann Olshausen, *Biblical Commentary on the New Testament* (New York: Sheldon, Blakeman & Co., 1858).

Robinson

J. Armitage Robinson, *St. Paul's Epistle to the Ephesians* (London: James Clarke & Co., n.d.).

TDNT

*Theological Dictionary of the New Testament,* ed. by Gerhard Kittel and Gerhard Friedrich (9 vols.; Grand Rapids: Eerdmans, 1964-73).

Thayer

Henry Thayer, *A Greek-English Lexicon of the New Testament* (New York: American Book Co., 1886).

Trench

R. C. Trench, *Synonyms of the New Testament* (Grand Rapids: Wm. B. Eerdmans Publishing Co., 1947 [reprint]).

VGT

J. H. Moulton and George Milligan, *Vocabulary of the Greek Testament, Illustrated from the Papyri and Other Non-literary Sources* (Grand Rapids: Eerdmans, 1949).

Vincent

Marvin Vincent, *Word Studies in the New Testament* (4 vols.; Grand Rapids: Eerdmans, 1946 [1887]).

Westcott

B. F. Westcott, *St. Paul's Epistle to the Ephesians* (Grand Rapids: Wm. B. Eerdmans Publishing Co., 1950 [reprint]).

# 1 CORINTHIANS

## Sanctified . . . Saints (1:2)

In the light of 3:1, where Paul says the Corinthian "brethren" are not spiritual but carnal, it is obvious that "sanctified" here is used in a restricted sense. It expresses a relationship of having been set apart to God. Findlay puts it well: "This initial sanctification is synchronous with justification" (EGT, 2:758).

These born-again believers were "called to be saints" (cf. Rom. 1:7). The term "saints" is the plural of *hagios,* "holy," which is the root of the verb "sanctified" *(hagi-azō).* So saints are literally "holy ones." Again, the term is used in its limited, sacramental sense of "belonging to God." This is the main meaning of "holy" in the Old Testament, though the personal and ethical meaning comes to the front in Isaiah and some other prophets and becomes dominant in the New Testament. However, it is clear that Paul here uses the term "saints" for all Christians, as those who are called to belong to God.

## Coming or Revelation? (1:7)

The Greek word is *apocalypsis,* which literally means an "uncovering," and so "revelation." That is the way it is usually translated in the KJV (12 out of 18 times). Only in this passage is it rendered "coming."

The Second Coming will be a revealing of Christ, who for over 1,900 years has been veiled from sight. We are told that when He comes again, "every eye shall see him," even "they also which pierced him" (Rev. 1:7; cf. John 19:37).

## Divisions (1:10)

This is a strong word in the Greek, *schisma,* from which we get our word "schism." The noun comes from the verb *schizō,* which means "split, divide, separate, tear apart, tear off" (AG, p. 805). It is used literally for a "rent" in a garment (Matt. 9:16; Mark 2:21). Elsewhere in the NT it is used figuratively, where it is translated "division" five times and "schism" once (1 Cor. 12:25).

Division was the main problem in the church at Corinth. There were four parties or cliques in the congregation (v. 12), and Paul devotes the first four chapters of this epistle to dealing with that crucial situation.

## Perfectly Joined Together (1:10)

Instead of being divided into quarreling cliques, Christians should be "perfectly joined together"—all one word in the Greek, *katērtismenoi,* the perfect passive participle of *katartizō.* This verb literally means "put in order, restore . . . restore to its former condition" (AG, p. 418). It is used of fisherman "mending" their nets (Matt. 4:21; Mark 1:19). Here in Corinthians it means "make one what he ought to be" (Thayer). Lias (CGT) says the idea is that of being *"fitted together,* as the fragments in a piece of mosaic, in which each minute portion exactly fills its proper place" (p. 34).

Perhaps Alford is a little closer to the true picture when he comments: *"katartizō* is the exact word for the healing or repairing of the breaches made by the *schismata" (Greek Testament,* 2:476).

In the ICC volume on 1 Corinthians, Robertson and Plummer write: "The word is suggestive of fitting together what is broken or rent (Matt. iv. 21). It is used in surgery for setting a joint (Galen), and in Greek politics for composing factions (Hdt. v. 28)" (p. 10). All three of these uses apply well to this passage.

## Judgment or Purpose? (1:10)

Of the Greek word used here, Lias says: *"gnōmē* is usually employed in the sense of *opinion.* But it has also the sense of *purpose* or *consent."* After citing a passage in Polybius, he affirms: "There, as here, the decision of the mind is meant, rather than the opinion on which it was formed" (p. 34). For this passage Arndt and Gingrich suggest "purpose" or "intention."

## Contentions or Quarrels? (1:11)

The word *eris* means "strife, wrangling, contention" (A-S, p. 180). Arndt and Gingrich suggest that in the plural, as here, it means "quarrels." Robertson and Plummer say, "The divisions became noisy" (p. 11). Findlay writes: *"erides* signifies the personal *contentions,* due to whatever cause, which lead to *schismata"* (EGT, 2:763). And so it is today that church quarrels lead to church splits.

## Preach the Gospel (1:17)

This is one word in the Greek, *euangelizō*. Paul declares: "Christ sent me not to baptize, but to evangelize." That is the main mission of the church.

## Preaching or Word? (1:18)

Paul says that "the preaching of the cross" is foolishness to those that perish. But the Greek word for "preaching" is simply *logos,* which is translated "word" 218 out of the 330 times it occurs in the NT. It is "the word of the Cross" (that is the word about the Cross) that perishing sinners despise. What the world still ridicules is the message of the Cross, the Good News of salvation through Christ's death for us at Calvary. Too many people would rather try to save themselves than to let Christ save them.

## Preaching or What Is Preached? (1:21)

*Kērygma* is still another word that is translated "preaching" in the KJV. It has become established in theological circles as an English term in good standing.

The word comes from the verb *keryssō*, which means "herald" or "proclaim." In classical Greek the noun meant "that which is cried by a herald, a proclamation" (A-S, p. 246). In the NT it is used in the sense of "proclamation" or "message," "that is, the substance as distinct from the act" *(ibid.).* Lightfoot declares: "It refers . . . to the subject, not to the manner of preaching" (*Notes,* p. 161). Lias comments: "The word translated *preaching* should rather be rendered *what is preached"* (p. 38). In agreement with all this, Findlay writes that *kerygma* "signifies not the act of proclamation, but *the message proclaimed* by God's herald" (EGT, 2:769).

On the basis of the KJV rendering many have thought that it is the *method* of preaching that is considered foolish. Rather, it is the *message*.

In Kittel's *Theological Dictionary of the New Testament,* Friedrich spells out what this message is. He writes:

> At the heart of the New Testament *kērygma* stands the lordship of God. Preaching is not a lecture on the nature of God's kingdom. It is proclamation, the declaration of an event (3:710).

Friedrich goes on to point out that the central emphasis of apostolic preaching was not the words of Jesus, but the historical fact of His life, death, and resurrection. He says:

> The reality of the resurrection constitutes the fulness of the early Christian *kērygma*. This is a fact which cannot be apprehended like other historical events. It has to be continually proclaimed afresh (3:711).

Commenting on 1 Cor. 1:21, he affirms: "The foolish message of Jesus crucified saves those who believe" (3:716). That is what the gospel is. And that is the Good News which every preacher is commissioned to proclaim.

## Require or Demand? (1:22)

The verb is *aiteō*. Basically it means "ask for something." Thayer lists this as one of the passages in which it probably carries the stronger sense of "demand," a meaning which Arndt and Gingrich support.

## Sign or Miracles? (1:22)

The first thing we would note is that in the oldest and best Greek manuscripts, the word *semeia* is plural, not singular. This term literally means "signs." It first refers to a distinguishing "mark" by which something is known.

But it also means *"a sign, prodigy, portent,* i.e., an unusual occurrence, transcending the common course of nature" (Thayer, p. 573). It is used "of miracles and wonders by which God authenticates the men sent by him, or by which men prove that the cause they are pleading is of God" *(ibid.).* When it is used in this way, Arndt and Gingrich would simply translate it as "miracle" (cf. NEB: "Jews call for miracles"). Perhaps a more adequate translation would be "miraculous signs" (NIV).

This tendency of the Jews to demand a miraculous sign is vividly illustrated by an incident related to us some years ago by the superintendent of a Hebrew Mission. He told of a young lady who had almost come to the place of accepting Jesus as her Savior, but she wanted to be certain that this Jesus was really the promised Messiah.

Right in the midst of her crucial struggle one day the superintendent and his wife were out for a drive with the young lady in the back seat. Suddenly, out of the clear sky, a ball of fire hit the highway in front of the car, causing the startled superintendent to jam on his brakes. But from the rear seat came the joyous exclamation: "Thank You, Lord, for giving me this proof; now I know that Jesus is Your Messiah." She then told how that very morning she had prayed: "O God, if Jesus is the true Messiah, give me a sign today to prove it." Evidently the Lord accommodated himself to her "demand." From that time on she was a devoted, faithful Christian, even though disowned and persecuted by her family.

In contrast to the Jews, said Paul, the Greeks "seek" or "look for" wisdom. They wanted intellectual evidence; for them logic was stronger proof than miracle. Actually, neither one is absolute evidence. The greatest proof of the truth of Christianity is the conscious presence of the living Christ in our hearts.

## Preaching (1:23)

This verse has an important message for all preachers. Paul said: (1) "we *preach*," not just talk, explain, teach; (2) "we preach *Christ*," not our own opinions, or even just principles and propositions; (3) "we preach Christ *crucified*," not just Christ as our example, but as our crucified Redeemer.

## Noble or Well-born? (1:26)

One of the besetting sins of the church members at Corinth was pride. This was a leading cause of their divisions. So Paul reminds them that not many of them were "wise according to worldly standards" (RSV), not many were "mighty"—*dynatoi*, "powerful," perhaps meaning "of the ruling class" (Phillips)—not many were "noble." The Greek word is *eugenēs*, which literally means "well-born," that is, "high-born" or from families of the nobility. "Noble" might mistakenly be taken as meaning "of noble character." The idea here is rather "of noble birth."

## Confound or Shame? (1:27)

The Greek word is *kataischynō*. It means "to disgrace, dishonour, put to shame" (A-S, p. 233)—which is hardly what we mean now by "confound." Most modern translations correctly have "shame."

## Base or Low-born? (1:28)

The word is *agenēs*, which is the opposite of *eugenēs* (v. 26). The latter is compounded of *eu*, "well," and *genēs*, "born." The former is composed of *a*, "not," and *genēs*, "born." Thayer defines *agenēs* thus: *"of no family,* a man of base birth, a man of no name or reputation; often used by profane writers, also in the secondary sense *ignoble, cowardly, mean, base.* In the New Testament only in I Cor. i. 28, *ta agenē tou cosmou,* i.e., those who among men are held of no account" (p. 6). Arndt and Gingrich say that its original meaning, as used by Xenophon and Plato of the fourth century B.C., was "not of noble birth," but that it was used "more commonly" in the secondary sense of "base, low, insignificant" (p. 8).

The adjective *agenēs* is in the neuter here. So most translations take it as referring to things, as in the KJV. But some translators follow Thayer in giving it a personal application. For instance, the *Berkeley Version* has: "God also has chosen the world's low-born and contemptibles and nobodies."

## Glory or Boast? (1:29, 31)

Once in verse 29 and twice in verse 31 we find the verb "glory." The Greek *kauchaomai* comes from the noun *kauchēma,* which means "boast." So the simplest translation of the verb is "boast," which is probably clearer today than "glory."

## Wisdom (1:30)

We read that God has made Christ Jesus to be to us "wisdom, and righteousness, and sanctification, and redemption." However, the Greek reads literally: "But of him you are in Christ Jesus, who has been made wisdom to us from God, both righteousness and sanctification and redemption." That is, the last three terms are additional explanations of "wisdom." God's wisdom in Christ is shown in our righteousness, sanctification, and redemption. Godet suggests that "wisdom" here means "the *understanding* of the Divine plan communicated to man by Jesus Christ" (*1 Corinthians*, p. 118). This divine plan is our salvation in Christ Jesus as He becomes our "righteousness" *(dikaiosyne)*, "sanctification" *(hagiasmos)* and "redemption" *(apolytrōsis)*.

Godet defines "redemption" as "our complete and final deliverance" (cf. Rom. 8:18-30). One could almost suggest that we find here the "three works of grace" in salvation: justification, sanctification, and glorification. The first two are available to us in this life; the third will come in the next.

## Enticing or Persuasive? (2:4)

The adjective *peithos* occurs only here in the NT. Not only that, but it has not been found anywhere else in Greek literature. It is formed from the verb *peithō*, which means "persuade." So it clearly means "persuasive," with none of the negative overtones that "enticing" suggests. The apostle was not using mere human persuasiveness nor superstitious manipulation.

The word *Peithō* was also the name of a Greek goddess, "Persuasion." Some of the Early Church fathers (Origen, Eusebius) thought that Paul here intended a reference to this goddess.

## Demonstration or Proof? (2:4)

The Greek word *apodeixis* is found only here in the NT. It first meant a "display" or "showing off." Then it came to be used for "demonstration," in the sense of conclusive proof. All scholars agree that this is its meaning here.

Findlay says that *apodeixis* was "the technical term for a proof drawn from facts or documents, as opposed to theoretical reasoning; in common use with the Stoics in this sense" (EGT, 2:776). Godet writes: "The word *apodeixis* indicates a clearness which is produced in the hearer's mind, as by the sudden lifting of a veil; a conviction mastering him with the sovereign force of moral evidence" (1:129). Such conviction comes only from "the Spirit" who works on our hearts in "power." Lias comments: "The 'power' of which he speaks was not so much that of working miracles in the ordinary sense of the word, as of touching the heart. He is referring to that conviction of sin, righteousness and judgment (John xvi. 8), which the Spirit of God produces in the spirit of man, and of the power to produce a change of heart and life which is the leading characteristic of the Gospel" (p. 43).

Robertson and Plummer make this helpful observation: "St. Paul is not dealing with scientific certainty; but he claims that the certitude of religious truth to the believer in the Gospel is as complete and as 'objective'— equal in degree, though different in kind—as the certitude of scientific truth to the scientific mind" (p. 33). Those who experience the reality of Christ's presence within and the illumination of His Spirit can surely say a hearty "Amen" to this.

In relation to the preaching of Paul in the context here, the words "demonstration of Spirit and power" mean "a proof by the Spirit and power of God, operating in me, and stirring in the minds of my hearers the most holy emotions and thus persuading them" (Thayer, p. 60).

In view of the current use of the word "demonstration" in our country, it would seem that "proof" would be a better translation here. It is also clearer and simpler. Then too, "demonstration" in religious circles means something outward, whereas the "proof" of the Spirit's power here is an inward conviction of one's sin and of the truth of the gospel.

## Perfect or Mature? (2:6)

The adjective *teleios* is translated "perfect" (KJV) 17 out of the 19 times it occurs in the NT. In 1 Cor. 14:20 it is rendered "man," and Heb. 5:14 "of full age."

It comes from *telos,* "end." So it really means "having reached its end, finished, mature, complete, perfect" (A-S, p. 442). In Heb. 5:14 it refers to persons who are physically full grown. In our passage here, and in 14:20, it is used for those who are "spiritually mature." That is probably the best translation here (cf. Phillips).

The objection to the word "perfect" is that it is often misunderstood. Some people say we should use it because "it's in the Bible." But that is begging the question. It is in the KJV, to be sure, but whether or not it is a precise translation of *teleios* is a matter of question. The term "perfect" has been much misunderstood as meaning that everything one does is beyond criticism. We are all human still and subject to faulty judgment and action. What is called "Christian Perfection" takes this into account. It is the inner, heart relationship to God which is to be perfect.

It is often said that we can receive purity in a moment, but that it takes time to reach maturity. There is much truth in this, of course. But it might also be affirmed that every Spirit-filled Christian is in a real sense "spiritually mature" because he is under the guidance of the Holy Spirit. In any case, the idea of maturity fits the present passage very well.

## Spiritual Things with Spiritual (2:13)

The Greek says: *pneumaticois pneumatica.* The word for "spirit" is *pneuma* and so the adjective *pneumaticos* simply means "spiritual."

The second form here, *pneumatica,* is clearly neuter

(both are plural). But the first word is in the dative case, which has the same form for both the masculine and neuter. This makes for ambiguity because *pneumaticois* may be translated "with" (or, "to") "spiritual things" or "spiritual people."

The KJV takes it as neuter and says "spiritual things." Weymouth also assumes the neuter but gives a more specific rendering: "adapting spiritual words to spiritual truths." The TDNT similarly has: "and so we explain spiritual things in spiritual language." Goodspeed is basically the same: "giving spiritual truth a spiritual form."

But many recent versions take *pneumaticois* as masculine. The RSV has: "interpreting spiritual truths to those who possess the Spirit" (cf. NEB). More simply, Phillips puts it this way: "explaining spiritual things to those who are spiritual." This was the way it was handled in the earliest English Bible by Wyclif (1382).

## Natural or Unspiritual? (2:14)

The Greek word is *psychicos,* from which we get "psychical." It is here, as in Jude 19, placed in contrast to *pneumaticos,* "spiritual." In James 3:15 it is equivalent to *epigeios,* "earthly." In both these places the KJV translates it "sensual." These are the only two places in the NT where *psychicos* is used outside 1 Corinthians. Besides our present passage, it occurs three times in chapter 15 (vv. 44, 46). There it refers to the "natural body" which is buried in the grave, in contrast to the "spiritual body" we shall receive in the resurrection.

How should *psychicos* be translated here? Lias thinks that "natural" is "fairly satisfactory," and then adds: "But the term 'worldly,' as used by the divines, seems most nearly to approach to the precise meaning of the

Apostle" (p. 47). Findlay says that the term "describes to the Corinthians the unregenerate nature *at its best*" (EGT, 2:783). Robertson and Plummer say: "The *psychicos* is the 'unrenewed' man, the 'natural' man (AV., RV.), as distinct from the man who is actuated by the Spirit" (p. 49). Perhaps the best translation is "the unspiritual man" (AG, RSV, Phillips, NEB).

## Carnal or Fleshly? (3:1-4)

The term "carnal" occurs four times (KJV) in these four verses. The difficulty of understanding the Greek word here is evidenced by the variety of renderings found in modern translations.

The confusion begins in the Greek text. The Textus Receptus (basis of KJV) has *sarkicos* in all four places. But the Textus Criticus, derived from the oldest and best Greek manuscripts, has *sarkinos* in verse 3 (twice) and *anthrōpos* (man) in verse 4.

What is the relation of *sarkicos* to *psychicos* (2:14)? Trench calls attention to the difference between classical and NT usage at this point. He writes: *"Psychicos,* continually used as the highest in later classical Greek literature—the word appears first in Aristotle—being there opposed to *sarkicos . . .* and constantly employed in praise, must come down from its high estate, another *pneumaticos* so much greater than it being installed in the highest place of all" (*Synonyms,* p. 268). He goes on to say: "According to Scripture the *psychē* (soul), no less than the *sarks* (flesh), belongs to the lower region of man's being . . . and it is at any rate plain that *psychicos* is not a word of honour any more than *sarkicos,* being an epithet quite as freely applied to this lower" (pp. 268-69). He concludes: "The *psychicos* of Scripture is one for whom the *psychē* is the highest motive power of life and action; in whom the *pneuma,* as the organ of the divine *Pneuma,* is suppressed, dormant . . . whom the operations of this divine Spirit have never lifted into the region of spiritual things" (p. 269).

What is the difference between *sarkicos* and *sarkinos?* Trench notes that words ending in *-inos* designate "the stuff of which anything is made," and so *sarkinos* properly means "fleshy," "that is, having flesh for the substance and material of which it is composed" (p. 272). *Sarkicos* is a more ethical term, meaning "fleshly." Trench says: "'Fleshly' lusts . . . are lusts which move and stir in the ethical domain of the flesh, which have in that rebellious region of man's corrupt and fallen nature their source and spring" (p. 273).

Findlay makes this same distinction. He comments: "*-inos* implying nature, *-icos* tendency or character" (EGT, 2:785). Arndt and Gingrich agree with this. They say: "*sarkicos* means 'belonging to the sarks', having the nature and characteristics of *sarks* . . . 'fleshly'; on the other hand, *sarkinos* is 'consisting' or 'composed of flesh', 'fleshy'" (p. 750).

Thayer suggests that *sarkicos* means "governed by mere human nature." Of the use of *sarkinos* in the best text of 3:1 he says that "unless we decide that Paul used *sarkicos* and *sarkinos* indiscriminately, we must suppose that *sarkinos* expresses the idea of *sarkicos* with an emphasis: *wholly given up to the flesh, rooted in the flesh as it were*" (p. 569).

Vincent translates *sarkinos* in verse 1 as "made of flesh" and *sarkicos* in verse 3 as "having the nature of flesh." He comments on verse 3: "Here the milder word is used. . . . In verse 1, Paul would say that he was compelled to address the Christians as unspiritual, *made of flesh.* Here he says that though they have received the Spirit in some measure, they are yet under the influence of the flesh" (*Word Studies,* 3:200). But as we shall note in a moment, it may well be that *sarkinos* (v. 1) was intended as the milder term—"merely human"—while *sarkicos* (v. 3) was a stronger word of condemnation: "You are still somewhat under the domination of your lower nature; instead of letting Christ be Lord of all in your lives." This is what we mean by a "carnal" Christian.

Schweizer thinks that Paul uses the two terms interchangeably in this passage (TDNT, 7:144). Grosheide thinks the difference between the two "is not great, but suggests that Paul may have used *sarkinos* in verse 1 in an attempt to avoid a stronger term at this point" (p. 78, n. 1). That is, he softened his approach to the Corinthians in denouncing them for their carnal attitudes.

What is the meaning of *anthrōpoi* (men) in verse 4, in comparison with *sarkicoi* (v. 3)? Robertson and Plummer comment: "The Corinthians were *anthrōpoi* in failing to rise to the higher range of motives; they were *sarkicoi* in allowing themselves to be swayed by the lower range" (pp. 54-55). They would translate the clause: "Are ye not mere human creatures?"

## Husbandry or Field? (3:9)

The term *geōrgion* is found only here in the NT. It means "cultivated land" or "field." Bengel says it is "a word of wide and comprehensive meaning, comprising the field, the garden, and the vineyard" (*Gnomon,* 3:218). The Christian congregation at Corinth is pictured in this verse as "God's farm, God's building" (Goodspeed). The first of these two metaphors looks back to verses 6-9: Paul planted, Apollos watered, God made the seed grow. The second metaphor looks forward to verses 10-17: Paul laid the foundation, Jesus Christ; let everyone be careful how he builds on that foundation.

Both the pastor and the people of every church need to face the implications of these two figures used by Paul. The pastor is to plant the seed of God's Word, see that it is watered with the showers from heaven (God's blessing on the services) and cultivate carefully the tender plants that grow. The verb *potizō,* "watered" (v. 6), was used in ancient Greek for irrigating a field. So we may think of preaching as also watering the hearts of the listeners. By faithful attendance and a spirit of cooperation and response, the people will benefit by his ministry.

But the congregation is also a building erected as a "temple of God" (v. 16). It should be a fit temple for Him to dwell in.

## Masterbuilder (3:10)

The Greek word (only here in NT) is *architectōn,* from which we get "architect." Of this term Plato writes: "The architect does not work himself, but is the ruler of workmen" (*Statesman,* p. 259).

But probably our concept of an architect today does not fit this passage. Findlay writes: "The Gr. *architectōn* was not a designer of plans on paper; he was like the old cathedral builders, the *master-mason,* developing his ideas in the material" (EGT, 2:790). Godet says: "The *master builder* is not only he who draws the plan of the building—in this sense the title would revert to God—but also the man who directs its execution" (1:179-80).

In the NT, God has furnished us the plan for the building. We are to carry out that plan in working with Christ in building His church—including the local congregation, as here.

Because the modern term "architect" could be misleading, almost all English versions have "master builder." That is what Paul was. J. I. Packer says that this word means "a head builder, masterbuilder, contractor, or director of works" (*The New International Dictionary of New Testament Theology*, 1:279).

## Try or Test? (3:13)

Paul declares that "the fire shall try every man's work." The verb is *dokimazō*. The first definition given by Thayer is: "to *test, examine, prove, scrutinize* (to see whether a thing be genuine or not), as metals" (p. 154). Trench comments: "As employed in the New Testament *dokimazein* almost always implies that the proof is victoriously surmounted, the *proved* is also *approved*" (p. 278). For this latter emphasis he cites 2 Cor. 8:8; 1 Thess. 2:4; 1 Tim. 3:10.

But this does not seem necessarily to attach to this passage. For the apostle presents two possible results of the testing. If any man's work stands the test, he will receive a reward (v. 14), but "if any man's work shall be burned, he shall suffer loss" (v. 15). Both alternatives are possible.

To understand what he is talking about, we have to go back to verse 11. There is only one foundation, Jesus Christ. But on this foundation people build with different materials. Some build solidly with "gold, silver, precious stones." These are the works that will "abide" (remain) through the testing by fire (v. 14). But other people build foolishly with "wood, hay, stubble." These inflammable materials will be burned up—"but he himself shall be saved; yet so as by fire" (v. 15). This suggests that some Christians whose experience is actually founded on Christ will waste their lives in useless endeavor, so that all their flimsy works will be in vain. It is a sad thing to contemplate a person working all his life without producing some permanent results. Winning souls is the kind of work that will survive the test by fire.

## Temple or Sanctuary? (3:16)

Paul writes that the Corinthian congregation is "the temple of God," because the Spirit of God dwells in them. It was His presence that made them sacred.

Two different Greek words are translated "temple" in the NT. (A third word, meaning "house," is incorrectly translated "temple" in Luke 11:51.) The first is *hieron,* which means a sacred place. It occurs 70 times in the Gospels and Acts—where it refers to the Temple area—and once elsewhere (1 Cor. 9:13). The second, *naos,* refers to the sanctuary itself, containing the holy place and the holy of holies. It is found 46 times scattered throughout the NT, most frequently in Revelation (16 times). *Naos* is the word used here. In a sense it could be said that the Christians together constituted God's dwelling place in Corinth. What a high view of the local church!

## Defile or Destroy? (3:17)

The first part of verse 17 reads: "If any man defile the temple of God, him shall God destroy." But in the Greek both verbs are the same. The correct translation is: "If anyone destroys the sanctuary of God, God will destroy him."

It must be remembered that this passage is a part of Paul's discussion of the problem of division in the church at Corinth. He devotes the first four chapters of the Epistle to this subject. What he means here, then, is that those who are dividing the church are destroying it.

This is because the church of Jesus Christ is a living organism, not just an organization. You can divide a pie into six pieces without destroying it; you are just preparing to serve it. This is because a pie is an organization. But if you divide a dog in two, you have destroyed him, because he is an organism. The Corinthian church was being divided into four cliques or parties (1:12). Thus it was in danger of being destroyed.

This passage sounds a solemn warning against those who would do anything to bring about a church quarrel, leading to a church split. In God's sight they have murdered a living organism.

The time to take care of problems is in the earliest stage, when they are small. At first in a personal quarrel only two people are involved, and that is all the pastor has to deal with. But if he ignores the problem and lets the quarrel continue, others get involved, and a church fuss is in the making. The problem is much more difficult to handle, because relatives and close friends have formed strong feelings about the situation. The pastor will have to straighten out two groups of people.

We could illustrate it this way. When a lion is a little cub, a man might play around with it freely. But when the lion is a year or two old, it isn't as safe to handle! Problems are like that; they get out of hand. And the pastor who tries to handle a church split is likely to get hurt in the process.

## Taketh or Catches? (3:19)

The verb *drassomai* is found only here in the NT, quoted from the Septuagint. It means "catch" or "seize" (AG, p. 205). Some recent versions have "trap."

## Craftiness or Cleverness? (3:19)

The noun *panourgia* originally meant "cleverness," almost always in a bad sense in classical Greek. It is sometimes translated "cunning." No matter how clever the "wise" men are, God traps them in their cleverness.

## Glory or Boast? (3:21)

We have already met this verb *kauchaomai* in 1:29. There we noted that "boast" is probably clearer—and, we might add, more contemporary—than "glory" (cf. 4:7).

Here we should like only to call attention to the fact that aside from twice in James (1:9; 4:16) this verb is used only by Paul (36 times). He uses it most frequently in 2 Corinthians (21 times). It is found 5 times each in Romans and 1 Corinthians. These three epistles were written at the same period in Paul's life (A.D. 54-56), when he was greatly plagued in spirit by the boastful attitude of the quarreling Corinthian church members.

## Ministers or Servants? (4:1)

The noun is *hyperetēs,* used by Paul only here. Literally it means "under-rower." So the basic emphasis is on one who is subordinate. Thayer defines it thus: "Any one who serves with his hands; a servant," and adds that it is used "in the N.T. of the officers and attendants of magistrates" (p. 641). Arndt and Gingrich say it means *"servant, helper, assistant,* who serves a master or a superior" (p. 850).

Occurring 20 times in the NT, this word is translated "officer" 11 times, "minister" 5 times, and "servant" 4 times. Probably "servant" is the best translation in most instances, though the sense of police "officers" fits well in many cases—for instance, of the "officers" (policemen) employed by the Sanhedrin. The term is used twice each in the three Synoptic Gospels, 9 times in John, and 4 times in Acts. The only places where it can possibly be translated "minister," meaning pastor or preacher, are Luke 1:2 and Acts 26:16.

## Stewards (4:1)

The word *oikonomos* occurs only 10 times in the NT and is correctly translated "steward" in all places except Rom. 16:23 ("chamberlain") and Gal. 4:2 ("governors"). It should be "steward" always.

The word comes from *oikos,* "house," and *nemō,* "manage." So it literally means "a house manager." Wealthy men employed slaves or freedmen to manage their households for them. It is used in this literal sense four times in Luke (three times in the Parable of the Unjust Steward, 16:1-8). In the present passage (1 Cor. 4:1-2) it is used metaphorically for those who are stewards of God's grace, responsible for giving it out to people. The same usage is found in Titus 1:7 and 1 Pet. 4:10.

## Judgment or Day? (4:3)

Paul said that it was a very little thing for him to be judged by the Corinthians, or by "man's judgment." The Greek literally says "by human day" *(hypo anthrōpines hēmeras).* This is clearly in contrast to the statement in 3:13, "Every man's work shall be made manifest; for the day shall declare it"; that is, the day of divine judgment. All of us face that Judgment Day. But Paul says he is not concerned about man's judgment day. He is not answerable to that, but only to God.

In the light of the whole picture here Abbott-Smith suggests the rendering "human judgment." But Lightfoot writes: "The word is put here because it is in opposition to *hē hēmere* of iii. 13 'The Lord's day.' The meaning is 'by any day fixed by man.' The idea of a day as implying judgment is common in Hebrew, and would be directly assisted by such expressions as 'diem dicere,' 'to fix a day for judgment.' Compare the English 'daysman' [Job 9:33, judge], which contains the same idea" *(Notes,* p. 198).

## By or Against? (4:4)

Lightfoot correctly observes that "'I know nothing by myself' is simply an archaism" *(ibid.)*. The context clearly demands the translation, "I know nothing against myself." In the Greek "myself" *(emautō)* is in the dative case without any preposition. But the meaning is obvious. In the time of King James (1611) "by" was used in the sense of "against," but such a usage now is misleading.

## Transferred or Applied? (4:6)

"I have in a figure transferred" is all one word in the Greek, *meteschēmatisa.* Its usual meaning is *"to change in fashion* or *appearance"* (A-S). But here (alone in NT) it has a specialized sense. Thayer spells it out very well; "to shape one's discourse so as to transfer to one's self what holds true of the whole class to which one belongs, i.e., so as to illustrate by what one says of himself what holds true of all: 1 Co. iv. 6, where the meaning is, 'by what I have said of myself and Apollos, I have shown what holds true of all Christian teachers'" (p. 406). Arndt and Gingrich translate the passage, "I have applied this to Apollos and myself." They say that it means, "I have given this teaching of mine the form of an exposition concerning Apollos and myself" (p. 515).

## Differ or Prefer? (4:7)

In the Greek "maketh . . . to differ" is *diacrinei.* The essential idea of this verb is "to separate," and so "to distinguish, discriminate" (A-S). Thayer thinks that here the verb means "to prefer," that is, "yield to him the preference or honor." Arndt and Gingrich translate it in this passage, "Who concedes you any superiority?"

In similar fashion Robertson and Plummer suggest:

"For who sees anything special in you?" They go on to say: "The verb has a variety of meanings . . . and these meanings are linked by the idea of 'separate' in one sense or another; here it means to distinguish favorably from others." The next question, "What hast thou that thou didst not receive?" they paraphrase: "Let us grant that you have some superiority. Is it inherent? You know that you have nothing but what you have received. Your good things were all of them *given* to you" (p. 82).

There are three questions in verse 7. Concerning the first, Findlay writes: "This question stigmatises the partisan conceit of the Corinthians as *presumptuous;* those that follow . . . mark it as *ungrateful;* both ways it is egotistic" (EGT, 2:800).

## Full or Satisfied? (4:8)

The first half of this verse consists of three ironical statements: "Now ye are full, now ye are rich, ye have reigned as kings without us." The verb "full" is *corennumi.* It is found only here (in a metaphorical sense) and in Acts 27:38 (in a literal sense). It comes from *coros,* "surfeit," and so in the passive means "be satisfied." The tragic thing about these Corinthians was that they were too well satisfied with themselves.

Robertson and Plummer reveal the attitude of the Corinthians. They write: "The Apostle now directly attacks the self-esteem of his readers in a tone of grave irony. 'You may well sit in judgment upon us, from your position of advanced perfection, whence you can watch us struggling painfully to the heights which you have already scaled'" (p. 83).

## I Would to God or Would That? (4:8)

The Greek text has nothing in it about God. All this

expression in English is one word in Greek, *ophelon,* which simply means "would that."

## Set Forth or Exhibited? (4:9)

The verb *apodeiknymi* was used for exhibiting gladiators in the arena of the amphitheater. Paul says it seems as though God has exhibited us apostles "last," that is, "to make the best sport for the spectators." Lightfoot adds: "The Apostles were brought out to make the grand finale, as it were" (*Notes,* p. 200). Godet writes: "Down to the end of the verse the apostle is alluding to the gladiators who were presented as a spectacle in the games of the amphitheatre, and whose blood and last agonies formed the joy of a whole population of spectators" (1:224).

Another possible picture is suggested in Goodspeed's translation: "God has exhibited us apostles at the very end of the procession." This might refer to the triumphal procession at Rome, when the emperor or a general would have his captives of war led in a long parade to humiliate them and exalt his own prowess. The ones at the end of the procession would be the most despised ones, left until the last.

Findlay combines the two ideas in his explanation. He writes: "One imagines a grand procession, on some day of public festival; in its rear march the criminals on their way to the arena, where the populace will be regaled with their sufferings" (EGT, 2:801). In a similar vein Robertson and Plummer say: "There is a great pageant in which the Apostles form the ignominious finale, consisting of doomed men, who will have to fight in the arena until they are killed" (p. 85).

## Appointed to Death (4:9)

This is one word in Greek, the adjective *epithanatios*

(only here in NT). In the apocryphal additions to the Book of Daniel it is used in the story of Bel and the Dragon to describe "condemned conspirators who were thrown to the lions, two at a time, daily . . . Dionysius of Halicarnasus, about B.C. 8, uses it of those who were thrown from the Tarpeian rock" *(ibid.)*. Lightfoot suggests that the adjective should be translated "condemned criminals." Moffatt renders the clause: "Like doomed gladiators in the arena." That seems to catch the picture here.

## Naked or Scantily Clothed? (4:11)

The verb *gymniteuo* occurs only here in the NT. It means to be scantily clad. Arndt and Gingrich give only the definition: "be poorly clothed."

## Buffeted or Beaten? (4:11)

The verb *kolaphizō* comes from the noun *kolaphos,* meaning "a fist." So it literally means "to strike with the fist." Moffatt translates it: "knocked about." It would seem that "buffeted" is a little weak (cf. "brutally treated," NIV).

## Have No Certain Dwellingplace (4:11)

Again this is one word in Greek, the verb *astateō.* It comes from the adjective *astatos,* which means "unstable." So it signifies: "to be unsettled, be homeless, lead a vagabond life" (A-S, p. 65). It could be translated "are vagabonds," or "are homeless" (NIV).

## Suffer or Endure? (4:12)

The verb *anechō* literally means "hold up." In the NT it is always in the middle voice and carries the idea of "bear with" or "endure." The rendering "suffer" gives a somewhat different connotation to the modern reader.

## Defamed or Slandered? (4:13)

The verb *dysphēmeō* is found only here in the NT. It means to speak ill of somebody. In 1 Macc. 7:41 it is used of the insults hurled at the Jews by Rabshakeh, the representative of King Sennacherib. Probably "slandered" (NIV) gives the best meaning today.

## Filth and Offscouring (4:13)

Both Greek words, *perikatharmata* and *peripsēma,* are found only here in the NT. Arndt and Gingrich define the first term as meaning *"that which is removed as a result of a thorough cleansing, i.e. dirt, refuse, off-scouring,* also as a designation of the 'off-scouring' of mankind (Epict. 3, 22, 78)" (p. 653).

The second term comes from the verb meaning "to wipe off all around." So it means "that which is wiped off, off-scouring" (A-S, pp. 358-59).

Of these two words Godet writes: "The term *perikatharma, filth,* denotes literally what is collected by sweeping all around the chamber *(peri);* and *peripsēma* the dirt which is detached from an object by sweeping or scraping it all around" (p. 228).

Lightfoot says that the first term means "sweeping, offscourings." He then comments:

> This is the primary meaning of the word. But the Apostle is carrying on the metaphor of *epithanatiois* above. Both *perikatharmata* and *peripsēma* were used especially of those condemned criminals of the lowest classes who were sacrificed as expiatory offerings, as scapegoats in effect, because of their degraded life. It was the custom at Athens to reserve certain worthless

persons who in case of plague, famine or other visitations from heaven might be thrown into the sea, in the belief that they would cleanse away, or wipe away, the guilt of the nation (*Notes,* pp. 200-201).

Arndt and Gingrich feel that the first of these two terms may have the meaning of "propitiatory offering." They say that "it is probably better to translate *scapegoats for the world*" (p. 653), in this passage (for "filth of the world"). Phillips' rendering is colorful: "We are the world's rubbish, the scum of the earth."

## Instructors or Tutors? (4:15)

The word *paidagōgos* occurs only here and in Gal. 3:24-25 (see notes there). It comes from *pais,* "child," and *agōgos,* "a leader," and so literally means "a child leader"; that is, a guide and guardian of boys. Both Thayer and Abbott-Smith give just one definition, "tutor."

Thayer has a rather full treatment of this term, which is worth quoting. He writes:

> Among the Greeks and Romans the name was applied to trustworthy slaves who were charged with the duty of supervising the life and morals of boys belonging to the better class. The boys were not allowed so much as to step out of the house without them before arriving at the age of manhood . . . The name carries with it an idea of severity (as a stern censor and enforcer of morals) in 1 Cor. iv. 15, where the father is distinguished from the tutor as one whose discipline is usually milder, and in Gal. iii. 24 f. where the Mosaic law is likened to a tutor because it arouses the consciousness of sin, and is called *paidagōgos eis Christon,* i.e., preparing the soul for Christ, because those who have learned by experience with the law that they are not and cannot be commended to God by their works, welcome the more eagerly the hope of salvation offered them through the death and resurrection of Christ, the Son of God (p. 472).

## Followers or Imitators? (4:16)

Our words "mimic" and "mimeograph" both come from the Greek word here, *mimetai,* which occurs seven times in the NT (cf. 11:1; Eph. 5:1; 1 Tim. 1:6; 2:14; Heb. 6:12; 1 Pet. 3:13). It always means "imitators," which is a stronger term than "followers." Paul wanted the Corinthian Christians to imitate him, as he was imitating Christ (11:1).

## Puffed Up or Arrogant? (4:18)

The verb *physioō* is used six times in this epistle—three times in this chapter (4:6, 18, 19; 5:2; 8:1; 13:4)—and only once elsewhere in the NT (Col. 2:18). This reflects the spiritual pride of the Corinthians, which was their main problem.

The word comes from *physa,* which means "bellows." So it means *"to puff up* or *blow up,* inflate" (A-S). In the New Testament the verb is always used metaphorically in the sense of being puffed up with pride.

The context suggests that "arrogant" (Weymouth, RSV) may be the best translation here. Some members of the Corinthian congregation were carrying on arrogantly, assuming that Paul would not come and straighten things out.

## Word or Talk? (4:19, 20)

"Speech" (v. 19) and "word" (v. 20) are both translations of *logos.* The RSV is consistent in having "talk" in both places. This is perhaps the best rendering. Paul's opponents in Corinth were doing a lot of talking, but they lacked real power. The apostle asserts that the kingdom of God is not mere talk; it is the power of the Holy Spirit, which these self-inflated Corinthians sadly lacked.

## Excommunication? (5:5)

Chapter 5 deals with a case of flagrant immorality in the church at Corinth. One of its members was living with his stepmother. This is what is called "incest," and it was particularly abhorrent even to the pagans of that day. So this sin in the church was bringing serious reproach on the name of Christ. Yet the proud, stubborn Corinthians were arrogant when they should have been repentant.

In verse 2 Paul says that they should have put the guilty person out of church, should have excluded him from their fellowship. He concludes his discussion of this problem by saying that the "wicked person" should be "put away from among you" (v. 13). This rather clearly means excommunication.

But what is the apostle talking about in verses 3-5? He says that he has already rendered a judgment in the case. With apostolic authority he has moved "to deliver such an one unto Satan for the destruction of the flesh, that the spirit may be saved in the day of the Lord Jesus" (v. 5). Paul uses similar language in 1 Tim. 1:20.

H. A. W. Meyer writes helpfully on this passage. He suggests that while the church could excommunicate an erring member, it was the prerogative of only the apostles to consign a man to Satan. He calls the latter "the *intensified* penalty of excommunication" (*Critical and Exegetical Handbook to the Epistles to the Corinthians,* p. 112).

Meyer also calls attention to the fact that what is to be destroyed is the *sarx,* "the flesh," not the body. The object of Paul's judgment of the man was that "his *sinful fleshly nature,* which is turned to account by the indwelling power of sin as the workplace of his desires and lusts, might be emptied of its energy of sinful life by the pains of bodily sickness, and might in so far perish and come to nought. It is not his *soma* (body) that is to *die,* but his *sarx* (flesh)" (p. 113). He goes on to say: "Observe that it is with an *anti-Christian purpose* that Satan smites the man delivered over to him with bodily misery, but that against his own will this purpose of his is made to *serve God's* aim of *salvation*" (pp. 113-14). The delivering to Satan was penal, but it had a remedial purpose.

## Leaven or Yeast? (5:6)

Paul quotes an old proverb: "A little leaven leavens all the dough." To regular readers of the KJV the term "leaven" is familiar. But many readers of the Bible today might not be aware of the fact that "leaven" means "yeast." Of course, in this day when very little baking is done at home, probably most young people would not even know what yeast is! It is true that "leaven" has become deeply ingrained in our language as a symbol of evil, although it is sometimes used for a good influence. Basically it means what affects the whole group or society.

## Fornicators or Immoral? (5:10)

In verses 10 and 11 the apostle mentions various types of sinful people. He says that we cannot avoid associating with such people in this world, but we are not to tolerate them in the church.

We have already noted that the Greek word translated "fornication" can refer to many kinds of immorality, including adultery and probably homosexuality. So "fornicators" *(pornois)* here should be rendered as "the immoral."

## Covetous or Greedy? (5:10, 11)

The noun *pleonektēs* occurs in both these verses and

in 6:11. Elsewhere in the NT it is found only in Eph. 5:5. It refers to a "greedy" person, as we would say today.

## Extortioners or Robbers? (5:10)

The adjective *harpax,* used here as a substantive, comes from the verb *harpazō,* which means "to seize, catch up, snatch away, carry off by force" (A-S, p. 60). So the reference here is to what we would call "robbers" (RSV) or "swindlers" (NEB, NIV).

## Railer or Abusive? (5:11)

The noun *loidoros* is found only here and in 6:10, where it is translated "reviler" in KJV. It comes from the verb *loidoreō,* which means "to abuse, revile" (A-S). Perhaps the best contemporary translation would be "an abusive person."

## To Judge . . . Judgments (6:2, 4)

For the one who tries to translate the Greek of these verses there are obvious difficulties. Both the above expressions render *criterion,* which basically has the same meaning in Greek as we have given it in English. Thayer defines it thus: "1. properly *the instrument* or *means of trying* or *judging anything; the rule by which one judges* (Plat., Plut., al). 2. *the place where judgment is given; the tribunal of a judge; a bench of judges:* plur. I Co. vi.2: Jas. ii.6.3. in an exceptional usage, *the matter judged, thing to be decided, suit, case:* plur. I Co. vi.4" (p. 362).

This definition helps out in translating verse 4. But "tribunals" hardly seems to fit verse 2, unless we render it: "Are you unworthy of being tribunals for smallest matters?"

This is the way Meyer takes it. He writes: *"Criterion* does not mean *matter of dispute, case at law,* as most expositors . . . wish to take it, with no evidence at all from the usage of the language in their favour, but *place of judgment* (*tribunal, seat of justice,* Jas. ii. 6) . . . or *judicial trial* which is held . . . The latter sense, *judicial trial* . . . is the true one here, as is evident from ver. 4. We render therefore: *Are ye unworthy to hold very trivial trials?* i.e. trials in which judgment is to be given upon very insignificant matters" (p. 129).

There is no question that "tribunal" or "judgment seat" fits very well in Jas. 2:6, the only other passage in the NT where this word occurs. There Arndt and Gingrich would translate the passage, "drag you into court." But they continue: "It is not easy to fit this meaning into the two other passages in our literature where *criterion* is found." They hold that the clause in verse 2 "could perhaps mean: *are you unfit to form even the most insignificant courts* (i.e. those that have jurisdiction over the petty details of every-day life)?" For verse 4 they suggest: *"if you have* (need for) *courts for the matters of everyday life, do you appoint insignificant men* (as judges)?" Then they add: "However, in both cases the tendency is now to prefer for *criterion* the sense . . . *lawsuit, legal action"* (p. 454). The idea then would be: "Are you unworthy (*anaxios,* only here in NT) to take care of the least important legal actions?" (v. 2).

The problem still remains: Is verse 4 to be taken as a command (KJV) or as a question (most Greek texts)? If the former, Paul must be speaking ironically. For instance, Findlay suggests: "Paul says in sarcasm, 'If you have lawsuits in secular affairs, set up the lowest amongst you (for judges of these low matters)!'" Actually, Findlay agrees with Meyer in insisting that *criterion* "signifies *place* rather than *matter* of judgment" (p. 814), and so prefers the

1 Corinthians / 43

translation: "Well then, for secular tribunals—if you have men that are made of no account in the Church, set these on the bench!" (EGT, 2:815).

Robertson and Plummer (ICC) have a full treatment of the matter. They write:

> If *cathizete* (set) is imperative, then these words mean "those in the Church who are held of no account," i.e. the least esteemed of the Christians. The apostle sarcastically tells them that, so far from there being any excuse for resorting to heathen tribunals, any selection of the simplest among themselves would be competent to settle their disputes about trifles. Let the insignificant decide what is insignificant.
>
> If *cathizete* is indicative [the same Greek form is used for both in second person plural of the present tense] and the sentence interrogative, then these words mean, "those who, in the Church, are held of no account," viz. the *adikoi* (unjust) of v. 1.

They add: "Both constructions are possible, and both make good sense."

After listing many authorities on both sides, they conclude: "We must be content to leave the question open. The general sense is clear. The Corinthians were doing a sameful thing in going to heathen civil courts to settle disputes between Christians" (pp. 113-14).

## Fault or Defeat? (6:7)

The word *hēttēma* occurs only here and in Rom. 11:12. The translation "fault" (KJV) is inaccurate in terms of what that means today. The Greek word means "loss" or "defeat." The latter is its use in the OT (LXX). Arndt and Gingrich translate this passage: "it is an utter defeat for you" (p. 350).

Lightfoot seems to capture the real significance. He translates: "it is a loss to you, a defeat." That is, "You trust to overreach, to gain a victory: it is really a loss, a defeat, before the trial even comes on" (*Notes,* p. 212). Even if a Christian won money in a damage suit against a fellow Christian, he had already sustained a great spiritual loss, perhaps even the loss of his own soul. This has happened many times. Paul goes on to suggest, "Better sustain a material loss than lose your salvation."

## Defraud or Rob? (6:7, 8)

The verb *apostereō* means *"to defraud, deprive of, despoil* (in classical Greek, chiefly of the misappropriation of trust funds)" (A-S, p. 54). Thayer even gives the meaning "rob," and Arndt and Gingrich give, "steal, rob." Goodspeed translates verse 8: "But it is you who wrong and rob others, and your own brothers at that!"

What Paul is saying to the Corinthian Christians is: "Better to be robbed than to rob. But you are actually robbing each other by unjust lawsuits against each other." The church at Corinth was a constant heartache and heartbreak to the apostle who had founded it.

## Homosexuals (6:9)

Two Greek words at the end of verse 9 seem to refer to much the same thing. The first is *malakos,* translated "effeminate." This adjective, in the plural here, literally means "soft" and was properly used of what is soft to touch. It occurs elsewhere in the NT in only two parallel passages (Matt. 11:8; Luke 7:25) where it describes "soft clothing."

But, as Arndt and Gingrich note, it was also used "of persons *soft, effeminate,* especially of *catamites,* men and boys who allow themselves to be misused homosexually" (p. 489). This was a common thing in that day. Deissmann gives a photographic facsimile of a third-century papyrus letter from a wealthy Egyptian to a police official, asking that "Zenobius the effeminate," a musician, be sent to him (LAE, p. 164).

"Abusers of themselves with mankind" is all one word in Greek, *arsenokoitai* (only here and 1 Tim. 1:10). It is compounded of *arsēn*, "male," and *koitē*, "bed," and so means "one who lies with a male as with a female, a sodomite" (Thayer, p. 75). The same sin is described graphically in Rom. 1:27.

Because these two words evidently refer to the same type of person, they are combined in many modern translations. In the Berkeley Version we find simply "partakers in homosexuality." The RSV followed suit with only one word, "homosexuals," but a footnote explains: "Two Greek words are rendered by this expression." The NEB ties these two words in with the previous term and reads: "none who are guilty either of adultery or of homosexual perversion."

In keeping with its policy of representing every Greek word in the English translation, NASB has both "effeminate" and "homosexuals." But today "effeminate" is popularly used to describe a fellow who acts like a "sissy." So it is hardly a correct translation here. The Jerusalem Bible has "catamites, sodomites," but it is doubtful if either of those terms would convey much to the average reader today. The New American Bible represents both terms together by "sodomites." The NIV has: "nor male prostitutes nor homosexual offenders."

In much of modern society in America and Europe homosexuality is no longer even frowned upon. Several church denominations have officially stated that homosexual relations between consenting adults should no longer be considered a crime. Congregations of homosexuals have sprung up in this country and have even formed themselves into an association like a denomination. Marriages of two men or two women are not uncommon. These homosexual "Christians" claim that they should be recognized as God's children just as readily as those who prefer the traditional way of life.

In the face of all this permissiveness we need to realize afresh what God's Word says about this practice. In both the Old Testament and the New it is categorically condemned. Certainly we need to be sympathetic with those who have a psychological problem at this point. But the Scriptures label homosexuality as a sin. Paul states very clearly here that no homosexual will inherit the kingdom of God. The same thing is implied in Rom. 1:27. Sodomy was the sin for which God destroyed ancient Sodom.

## Sanctified (6:11)

Paul writes: "And such were some of you: but ye are washed, but ye are sanctified, but ye are justified in the name of the Lord Jesus, and by the Spirit of our God."

The first thing that should be noted is that in all three cases the verb is in the aorist tense, not the present, in the original. The Greek says: "You were washed . . . sanctified . . . justified." One of the main weaknesses of the translators working 350 years ago was their failure to accurately translate the Greek tenses.

In the second place, it will be observed that "sanctified" occurs between "washed" and "justified." The order of the terms would suggest that the verb *hagiazō* has here its lesser meaning of "set apart to God." All three terms seem to refer to the initial experience of conversion. At that time those to whom Paul is writing had their sins washed away—the compound verb *apolouō* (only here and Acts 22:16) means "wash off" or "wash away"—they were set apart to God, and they were "justified" (made and declared righteous in God's sight).

## Corinthian Antinomianism (6:12-18)

Paul twice writes: "All things are lawful for me." But it seems clear that he is quoting his critics. So the statement should be put in quotation marks both times (cf. RSV, NIV). In each case the apostle gives his answer to the proud claim of those who wanted to do as they pleased. The same goes for the first part of verse 13: "Food for the stomach, and the stomach for food" (literal translation).

It appears that there were those in the church at Corinth who gloried so much in their freedom from the Mosaic law and their liberty in Christ that they had become almost libertines. This is evidently the reason for the apostle's strong castigation of immorality in the preceding verses. He goes on to warn against participation in the pagan worship that involved relations with sacred prostitutes in the temple (vv. 15-16). He warns them to "flee immorality" (v. 18). Corinth was perhaps the most wicked city of that day, and the Christians needed to be particularly careful.

## Body and Spirit? (6:20)

Paul concludes his discussion by reminding his readers that they have been "bought with a price," the precious blood of Christ, and so they are to "glorify God in your body." The added words, "and in your spirit, which are God's," are not in any of the oldest and best Greek manuscripts—from the third, fourth, and fifth centuries. They must have been inserted in the text by a later scribe.

Gnosticism taught that all matter is evil; only spirit is good. Therefore the human body is essentially evil. Unfortunately, Gnostic ideas crept into the Early Church, causing an unwholesome emphasis on asceticism. To tone down the strong admonition here to glorify God in our bodies, a copyist added "and in your spirit." (All modern translations correctly end the chapter with "body.")

The teaching of both the Old Testament and the New is that our physical bodies were made by God and so are good. It is how we use them that matters. They can be used for sinful purposes. But they can also be used for holy purposes, and so glorify God.

## Fornication or The Fornications? (7:2)

"Nevertheless, to avoid fornication, let every man have his own wife, and let every woman have her own husband." This seems to suggest a low motive for marriage. But instead of "to avoid fornication," the Greek reads: "on account of the fornications." The NASB renders it correctly, "because of immoralities;" *porneia* is used in the NT for all kinds of immorality, including adultery and homosexuality. The NIV reads: "But since there is so much immorality."

The reason for Paul's admonition was that Corinth was at that time perhaps the most immoral city in the world. Cases of immorality were to be seen on every side. The Christians at Corinth were safer to be married, since they had to live in such immoral surroundings.

## Due Benevolence (7:3)

The Greek is simply *tēn opheilēn*. This comes from the verb *opheilō*, which means "I owe." So it means "one's due." The correct translation is "what is due her" (NEB). The context suggests that the reference is to her conjugal rights, that is, normal marriage relationships. Both husband and wife owe this to each other. People who are not prepared to do this should not be married.

## Defraud or Deprive? (7:5)

The verb is *apostereō*. Its earliest meaning was "steal, rob." Then it came to signify "defraud," as we use that term today. But the context (cf. v. 3) suggests that Paul is saying, "Do not deprive each other" (NIV). Phillips, with his paraphrase, spells it all out: "Do not cheat each other of normal sexual intercourse." This is the correct meaning.

## Consent or Agreement? (7:5)

It is the adjective *symphōnos,* which is compounded of *syn,* "together," and *phōnē,* "sound." So the literal meaning is "agreeing in sound." Metaphorically it is used in the sense of "harmonious, agreeing." So the phrase here means "by agreement."

This adjective occurs only here in the NT. The same is true of the noun *symphōnia* (Luke 15:25), which meant a musical symphony. The language suggests that our married life should be a true symphony, with no jarring, discordant sounds. It's the "sour notes" in marriage that ruin the symphony. We keep in tune with each other when we both follow the maestro, Christ.

## Give or Devote? (7:5)

We do not find here the common word for "give"—*didōmi.* Rather the verb is *scholasēte,* from which we get "scholastic." What's the connection?

The verb *scholazō* comes from the noun *scholē.* Originally this meant "freedom from labor, leisure." In later Greek it was used for "a place where there is leisure for anything, a school" (Thayer, p. 610). This is its meaning in the only place where it is found in the NT (Acts 19:9). Learning takes time. Someone has said, "Without leisure there is no true education." Probably that is the reason there are so few really educated people today! Most of us don't take time to think.

The verb used here originally meant "to cease from labor," then "to be free from labor, to be at leisure . . . to have leisure for a thing, i.e. to give one's self to a thing" (Thayer, p. 610). Abbott-Smith spells it out even more clearly: *"to be at leisure,* hence, to have time or opportunity for, *to devote oneself to,"* (p. 436). The best translation here is "devote" (NIV).

## Fasting? (7:5)

Paul says that the husband and wife should not deprive each other of normal married relationship except by mutual agreement for a short time, "that ye may give yourselves to fasting and prayer." But the oldest and best Greek manuscripts—the third-century Papyrus 46, together with all the fourth- and fifth-century manuscripts and the earliest versions—do not have "fasting" here. They simply mention "prayer." The strong emphasis on fasting was a part of the development of asceticism in the Early Church, under the evil influence of Gnosticism. This heresy taught that all spirit is good and all matter is evil: so the physical body must be suppressed as an evil thing.

The first chapter of Genesis teaches that God created matter and called it "good." When He crowned it all with the creation of man He surveyed the results and pronounced them "very good" (Gen. 1:31). Asceticism is a denial of biblical theology.

## Incontinency (7:5)

This is an archaic translation of *akrasia* (only here and Matt. 23:25). The proper rendering today is "lack of self-control" (Weymouth, RSV, NEB, NASB, NIV).

## Permission or Concession? (7:6)

The apostle states that in the advice given in verse 5 he speaks "by permission and not of commandment." The noun *syngnōmē* means "concession." Robertson and Plummer write: "The word occurs nowhere else in N.T. and is very rare in LXX." In a footnote they comment: "'By permission' (A.V.) is ambiguous: it might mean, 'I am permitted by God to say as much as this' . . . It means 'By way of concession': he is telling people that they may marry, not that they must do so" (p. 135).

## Contain or Have Self-control? (7:9)

The verb *engkrateuō* occurs only here and in 9:25. It means "to exercise self-control," and that is the way to translate it here.

## Burn or Be Aflame? (7:9)

On the surface this verse could be taken as meaning: "It is better to marry than to burn forever in hell." It is true that the verb *pyroō* (from *pyr*, "fire") means "to be set on fire, to burn" (A-S, p. 394); it is always passive in the NT. But almost all the modern translations agree that the correct meaning is "to be aflame with passion" (RSV). Weymouth has: "For marriage is better than the fever of passion." As usual, the NASB gives a literal rendering, "to burn," but it adds in the margin: "i.e., *burn with passion*" (cf. NIV).

Robertson and Plummer call attention to the fact that the verbs "contain" and "burn" are in the present tense of continuous action. They comment: "A prolonged and painful struggle seems to be intended, a condition quite fatal to spiritual peace and growth" (p. 139).

It is true that in our day, as in ancient Corinth—when

the Christian is surrounded by flagrant, blatant immorality—the safest condition for most people is a normal married life. That was what God ordained in Eden, and it is still His pattern for human beings.

## Put Away . . . Put Away . . . Leave (7:11, 12, 13)

These are the translations found at the end of these verses. But in the Greek the verb is the same in all three places. It is *aphiēmi,* which means "send away" and is so translated in all three places in NASB. Since in the context here this would mean "divorce," the word is rendered that way in RSV and NIV. Among the Jews a woman could not divorce her husband. This fact probably accounts for the change in translation in KJV for verse 13. But 1 Corinthians was written to a Gentile church, and we know that Greek and Roman women could divorce their husbands. Many modern translators use "divorce" here.

## Distributed or Assigned? (7:17)

Paul says that each man should keep the place in life which the Lord has "distributed" to him. It is true that the verb *merizō* means "to divide" or "distribute." But the meaning that fits this passage is "assigned" (NIV).

## Servant or Slave? (7:21)

The noun *doulos* comes from the verb *deō,* which means "bind." So the noun means a bond-servant, or slave. This is clearly the connotation here, for it speaks of being "made free," not fired.

The last clause of this verse is somewhat ambiguous in the Greek. What does "use it rather" mean? By equally competent scholars it has been taken with opposite meanings.

Weymouth (1902) rendered the last two clauses: "And yet if you can get your freedom, you had better take it." Moffatt (1913) similarly has: "If you do find it possible to get free, you had better avail yourself of the opportunity." But Goodspeed (1923) goes in the other direction: "Even if you can gain your freedom, make the most of your present condition instead."

The majority of recent translations have followed Weymouth and Moffatt, rather than Goodspeed. But both RSV and NEB give the alternative rendering in the margin, since there is no way of being certain which was intended in the original. The NIV follows the majority: "although if you can gain your freedom, do so."

Among the commentators there is likewise a division of opinion, with equally good authorities lined up on each side. But Robertson and Plummer make a strong case for the view adopted above. The aorist tense of "use" suggests a new condition. They conclude: "The advice, thus interpreted, is thoroughly in keeping with the Apostle's tenderness of heart and robustness of judgment" (p. 148).

## Abuse or Use Up? (7:31)

"And they that use this world, as not abusing it." This is a good attempt to bring over into English the play on words in Greek. "Use" is the verb *chraomai*, "abuse" is *katachraomai*. The prepositional prefix *kata* has the intensive force. So the compound verb means "to make full use of, use to the uttermost, use up" (A-S, p. 240). This is expressed well in NEB: "Nor those who use the world's wealth on using it to the full." We are to use the material resources of this world for the good of the Kingdom, but we must not use them selfishly upon ourselves. To do so is to abuse our privileges, rather than use them.

## Carefulness or Anxiety? (7:32)

The adjective *amerimnos* occurs only here and in Matt. 2:14. It means "free from anxiety." Paul is not telling us to be "without carefulness." One of the most important of the ABCs of life is: "Always Be Careful!" But he does express the wish that his readers should be "without anxiety," or "free from anxious care."

## Snare or Restraint? (7:35)

The word *brochos* is found only here in the NT. Thayer defines it as *"a noose, slip-knot,* by which any person or thing is caught, or fastened, or suspended." Used with the verb *epiballō*, as here, the phrase means *"to throw a noose upon one,* a figurative expression borrowed from war (or the chase) . . . i.e., by craft or by force to bind one to some necessity, to constrain him to obey some command" (p. 106).

Metaphorically it means "restraint," as here. Robertson and Plummer comment: " 'Cast a snare upon you' (AV., RV.) gives a wrong idea: *brochos* is a halter or lasso, not a trap . . . He has no wish to curtail their freedom, as one throws a rope over an animal that is loose, or a person that is to be arrested" (p. 158).

## Comely or Proper? (7:35)

The adjective *euschēmon* literally means "elegant, graceful, comely." But here it is used in its moral sense of "seemly, becoming." The simplest translation is "proper."

## Attend . . . Without Distraction (7:35)

This verse has three words used only once in the NT. We have already noted *brochos*. Two more occur near the

end of the verse. The first is *euparedros,* "constantly attendant or waiting on." The second, *aperispastōs,* is an adverb
meaning "without distraction." It comes from *a*-negative
and the verb *perispaō,* "distract," found only in Luke
10:40. There we read that Martha was "cumbered" (distracted) with much serving. Paul wished that workers in
the church might sit at the Master's feet, as did Mary, not
be distracted as Martha.

The great apostle was so wrapped up in the business
of the Kingdom that he had no time for anything else. He
would liked to have applied this ideal to everybody. But in
reading this paragraph (vv. 25-40) we should always keep
in mind the opening verse: "Now concerning virgins I have
no commandment of the Lord: yet I give my judgment, as
one that hath obtained mercy of the Lord to be faithful"
(v. 25). He also closes the discussion by saying that he is
giving his own judgment (v. 40). So the guidelines he suggests here are not binding on the Christian—they state
Paul's own preferences, as he is careful to tell us. It should
also be noted that he was dealing with a special, abnormal
type of situation in Corinth. That the apostle had a high
view of marriage is clearly seen in Eph. 5:25-27.

## Virgin or Virgin Daughter? (7:36, 37)

The English Revised Version (NT, 1881), the ASV
(1901) and the NASB (NT, 1963) all have "virgin *daugh-
ter.*" The older commentaries (e.g., CGT, ICC, EGT)
support this rendering, mainly because of the expression
"giveth her in marriage" in verse 38. Thayer's *Lexicon*
takes it that way.

The Greek simply has *parthenos.* Under *gamizō,*
"give in marriage," Arndt and Gingrich note that the verb
may here be used for *gameō,* "marry." They go on to say:
"In the context of vv. 36-8 *parthenos* would then mean

either a Christian's fiancee . . . or perhaps even his 'spiritual bride,' who lived with him as a virgin" (p. 150). The RSV takes it in the former way—"If anyone thinks he is not behaving properly toward his betrothed" (v. 36). The NEB adopts the other view: "But if a man has a partner in celibacy" (v. 36) . . . "and if he has decided in his own mind to preserve his partner in her virginity" (v. 37). Probably the NIV rendering is best: "the virgin he is engaged to" (v. 36), "the virgin" (vv. 37, 38).

## Things Offered unto Idols (8:1)

This is all one word in Greek, *eidolothyta*. It is compounded of *eidolon,* "idol," and *thyō,* "sacrifice." So it literally means "things sacrificed to idols." The term is used four times in this chapter (vv. 1, 4, 7, 10), twice in chapter 10 (vv. 19, 28), twice in Acts (15:29; 21:25) and twice in Revelation (2:14, 20). Thayer says that it denotes "the flesh left over from the heathen sacrifices; it was either eaten at feasts, or sold (by the poor and the miserly) in the market" (p. 174). Arndt and Gingrich (p. 220) note: "From the Jewish viewpoint it was unclean and therefore forbidden" (cf. Num. 25:2; Ps. 106:28). Dean Stanley observes: "This identification of a sacrifice and a feast was carried to the highest pitch among the Greeks. Sacrifices are enumerated by Aristotle and Thucydides amongst the chief means of social enjoyment" (Quoted by Lias, *Romans,* p. 94).

## Edifieth or Builds Up? (8:1)

The Greek word is *oikodomeō,* which literally means "build a house," and so more generally "build." One could translate the last part of this verse: "Knowledge blows up, but love builds up." The first verb is *physioō,* which comes from *physa,* "bellows." So it means "blow up" or "inflate."

The picture here is a striking contrast. Intellectualism often inflates a person with pride. We can blow up a balloon in a minute or two, and collapse it in a second with a pin prick. So it is with self-important intellectuals. They can be deflated with a single remark.

But building up with love is something else. Just as one has to lay stone on stone or brick on brick in order to construct a solid building, so we must lay one loving deed on another if we would build a solid life that will last.

## Answer or Defense? (9:3)

The word is *apologia,* from which we get "apology." But the Greek term means "a speech in defense." Actually the original meaning of "apology" in English was "defense."

## Power or Right? (9:4)

The term used here (vv. 4, 5, 6, 12, 18) is not *dynamis,* "power," but *exousia,* "right, privilege, authority." Paul first asks "Have we not power to eat and to drink?"—that is at the church's expense. Some evidently insisted that because Paul was not one of the original 12 apostles, he had no right to be maintained by the church.

In the second place, Paul asks if he does not have just as much right to be accompanied by a wife as had other apostles and the Lord's brothers and Peter. The third question the apostle asked is: "Or I only and Barnabas, have we not power to forbear working?" (v. 6). The last two words are literally "not to work." What Paul is asking is this: "Are Barnabas and I the only ones who do not have the right to refrain from working?"

Lias comments: "The reason why Paul and Barnabas

refused to accept payment for their services is not hard to discover. They went on a mission to the Gentiles, the other Apostles to the Jews. The latter fully understood that the ministers should be maintained by the offerings of the worshippers. The Gentiles, on the contrary, had so long known what it was to be plundered by greedy sophists who lived by their wits, that it was above all things necessary for the Apostles of Christ to avoid being confounded with such persons" (pp. 102-3).

## Goeth a Warfare (9:7)

This is one word in the Greek, *strateuetai*. The verb simply means "serve as a soldier." It is used literally here and in Luke 3:14 and 2 Tim. 2:4. In the other four occurrences in the New Testament (2 Cor. 10:3; 1 Tim. 1:18; James 4:1; 1 Pet. 2:11) it is used metaphorically of making war in a spiritual conflict.

## Charges or Expense? (9:7)

The word *opsōnion* meant "provisions, provision-money, soldier's pay" (A-S, p. 332). That is how it is used here and in Luke 3:14. In 2 Cor. 11:8 it is used in a more general sense for wages, and in Rom. 6:23 for the "wages" of sin. The general sense of "wages" is found in the papyri (Deissmann, *Bible Studies,* p. 148). The correct translation of the first question in verse 7 is: "Who at any time serves as a soldier at his own expense?" (NASB).

## Carnal or Material? (9:11)

Paul writes: "If we have sown unto you spiritual things *(pneumatica),* is it a great thing if we shall reap your carnal things *(sarkica)."*

*The Oxford English Dictionary* (2:123) indicates that the earliest meaning of "carnal" was "of or pertaining to the flesh or body; bodily, corporeal." But it labels this "obsolete." It then came to mean "pertaining to the body as the seat of passions or appetites; fleshly, sensual." This is the usual way that the word "carnal" is taken today, but obviously this is not what Paul is talking about here. Another definition, labeled "archaic," is "material, temporal, secular." That is the sense in which it is used here. The correct translation is "material things," or, "money." What the apostle is saying in this passage (vv. 11-14) is that the one who dispenses food for the soul should be paid for this just as is the grocer who furnishes food for the body.

## Live or Eat? (9:13)

Paul says that those who work at holy tasks in the temple "live of the things of the temple." Instead of "live" the Greek has "eat" *(esthiousin).* This refers to the fact that the priests were entitled to get their meat from the sacrifices offered in the temple, as ordered in the law of Moses (Num. 18:8-20). They shared ("partakers with") the food that was placed on the altar.

## Willingly . . . Against My Will (9:17)

In the Greek there is a play on words: *hekōn . . . akōn.* The latter is found only here in the New Testament; the former occurs only here and in Rom. 8:20. Obviously the translation should be: "willingly" . . . "unwillingly."

## Dispensation or Stewardship? (9:17)

The word *oikonomian* means "dispensation" in its original meaning of "a dispensing." Paul was dispensing the gospel to others. But today the term "dispensation" usually refers to a period of time, and so its use here is misleading. The proper translation is "stewardship."

## Servant or Slave? (9:19)

Paul declared that although he was free from domination by any man, yet he had made himself "servant" to all men, "to win as many as possible" (NIV). The verb *douloō* means "make (myself) a slave to" (see *Word Meanings,* 3:125). So probably the better translation here is "slave" (NASB, NIV).

## Gain or Win? (9:19)

The verb *kerdainō* regularly means to "gain," in the sense of gaining *things.* "That I might gain the more" (KJV) would most naturally be thought of as gaining more possessions. But with *persons* the correct word is "win"— "that I might win the more" (RSV, NASB). This applies to vv. 19-22.

## This or All? (9:23)

"This" (KJV) is *panta,* "all things." Whatever Paul did was for a definite purpose—"I do all this for the sake of the gospel" (NIV).

## The Stadium (9:24)

The Greek word for "race" in this passage is *stadion,* which was taken over into English in its Latin form "stadium." It means "a stadium, i.e. (1) a measure of length equal to 600 Greek feet or one-eighth of a Roman mile . . . this being the length of the Olympic course, (2) a racecourse: 1 Cor. 9:24" (A-S, p. 415). Later it came to mean the "arena . . . on or in which the foot races and other

public athletic contests were held" (AG, p. 771)—which is
what "stadium" means now.

## Striveth for the Mastery (9:25)

This is all one word in the Greek, *agōnizomenos*. The
verb *agōnizō* is used here in its literal meaning of "contend
for a prize" (A-S, p. 8). (It is used metaphorically in Col.
1:29; 4:12; 1 Tim. 4:10; 6:12; 2 Tim. 4:7). Here "competes
in the games" (NASB, NIV) translates the verb well.

"Is temperate" is better rendered "exercises self-
control." That is what athletes have to do in order to win.
And that is what Christians must do to win in the race of
life. The verb *engkrateuō* is found (in NT) only here and
7:9.

## Crown or Wreath? (9:25)

The Greek word is *stephanos*. It does not usually mean
a royal crown (Greek, *diadēma*) but the victor's crown.
This was a laurel wreath (NIV) given to the one who won
in an athletic contest, particularly the Marathon race.
Grundmann writes: "Like Philo . . . Paul draws on the
perishable crown which is given to the victor as an award
in the games . . . and he compares the Christian life to a
sporting contest. The point of comparison is the self-con-
trolled abstinence . . . which is practised for the sake of the
goal" (TDNT, 7:629).

## Uncertainly or Aimlessly? (9:26)

The adverb *adēlōs* (only here in NT) is compounded
of *alpha*-negative and *dēlos*—"visible, clear." While it
does have the general meaning "uncertainly," yet "aimlessly" fits better in connection with a race. Paul is saying

that he is running "not aimlessly, i.e., not as one who has no fixed goal" (AG, p. 16). Changing the figure, he says, "I do not box (*pykteuō,* only here in NT) as a man beating the air"—or, shadowboxing.

## Keep Under or Beat? (9:27)

The verb *hypōpiazō* is found only here and in Luke 18:5, where KJV has the very weak translation "weary." It literally means "to strike under the eye, give a black eye" (A-S, p. 463). Thayer defines it: "properly, to beat black and blue, to smite so as to cause bruises and livid spots." Here Paul is saying, "Like a boxer I buffet my body, handle it roughly, discipline it by hardships" (p. 646). Weiss says of Paul: "He has in view the physical mistreatment he has received, the scars this has left on his body, the hardships to which his body is constantly exposed, and the results of these" (TDNT, 8:591).

## Bring It into Subjection (9:27)

This is all one word in Greek, *doulagōgō* (only here in NT). Thayer defines this: "to lead away into slavery, claim as one's slave . . . to make a slave . . . to treat as a slave, i.e., with severity, to subject to stern and rigid discipline" (p. 157). The simplest translation is "make it my slave" (NASB, NIV). Paul believed that his spirit should dominate his body, not vice versa.

## A Castaway or Disqualified? (9:27)

The Greek word *adokimos* means "rejected after testing." Robertson and Plummer comment: "Manifestly exclusion from the contest, as not being qualified, is not the meaning; he represents himself as running and fighting: It is exclusion from the prize that is meant. He might prove to be disqualified" (p. 197). For that reason "disqualified for the prize" (NIV) may be a more adequate translation than simply "disqualified" (RSV, NASB).

Seneca, the pagan philosopher, has a passage that is amazingly appropriate to these verses of Paul's. He wrote: "What blows do athletes receive in their faces, what blows all over their bodies. Yet they bear all the torture from thirst of glory. Let us also overcome all things, for our reward is not a crown or a palm branch or the trumpeter proclaiming silence for the announcement of our name, but virtue and strength of mind and peace acquired ever after" (*Moral Epistles,* 78:16). How much greater the Christian's reward in heaven!

## Play (10:7)

The verb *paizō* (from *pais,* child) originally meant to "play like a child." Then it came to mean *"to play, sport, jest; to give way to hilarity,* especially by joking, singing, dancing" (Thayer, p. 473).

This is the only place where *paizō* occurs in the NT, and it is found here in a quotation from the Septuagint of Exod. 32:6. Bertram says, "There can be no doubt that Exod. 32:19 refers to cultic dances" (TDNT, 5:629). Similarly Robertson and Plummer write: "The quotation, therefore, indicates an idolatrous banquet followed by idolatrous sport" (p. 204). So "play" may be "indulge in pagan revelry" (NIV).

## Murmur or Grumble? (10:10)

The verb *gongyzō* is an onomatopoetic word; that is, its sound suggests its sense. The only trouble with "murmur" is that we use it now of speaking softly, and probably the Israelites were not that quiet! For this reason "grumble" is better. Both words are onomatopoetic.

## For Ensamples or As Types? (10:11)

It is odd that earlier translators adopted "ensamples" here in place of the more familiar "examples" of v. 6. The noun in v. 6 is *typos,* from which we get "types." In v. 11 it is the adverb *typicōs,* "typically." For this passage Arndt and Gingrich suggest, *"typologically, as an example* or *warning,* in connection with the typological interpretation of Scripture" (p. 837). For v. 6 they say for *typoi;* "of the *types* given by God as an indication of the future, in the form of persons or things" (p. 838). Lias thinks that both "examples" and "types" fit well (p. 113).

## A Way to Escape (10:13)

The Greek says *tēn ekbasin,* "the way out." Robertson and Plummer say this means "the necessary way of escape, the one suitable for such a difficulty" (p. 209).

## Bear or Bear Up Under? (10:13)

The verb *hypopherō* means "to bear up under, to endure patiently." Robertson and Plummer say: "Temptation is probation, and God orders the probation in such a way 'that ye may be able to endure it'" *(ibid.).*

## Idolatry (10:14)

Our English word comes directly from the Greek *eidōlatria* which is compounded of *eidōlon,* "image," and *latreia,* "worship." So idolatry is the worship of images.

## Communion (10:16)

The Greek word is *koinōnia*. It comes from the adjective *koinōnos,* which means "common," but when used as a substantive means "a partaker, sharer" (see "partakers," v. 18). So the noun *koinōnia* may here be translated "a sharing" (NASB) or "a participation" (RSV, NIV). These terms make Paul's point a little clearer. However, since the reference is probably to the Lord's Supper, "communion" is also meaningful here. Arndt and Gingrich suggest "participation." But they offer as an alternative: "a means for attaining a close relationship with the blood (body) of Christ" (p. 440). That is what the Communion service is supposed to be. Hauck says that *koinōnia* "denotes 'participation, fellowship,' especially with a close bond" (TDNT, 3:798).

## Shambles or Meat Market? (10:25)

The word *makellon* is found only here in the NT. "Shambles" (KJV) does not convey the correct meaning today. A more accurate rendering is "meat market" (RSV, NASB, NIV). But Schneider writes: "The word means not only a meat market but a food market in general. The meat market is part of the *makellon*" (TDNT, 4:371). When Pompeii was excavated, the Macellum (Latin form) was found to be a rectangular court of pillars, covered by a dome-shaped roof, with booths on the sides.

## Offered in Sacrifice (10:28)

This is all one word in Greek, *hierothyton,* which is compounded of the *hieros* ("consecrated to the deity, sacred") and the verb *thyō* ("sacrifice"). So it meant "offered in sacrifice." Arndt and Gingrich say that here, as a substantive, it denotes "meat sacrificed to idols" (p. 373). Schrenk points out that it was regularly used to indicate "the flesh of sacrificial animals" (TDNT, 3:252).

The KJV rendering, "offered in sacrifice unto idols," is based on the reading *eidōlothyton,* which is found in the late manuscripts. G. G. Findlay observes: "The genuine reading, *hierothyton* (slain as sacred, i.e., in sacrifice), takes the statement as from the mouth of unbelievers; a Jew or a Christian would presumably say *eidōlothyton"* (EGT, 2:868)—which is genuine in v. 19, but not here. So the translation "offered in sacrifice" (RSV, NIV) is more accurate than "meat sacrificed to idols" (NASB).

Incidentally, the repetition of "for the earth is the Lord's and the fulness thereof" (from v. 26) occurs only in a few, very late manuscripts. It is obviously a scribal addition, not a part of the original text.

## Give None Offence (10:32)

The translation "give no offense" (RSV, NASB) is practically the same as "Give none offence" (KJV). The Greek says, "Become *aproskopoi."* This Greek word is compounded of *a*-negative and the verb *proskoptō,* which in the transitive means "strike against" and in the intransitive "stumble." Abbott-Smith defines the adjective *aproskopos* as meaning "not causing to stumble." Probably the best translation is "Do not cause anyone to stumble" (NIV).

## Ordinances or Traditions? (11:2)

The Greek word *paradosis* comes from the verb *paradidōmi,* which in this verse is translated "delivered." The verb means "to hand down, hand on, or deliver verbally" (A-S, p. 339). So the noun refers to what has been handed down. Today we call these "traditions" (RSV, NASB). Probably Paul is referring primarily to the doctrines of the Christian faith, but also to apostolic injunctions for Christian conduct. The KJV renders *paradosis* as "traditions" in all the other 12 places where it occurs in the NT. Why an exception here?

## Shearing the Head (11:6)

Today we speak of shearing sheep. That is the way the verb *keirō* is used in Acts 9:32, in a quotation from Isaiah. But here it is used for cutting off a woman's hair ("be shorn"). So the better translation now is "have her hair cut off" (NASB, NIV). Paul was alluding to customs that were current in Corinth at that time.

## Power or Authority? (11:10)

The word is not *dynamis,* "power," but *exousia,* "authority." But what does it mean when it says that a woman should have authority on her head? The bare statement seems to require something additional in order to make sense. That is why we find "*symbol* of authority" (NASB) —the italics indicate there is no word in the Greek—or "sign of authority" (NIV). The RSV goes a step farther by saying, "That is why a woman ought to have a veil on her head," with the footnote: "Greek *authority* (the veil being a symbol of this)." That is probably the correct meaning, in keeping with the custom that Paul reflects here.

## Without or Independent of? (11:11)

The Greek preposition *chōris* means "separate from, apart from." The translation "without" seems a bit weak. Probably "independent of" (RSV, NASB, NIV) is more adequate, and so, more accurate. God originally created mankind "male and female" (Gen. 1:27). Husband and wife are to be "one flesh," not independent of each other. It should be noted that the words for "man" and "woman" mean "husband" and "wife," and they are often translated that way in the NT. That is the meaning here.

## Covering (11:15)

Abbott-Smith thinks that the word *peribolaion,* "that which is thrown around," means "a veil." But Robertson and Plummer translate the second half of this verse: "Long hair is a permanent endowment *(dedotai)* of woman, to serve as an enveloping mantle" (p. 235). They also make this comment on v. 14: "At this period, civilized men, whether Jews, Greeks, or Romans, wore their hair short" *(ibid.).* We would agree with their observation: "While fanaticism defies nature, Christianity respects and refines it; and whatever shocks the common feelings of mankind is not likely to be right" *(ibid.).*

## Contentious (11:16)

*Philoneikos* (only here in NT) is an adjective compounded of *philos,* "loving," and *neikos,* "strife." So it means "fond of strife" or "contentious." Unfortunately, most churches have some who are fond of strife, who, as we say, would rather argue than eat.

## Testament or Covenant? (11:25)

The Greek word is *diathēkē.* In the NT (KJV) it is translated "testament" 13 times and "covenant" 20 times. Most scholars agree that it means "covenant" in almost every case. It is claimed that the Hebrews did not make wills or testaments as the Greeks and Romans did. But they did make covenants, as we find in many places in the OT.

Robertson and Plummer translate here: "This cup is the new covenant, and it is so in virtue of My Blood." They go on to say: "The Atonement is implied, without which doctrine the Lord's Supper is scarcely intelligible. . . . The choice of *diathēkē,* rather than *synthēke,* which is the common word for covenant, is no doubt deliberate, for *synthēke* might imply that the parties to the covenant contracted on equal terms. Between God and man that is impossible. When He enters into a contract He disposes everything, as a man disposes of his property by will" (p. 247).

## Spiritual Gifts (12:1)

Here and in 14:1 the Greek says simply *tōn pneumaticōn,* "the spiritual (things)." But the use of gifts in vv. 4, 9, 28, 30, and 31 seems to show conclusively that "spiritual gifts" is a correct interpretation—as almost all versions have. The opening words of chapter 12, "Now concerning," clearly introduce a new problem, and unquestionably the problem of chapters 12—14 is that of spiritual gifts, or gifts of the Spirit.

## Accursed (12:3)

Paul declares that no one speaking "by" (or "in") the Spirit of God "calleth Jesus accursed"—literally, "says, *'Anathema Iēsous.'*" Furthermore, only by the Holy Spirit can one "say that Jesus is Lord"—literally, "say 'Lord Jesus.'" The Holy Spirit alone can enable us to submit to the Lordship of Christ.

The basic meaning of the Greek word *anathema* is

"something dedicated or consecrated to the deity." It was used first "of the consecrated offerings laid up in the temple," and second, for "something delivered up to divine wrath, dedicated to destruction and brought under a curse" (Behm, TDNT, 1:354). Paul always uses it in the latter sense—"the object of a curse" *(ibid.).*

Robertson and Plummer write: "The blasphemous *Anathema Iēsous* would be more likely to be uttered by a Jew than a Gentile. . . . It is not improbable that Saul himself used it in his persecuting days, and strove to make others do so (Acts 26:11). . . . Unbelievers, whether Jews or Gentiles were admitted to Christian gatherings (16:24), and therefore one of these might suddenly exclaim in the middle of public worship *'Anathema Iēsous.'* To the inexperienced Corinthians a mad shout of this kind . . . might seem to be inspired. . . . St. Paul assures them that this anti-Christian utterance is absolutely derisive. It cannot come from the Spirit" (261). *Anathema* "is one of the 103 words which in NT are found only in Paul and Luke" *(ibid.).*

## Diversities or Differences? (12:4, 5, 6)

In these three verses we find (KJV): "diversities . . . differences . . . diversities." In the Greek it is exactly the same word all three times—*diaireseis* (used only here in NT).

Thayer defines it as first, "division, distribution," and second, "distinction, difference," and then adds that in particular it means "a distinction arising from a different distribution to different persons" (p. 137).

Schlier, after noting the different meanings of *diairesis* (sing.), says: "So far as concerns 1C. 12:4 ff., this can be decided only from the context. The plural *diaireseis,* the opposition *to de auto pneuma* [but the same spirit], and the parallelism with the basic concept of *hē phanerōsis tou pneumatos* (v. 7) all favour 'distribution' rather than 'distinction.' The one Spirit is manifested in apportionments of gifts of the Spirit" (TDNT, 1:185).

The corresponding verb *diaireō* is used in v. 11, where "dividing" (KJV) should be "distributing." In His sovereign will—"as he will"—the Holy Spirit distributes His gifts to different individuals. It is not God's intention that everyone should have the same gift (see vv. 28-30). The failure to recognize this clearly stated truth has led to a great deal of confusion in our day. The strong emphasis of vv. 4-11 is on one Spirit distributing many gifts to many people.

## Administrations or Service? (12:5)

Here we find the common Greek word *diaconia*, which means "service." It is translated "administration" only here and in 2 Cor. 9:12. The most frequent translation is "ministry" (15 times). It is being increasingly recognized that in the church there are many types of ministries in which different members of the church should be involved.

## Operation or Working? (12:6)

In this verse "operations" is *energēmatōn* and "worketh" is *energōn*. Obviously these have the same basic root. Why not show in English this close connection in Greek? This is easily done: "There are different kinds of working, but the same God works all of them in all men" (NIV). It is interesting to note that the same noun is translated "working" in v. 10 (KJV). That fits best here too.

## Discerning (12:10)

One of the gifts is labeled "discerning of spirits." The

first word is *diacrisis.* It comes from the verb meaning to "judge." Buechsel says that in the NT it usually means "differentiation" (TDNT, 3:949). Thayer defines it as "a distinguishing, discerning, judging" (p. 139). Robertson and Plummer make this comment: "The gift of discerning, in various cases (hence the plural) whether extraordinary spiritual manifestations were from above or not; they might be purely natural, though strange, or they might be diabolical" (p. 267).

## Will or Determines? (12:11)

Paul declared that the Holy Spirit distributes the gifts "as he will." The Greek has *bouletai,* which is a strong verb meaning "to wish, desire, purpose" implying "the deliberate exercise of volition" (A-S, p. 84). So "just as he determines" (NIV) is a more adequate translation.

## Members or Parts? (12:12)

The Greek word is *melos,* which means a member, or part, of the body. In classical Greek it is used regularly in the plural for the parts of the body, and this usage is reflected in the Septuagint and the papyri.

The metaphor of Christians as members of the Body of Christ is introduced very effectively by Paul in Rom. 12: 4-5, with its application to differing functions in the church (vv. 6-8). In 1 Corinthians the apostle elaborates this figure, devoting 16 verses to it (12:12-27).

He declares that the body is not one member, but many (v. 14). No individual Christian should try to dominate the whole church. Paul illustrates this by the relation of the two most active parts outwardly, the hand and the foot (v. 15). Then he speaks of the ear and the eye (v. 16). There are "many members, yet but one body" (v. 20). All are needed (vv. 21-25).

Finally he makes the spiritual application: "Now you are the body of Christ, and each one of you is a part of it" (v. 27, NIV).

There are two arguments for using "part" rather than "member" as the translation. The first is that today we speak of "parts of the body" rather than "members of the body." The second is that when we use the expression "members of the body" we mean a person who is a member of a duly constituted body, such as the Congress. But the Body of Christ, the true Christian Church, is not an *organization;* it is an *organism.* It is not a social institution but a spiritual union. As Horst remarks, "Membership does not consist in belonging to a social body" (TDNT, 4:564). One of the great tragedies of history is that many people have thought that salvation comes by being a "member" of some church. We need to recapture Paul's emphasis on the nature of the church as a spiritual organism, with each true Christian functioning as a vital organ of Christ's Body. That is the main thrust of 1 Corinthians 12.

## Uncomely and Comely (12:23, 24)

The first word is *aschēmona* (plural adjective), the second *euschēmona.* The first prefix is *alpha*-negative. The second, *eu,* means "good" or "noble."

*Aschēmon* (singular) occurs only here in the NT. *Schēma* from which we get "scheme," means "figure" or "fashion." Schneider notes that it "always refers to what may be known from without" (TDNT, 1:954). *Aschēmon* is defined by Thayer as meaning "indecent, unseemly"— what is usually covered up, so that it cannot be seen.

*Euschēmona* is used here for "the comely parts of the body that need no covering" (Thayer, p. 263). Greeven says that the adjective literally means "of good external appearance" (TDNT, 2:771).

The application that Paul seems to be making is that the members of Christ's Body who do not receive much public honor are still necessary. Each Christian is an essential part of the Body of Christ.

## Apostles (12:28)

In this verse Paul mentions eight types of ministry in the church. The first is that of apostles.

Who were the apostles in the Early Church? Are there still apostles in the church of today? Neither of these questions is easy to answer.

The Greek noun *apostolos* comes from the verb *apostellō,* which means "send with a commission, or on service." So *apostolos* is "a messenger, one sent on a mission." Abbott-Smith continues his definition by saying: "In NT, an *apostle* of Christ *(a)* with special reference to the Twelve . . . , equality with whom is claimed by St. Paul . . . *(b)* in a wider sense of prominent Christian teachers, as Barnabas, Acts 14:14, apparently also Silvanus and Timothy, 1 Thess. 2:6, and perhaps Andronicus and Junias (Junia?), Rom. 16:7 . . . ; of false teachers, claiming apostleship" (p. 55). It is evident that the word has a variety of applications in the NT.

In his long article on *apostolos* in Kittel's *Theological Dictionary of the New Testament,* Rengstorf shows that in classical and early Hellenistic Greek there is no parallel to the NT use of this word. This is true even of the Septuagint, Josephus, and Philo (1:408).

The word is found 79 times in the NT. Paul and Luke (his close companion) each use it 34 times (68 out of the 79). It occurs three times in Revelation, twice in 2 Peter, and once each in Matthew, Mark, John, Hebrews, 1 Peter, and Jude. Paul has it at the beginning of 9 of his 13 Epistles.

*Apostolos* is used for messenger, "one sent" in John 13:16. In 2 Cor. 8:23 Paul applies this term to the commissioned representatives of local church congregations. "Finally, *apostoloi* is a comprehensive term for 'bearers of the NT message'" (TDNT, 1:422). It is used primarily for the 12 apostles chosen and commissioned by Christ. This is the dominant usage in Luke's Gospel and Acts.

Then we also find the wider spread suggested by Abbott-Smith. Paul and Barnabas were first of all apostles of the church at Antioch. But Paul calls himself, at the beginning of his epistles, "an apostle of Jesus Christ." Luke does not hesitate to speak of Paul and Barnabas as apostles (Acts 14:4, 14).

The first apostle was Jesus himself (Heb. 3:1), sent from God. Rengstorf comments: "Here the only possible meaning of *apostolos* is that in Jesus there has taken place the definitive revelation of God by God himself (1:2)" (TDNT, 1:423). All other apostles are direct representatives of Jesus.

Are there apostles today in the Church? In a general, unofficial, nontechnical sense, yes. But it may well be questioned whether apostolic authority as found in the first-century Church has carried over to subsequent centuries. Acts 1:21-22 indicates that an apostle was to be one who had been in close contact with Christ during His earthly ministry and who could be a witness of His resurrection. Paul fulfilled the latter requirement (1 Cor. 15:8), but not the former one. However, he was careful to state that he had "received" the necessary information (1 Cor. 15:3).

Charles H. Spurgeon was perhaps a bit severe when he characterized apostolic succession as laying empty hands on empty heads. But many of those who claim apostolic succession today hardly show themselves to be true representatives of the Christ of the NT.

## Prophets (12:28)

The Greek *prophētēs* comes from the verb *prophēmi,* which means "speak forth." So it signifies "one who acts as an interpreter or forth-teller of the Divine will" (A-S, p. 390). Contrary to popular usage today, the biblical meaning of "prophecy" is not foretelling, but forth-telling. Put in simplest terms, the prophet is one who speaks for God.

In Kittel's *Theological Dictionary of the New Testament,* Friedrich has a lengthy article on *prophētēs* and its cognate terms in the New Testament. He notes some differences between OT and NT prophets. He says that "prophecy is not restricted to a few men and women in primitive Christianity. According to Acts 2:4; 4:31, all are filled with the prophetic Spirit and, according to Acts 2:16 ff., it is a specific mark of the age of fulfilment that the Spirit does not only lay hold of individuals but that all members of the eschatological community without distinction are called to prophesy" (6:849).

But our present passage, as well as Eph. 4:11, shows that there was a special gift of prophecy in the Early Church. It is ranked first, as the best gift after "apostles," in our present passage as well as 14:1.

Has the gift of prophecy continued? In the second century the Montanists went to unfortunate extremes in their claims for this gift. Friedrich writes: "With the repudiation of Montanism prophecy came to an end in the Church" (6:860). On the other hand, many Bible scholars believe that the NT prophets were essentially preachers, and so this gift of the Spirit is present today.

## Helps (12:28)

The Greek word *antilēmpsis* (only here in NT) is used

in the Septuagint and papyri in the sense of "help." Abbott-Smith thinks that here it is used for the "ministrations of deacons" (p. 41). Cremer says that the word is "taken by the Greek expositors uniformly as answering to *deacons* (implying the duties towards the poor and sick)" (p. 386).

## Governments (12:28)

*Kybernēsis* is likewise found only here in the NT. It comes from the verb meaning to guide or steer. In classical Greek it referred to the piloting of a boat. Then it was used metaphorically for "government." Beyer writes that, in view of its literal meaning and attested usage, "The reference can only be to the specific gifts which qualify a Christian to be a helmsman to his congregation, i.e., a true director to its order and therewith of its life" (3:1036). The word may be translated "gifts of administration" (NIV).

## Tongues of Men (13:1)

The form *lalō*, "I speak," can be either indicative or subjunctive. But the *ean* at the beginning of the sentence shows that it is subjunctive. Charles B. Williams, in his translation *The New Testament* (1937), always makes a careful distinction between the Greek moods and tenses. He renders this: "If I could speak." F. F. Bruce, in his *The Letters of Paul: An Expanded Paraphrase* (1965), has: "I may speak."

The Corinthians prided themselves on their elegance and eloquence in public speaking. Paul, the Jew, was not their ideal. His opponents in the church at Corinth sneered: "His bodily presence is weak, and his speech contemptible" (2 Cor. 10:10). So Paul says, "If I could speak with the tongues of men."

## Tongues of Angels (13:1)

He did not stop with "men," but added: "even of angels." (The Greek *kai* can be translated by either "and" or "even.") It was a remote possibility—"but if."

Chapters 12, 13, and 14—all three—deal with the problem of speaking in tongues at Corinth. The abuse of this gift was causing confusion and division in the church. The Corinthian Christians were far more concerned about the gifts of the Spirit than the Giver of those gifts. They were forgetting the great Gift, the Holy Spirit (Acts 2:38). And so they were divided.

The place that chapter 13 occupies is clearly indicated by the last verse of chapter 12 and the first verse of 14. In 12:31 he says: "But covet earnestly the best gifts"—not tongues which is at the bottom of the list (vv. 28-30), but prophecy (cf. 14:1)—"and yet shew I unto you a more excellent way"—the way of love (c. 13). Then in 14:1, after describing love, he commands: "Follow the way of love" (NIV).

But the reference to speaking in the tongues of angels shows the connection also. Evidently some of those who spoke in tongues at Corinth claimed to be speaking the language of angels. A few years ago the official organ of a certain denomination made this claim for those who now speak in tongues. Such an attitude fosters spiritual pride— the worst pride of all—and causes schisms in the Church of Jesus Christ today, as it did in ancient Corinth.

## Charity or Love? (13:1)

Paul declared that even if he could speak in the tongues of men or angels, it would all be hollow and meaningless if he did not have "love." The word is *agapē*, the highest word for "love" in the NT.

The verb *agapaō* occurs 142 times in the NT. In the KJV it is translated "love" 135 times ("beloved" 7 times). The noun *agapē* is found 116 times. It is translated "love" 86 times and "charity" 27 times.

One of the most pronounced blunders of KJV translators was the use of "charity" for "love." Nearly 100 years ago Lias wrote: "The AV has unfortunately departed here from the earlier rendering *love* of Tyndale and Cranmer (which the Revised Version has restored) and has followed the Vulgate *caritas*. Thus the force of this eloquent panegyric on love is impaired, and the agreement between the various writers of the New Testament much obscured. . . . The English word *charity* has never risen to the height of the Apostle's argument. At best it does but signify a kindly interest in and forbearance towards others. It is far from suggesting the ardent, active, energetic principle which the Apostle had in view" (p. 146).

The KJV (1611) was largely a revision of the Bishop's Bible (1568) and since the bishops of the Church of England at that time were barely out of the Roman Catholic church, their love for the Latin Vulgate was still strong. So they used "charity," and 43 years later it was retained in the KJV.

The Greeks had three verbs for *love: eran, philein,* and *agapan* (to cite the infinitive forms). Stauffer writes: *"eran* is passionate love which desires the other for itself" (TDNT, 1:35). From the Greek noun *eros* we get *erotic,* with all its sensual connotations. That is why *eros* and *eran* are not found in the NT.

The second verb, *philein (phileō)* occurs 25 times. It is translated "love" 22 times and "kiss" 3 times. This shows that it refers to the love of the affections. The noun *philia* is found only once (James 4:4) and is translated "friendship." So *philia* is affectionate friendship.

We have already noted how frequently *agapē* and

*agapaō* occur in the NT. Of the relationship between this concept and that of *eros,* Stauffer says: *"Eros* is a general love of the world seeking satisfaction wherever it can. *Agapan* is a love which makes distinctions, choosing and keeping to its object. . . . *Agapan* relates for the most part to the love of God, to the love of the higher lifting up the lower, elevating the lower above others. *Eros* seeks in others the fulfilment of its own life's hunger. *Agapan* must often be translated 'to show love'; it is a giving, active love on the other's behalf" (TDNT, 1:37). He adds: "It is indeed striking that the substantive *agapē* is almost completely lacking in pre-biblical Greek" *(ibid.).* The Greek *agapaō* occurs about 275 times in the Septuagint, most often in the Psalms. *Agapē* is found only 20 times. In the NT it is the dominant word for "love." God is *agapē* (1 John 4:8, 16). His love for the world of sinners is expressed by the verb *agapaō* (John 3:16). We are commanded to love *(agapan)* God with all our being (Matt. 22:37) and to love our neighbor as ourselves (Matt. 22:39). Christian love is *agapē* love.

## Tinkling or Clanging? (13:1)

*Alalazon* is a participle of the verb *alalazō* (only here in NT). It comes from a battle cry of that day, *"Alala!"* So it literally means "raise a war cry." Obviously "tinkling" is too tame a translation. Robertson and Plummer write: *"Alalazon* imitates loud and prolonged noise" (p. 289). They go on to say:

> Cymbals are often mentioned in the OT, but nowhere else in the NT: and in St Paul's day they were much used in the worship of Dionysus, Cybele, and the Corybantes. Seeing that he insists so strongly on the unedifying character of the Tongues (XIV), as being of no service to the congregation without a special interpreter, it is quite possible that he is here comparing

unintelligible tongues in Christian worship with the din of gongs and cymbals in pagan worship. Or he may be pointing out the worthlessness of extravagant manifestations of emotion, which proceed not from the heart, but from hollowness. Cymbals were hollow, to increase the noise. Or he may be saying that tongues without Christian love are as senseless as the unmusical and distracting noise of a soulless instrument *(ibid.)*.

## Feed the Poor (13:3)

"Bestow . . . to feed the poor" is all one word in Greek, *psōmisō* (only here and Rom. 12:20). The verb comes from the noun *psōmos,* "a morsel." So it means *"to feed with morsels* (as children, or the sick), hence, generally in late writers, *to feed, nourish"* (A-S, p. 489). Lias suggests: "If I feed people one by one with all my goods" (CGT, in *loco*). C. B. Williams translates it: "If I should dole out everything I have for charity."

## Burn or Boast? (13:3)

C. B. Williams reads: "And give my body up to torture in mere boasting pride." Goodspeed has: "And give myself up, but do it in pride." What is the basis for this?

The answer is that the three oldest manuscripts of 1 Corinthians—Papyrus 46 (3rd century), Vaticanus and Sinaiticus (4th century)—have *kauchēsōmai* (to boast) rather than *kauthēsōmai* (to burn). (In the Greek the difference is only one letter.) But many feel there is stronger internal evidence for *kauthēsōmai* and so most versions have "burned."

## Longsuffering and Kind (13:4)

Having shown the absolute necessity of love (vv. 1-3),

the apostle now goes on to describe the characteristics of love (vv. 4-7). He first says that it "suffereth long, and is kind" (KJV). In the Greek this is: *makrothymei, chrēsteu-etai*. The first verb is from the adjective *makrothymos,* "long-tempered," and so means "is patient or long-suffer-ing." The second (only here in the NT) means to be kind. The first is passive—not retaliating. The second is active —bestowing benefits. The best translation is: "Love is patient, love is kind." The twofold statement stands as a daily challenge to every Christian.

## Vaunteth Not Itself (13:4)

The verb *perpereuomai* is found only here in the NT—or LXX. Robertson and Plummer translate: "Does not play the braggart." They add: "Ostentation is the chief idea." Today we would say, "it does not boast" (NIV).

## Unseemly (13:5)

"Behave itself unseemly" is *aschēmonei* (only here and 7:36, where it is translated "behaveth himself uncome-ly"). It means "act unbecomingly, behave dishonourably" (A-S). F. F. Bruce reads: "Never acts dishonourably." G. G. Findlay writes: "Love imparts a delicacy of feeling beyond the rules of politeness" (EGT, 2:899).

## Not Easily Provoked (13:5)

There is no basis in the Greek for the modifier "eas-ily." It has been suggested that it was added because King James had such a violent temper! The verb is *paroxynetai* (only here and Acts 17:16).

Robertson and Plummer comment: "Not merely 'does not fly into a rage' but 'does not yield to provocation'; it is

not embittered by injuries, whether real or supposed"
(ICC, *in loco*).

## Thinketh no Evil (13:5)

The verb is *logizomai,* which literally means "count"
or "reckon." Then it has the metaphorical sense of "take
into account." Thayer notes that it is "a favorite word with
the Apostle Paul, being used (exclusive of quotations)
some 27 times in his epistles, and only four times in the
rest of the NT" (p. 379). For this passage he suggests the
translation "to pass to one's account, to impute." So
the Greek literally says, "does not impute the evil"; that
is, "it keeps no records of wrong" (NIV).

## Beareth or Protects? (13:7)

The verb *stegō* is related to the noun *stegē,* which
means "a roof." Its literal meaning is "to cover closely, to
protect by covering" (A-S). In 1 Thess. 3:1, 5, and 1 Cor.
9:12 (its only other NT occurrences), it seems to mean
"endure." But Kasch says, "The most difficult passage is
1 Cor. 13:7" (TDNT, 7:586). He favors the translation
"covers all things" (*ibid.,* p. 587). Another rendering is "it
always protects" (NIV).

## Fail . . . Vanish Away (13:8)

After pointing out the Primacy of Love (vv. 1-3) and
the Perfection of Love (vv. 4-7), Paul now asserts the
Permanence of Love (vv. 8-13). He declares that love never
"fails." The Greek is *piptei,* which literally means "falls."
But here, as in some other places, it carries the idea of
falling into ruin.

This verse affords an illustration of a frequent translator's fault--translating two different Greek words by the same English word, and translating the same Greek word by two English words. "Faileth," as we have just noted, is the verb *piptō*. But "fail" is *katargeō,* which at the end of the verse is rendered "vanish away." The verb *katargeō* means "put out of action." Prophecies will disappear when the reality comes.

## Tongues (13:8)

In view of the discussion of the gift of tongues in chapters 12 and 14, the most natural way to take *glossai* would be as meaning speaking in tongues, which will finally cease. But the word also means "languages." So the reference could be to the fact that the various languages which began at Babel will come to an end in the beautiful unity of eternity. There will be no language barrier in heaven.

## Childish Things or Ways? (13:11)

The Greek could equally well be translated "things" or "ways." But the latter is much more meaningful. Many "adults" (chronologically, not psychologically) have put away their *things* of childhood—dolls and toys—but they have never given up their childish *ways* of reacting to life. They still throw a fit when they can't have their own way.

## Glass or Mirror? (13:12)

The Greek word *esoptron* is found (in NT) only here and in Jas. 1:23. It simply means "mirror." Findlay writes: "Ancient mirrors made of burnished metal—a specialty of Corinth—were poor reflectors; the art of silvering glass was discovered in the 13th century" (EGT, 2:901). So "mirror" is the better translation.

## Darkly (13:12)

This is two words in Greek, *en ainigmati*, "in an enigma, or riddle" (only here in NT). The Greek says: "For we see at present by means of a mirror in a riddle." When we can see only enigmatically we should be careful how we speak dogmatically!

## Pursuing Love (14:1)

"Follow after charity" (KJV). The Greek literally says, "Keep on pursuing love." A good paraphrase would be: "Make love your lifelong pursuit." The verb *diōkō* means "zealously to follow" (Oepke, *"diōkō,"* TDNT, 2:230).

This may suggest that love is a rather elusive thing. And this is true. We do not find love by wishful thinking or by halfhearted effort. We have to pursue it eagerly every day, if we are going to find it operating in our lives as it should. We must ask the Holy Spirit, who makes us perfect in love, to help us express that love to others constantly in a Christlike way. When one makes love his lifelong pursuit, he discovers that his capacity for loving those around him grows with the years.

## Unknown? (14:2)

We hear a great deal these days about speaking in unknown tongues. The supposed scriptural support for this is the fact that five times in this chapter (vv. 2, 4, 14, 19, 27) Paul talks about speaking "in an unknown tongue."

However, the word "unknown" is in italics in every case, indicating thereby that it is not in the Greek. So we have no right to quote it as support for argument. The Greek simply says, "in a tongue." This could mean a foreign language, as it clearly does in Acts 2:4-11. "No man understandeth him" would then mean that no one present understood this particular foreign language.

## Edification (14:3)

The Greek word is *oikodomē*. It comes from *oikos*, "house," and *demō*, "build." So it literally means "the act of building." In the NT it is used only in the metaphorical sense of "building up."

Does the word "edification" suggest to us the idea of "building up," as one would build a house? Perhaps not. Arndt and Gingrich (p. 561) say that *oikodomē* has the figurative sense of "spiritual strengthening" (cf. NIV). Michel writes: "In the N.T. *oikodomē* is a familiar figure of speech which is primarily used for the community" (TDNT, 5:145). This is clearly its context in verse 5, and probably throughout this chapter (vv. 3, 5, 12, 26). Paul had already said in 3:9, "Ye are God's building" *(oikodomē)*. So here he is pleading for the building up of the Corinthian congregation as a "temple of God" (3:16), where God can dwell and manifest himself. And here in verse 4 he declares that it is prophesying—that is, preaching the Word of God—which builds up the church, not speaking in tongues.

That is the main test of tongues in this chapter. In public worship we should have only what "builds up" the church.

## Exhortation (14:3)

The Greek word is *paraclēsis*. In the New Testament (KJV) this noun is translated "consolation" 14 times, "exhortation" 8 times, and "comfort" 6 times—plus "entreaty" once. Since the last word in this verse *(para-*

*mythia,* only here in NT) clearly means "comfort," some other translation is used for *paraclēsis.*

The meaning of this word oscillates between "exhortation" and "comfort." It would seem that "encouragement" (NIV) best spans the gap between these two senses, which are rather different in English.

This is a good example of the frequently illustrated fact that no two words in different languages have exactly the same meaning. Dr. Nida of the American Bible Society says, "Words in different languages do not have formal equivalence; they have only dynamic equivalence." Anyone who works at the job of translating soon discovers how true this is.

## Pipe or Flute? (14:7)

The word *aulos* (only here in NT) comes from *aō,* a verb meaning "to blow." So it refers to a "wind instrument," probably a flute. It is joined here with *kithara,* "harp." The two terms together, then, could be thought of as representing all the wind and stringed instruments of music.

## Easy to Be Understood (14:9)

This is one word in Greek, the adjective *eusēmon* (only here in NT). It literally means "good sign" (*eu,* "good," plus *"sēma,"* "sign"). So it indicates here a word that signifies something. It may be translated "intelligible" (NIV). G. Abbott-Smith says that it means "clear to the understanding, distinct" (p. 189). Arndt and Gingrich translate the whole phrase "utter intelligible speech" (p. 326).

## Without Signification (14:10)

The Greek word is *aphōnon.* It is composed of *alpha-*

negative and *phōnē*, "sound." So it literally means "sound-less" or "voiceless." But here it carries the connotation of "unintelligible" (A-S, p. 72).

## Barbarian (14:11)

The Greek word (twice here) is *barbaros*. Windisch says, "The basic meaning of this word . . . is 'stammering,' 'stuttering,' 'uttering unintelligible sounds.'" Then we have "the transition to the most important usage, i.e., 'of a strange speech,' or 'the one who speaks a strange language' (i.e., other than Greek)" (TDNT, 1:546).

It is in the first sense that the word is used here. The one who utters "unintelligible sounds" in a church service does not help anybody. Paul says, "Try to excel in gifts that build up the church" (v. 12, NIV).

## Understanding or Mind? (14:14-15)

The term *understanding* is found three times in these two verses. The Greek word is *nous*, "mind." Paul says that he will pray and sing not only with his spirit but also with his mind. God made us intelligent creatures, and He expects us to use that intelligence, not scuttle it. True worship involves the intellect, the emotions, and the will. It is the whole person worshiping God.

## Unlearned or Ungifted? (14:16, 23, 24)

The Greek word in all three of these verses is *idiōtēs*. Aside from here, it is found (in NT) only in Acts 4:13 ("ignorant") and 2 Cor. 11:6 ("rude").

The term comes from the adjective *idios*, which means "one's own," or "private." So it first meant a private individual as distinct from a public person or official. Schlier shows that in Greek usage it finally signified "the 'outsider' or 'alien' as distinct from a member" (TDNT, 3:216). He also notes that there is no fixed translation for this word; it takes its exact sense from the context.

What does it mean here in 1 Corinthians 14? Schlier says that it is "the one who does not have the gift of tongues or the interpretation of tongues. He is expressly described as one who 'does not know what thou sayest,' and who consequently cannot say Amen to the charismatic thanksgiving of the man who speaks with tongues" (TDNT, 3:217).

In vv. 23 and 24 the *idiōtēs* is linked with "unbeliever." On this basis Schlier writes: "The *idiōtai* are those who do not belong to the community though they join in its gatherings. They are first characterized as such by the fact that they do not understand speaking with tongues, and then by the fact that they are not members (v. 24)" *(ibid.)*.

## Understanding or Thinking? (14:20)

This is not the same word that is translated "understanding" in vv. 14-15 (see above). Rather, it is *phrēn* (only here in NT), which Thayer defines as "the faculty of perceiving and judging" (p. 648).

The literal meaning of the word was the physical diaphram which controls the breath. Bertram notes that the term "was early regarded as the seat of the intellectual and spiritual activity" (TDNT, 9:220). With regard to its use here, he says: "To give preference to speaking with tongues as an immediate utterance of the Spirit is childish, 1 Cor. 14:20. The Corinthians should use their reason, which includes emotion and will, and achieve perfection therein" (TDNT, 9:230). Probably the best translation is "thinking" (NASB, RSV, NIV).

## Malice or Evil? (14:20)

Today "malice" means "the desire to harm others, or to see others suffer" (Am. Heritage Dict., p. 790). But here the Greek word is simply *kakia*, which means "evil" (so in most modern versions).

## Be Ye Children (14:20)

This is one word in Greek, *nēpiazete* (only here in NT). It comes from *nēpios*, "infant," and so means literally "be an infant." Paul is urging the Corinthian Christians to stop being (pres. tense) childish in their thinking, but at the same time to be always (pres. tense) childlike in regard to evil: that is, be innocent.

## Men or Mature? (14:20)

The word translated "men" (KJV) is the adjective *teleios*, "complete," "perfect," or "mature." A good rendering of this verse is: "Brothers, stop thinking like children. In regard to evil be infants, but in your thinking be adults" (NIV).

## Doctrine or Teaching? (14:26)

The Greek word *didachē* occurs 30 times in the NT. In the KJV it is rendered "has been taught" once, and "doctrine" all the other times. But the noun comes from the verb *didaskō*, which is always correctly translated "teach" (97 times). So the noun should be "teaching." "Doctrine" is too theological a term.

## Judge or Weigh? (14:29)

Paul says that only two or three prophets should speak

in a service, and let the listeners "judge." The verb is *diakrinō*. Properly it means "distinguish, discriminate, discern," but Abbott-Smith goes on to suggest that here it means "settle, decide, judge" (p. 108). Arndt and Gingrich (p. 184) give for this place: "Pass judgment" (NASB). But "weigh" (RSV) or "weigh carefully" (NIV) seems to fit well. However, Buechsel suggests the meaning "assess," and comments: "The reference is not so much to what the prophets say as to the spirits of the prophets, 12:10" (TDNT, 3:947).

## Decently or Properly? (14:40)

Besides this place, the adverb *euschēmonōs* is found (in NT) only in Rom. 13:13 and 1 Thess. 4:12. In both places it is translated "honestly"—"walk honestly" (KJV). Arndt and Gingrich suggest for our passage "properly" (cf. NASB). The NIV translates this verse: "But everything should be done in a fitting and orderly way." This is the way we should conduct our church services.

## Keep in Memory (15:2)

The Greek has one word, *katechete.* The verb *katechō* means "hold fast" (NASB) or "hold firmly" (NIV). Paul clearly asserts here that our finally being saved depends on our holding firmly to the Word of the gospel.

## Rose or Was Raised? (15:4)

The verb is *egeirō*. Arndt and Gingrich say that it means "figuratively *raise, help to rise,* " as of a fallen or sick or dead person, and specifically "of the raising of Jesus" (p. 213).

Here and in v. 12 the form is the perfect passive,

*egēgertai,* which literally means "has been raised" (see v. 12, NASB, NIV). The English Revised Version (1881) reads "hath been raised." Vincent approves this and notes: *"Died* and *was buried* are in the aorist tense. The change to the perfect marks the abiding state which began with the resurrection. He hath been raised and still lives" (3:273). The perfect tense in Greek indicates completed action and a continuing state with primary emphasis on the continuation.

Paul's theology stresses the fact that God raised Christ from the dead (6:14; 15:15; 2 Cor. 4:14). That is the reason for the translation "was raised" in the NASB and NIV.

## Was Seen or Appeared? (15:5-8)

Four times in these four verses we have the expression "he was seen" (KJV). This is the literal translation of *ōphthe* (aorist passive of *horaō,* "see"). The aorist tense suggests a single event in each case—the Risen Christ was seen by different ones at different times.

This word may also be translated "appeared" (NASB, NIV). And so we find in 1 Corinthians (A.D. 55) the earliest list of the post-resurrection appearances of Jesus. (The four Gospels were written later.)

Paul begins with Christ's appearance to Peter (v. 5), although we know from the Gospels that He appeared first to the women who came early on Easter Sunday morning (John 20:11-18; Matt. 28:9). But Peter was the first prominent leader in the Early Church. It was he who assumed charge of the 120 in the Upper Room (Acts 1:15) and who delivered the sermon on the Day of Pentecost (Acts 2:14) that resulted in 3,000 being saved (Acts 2:41). The Lord used him in the healing of the cripple at the Beautiful Gate of the Temple (Acts 3:4-7) and in preaching the subsequent sermon (Acts 3:12-26). The same Peter who had denied his Lord, now filled with the Holy Spirit, stood boldly before the Sanhedrin and accused the Jewish leaders of murdering their Messiah (Acts 4:8-12).

The last appearance was to Paul ("me also," v. 8). The significant thing is that Paul uses the same verb that he used for the previous appearances. He thereby claims that he actually saw Jesus in visible form. It was no hallucination. That is why Paul emphasizes the Resurrection so strongly in his Epistles.

## Cephas (15:5)

This is a Greek transliteration of the Aramaic word for "stone" (see John 1:42; Matt. 16:18).

## One Born out of Due Time (15:8)

In the Greek this is simply the definite article with the noun *ektrōma* (only here in the NT). It may be translated "one untimely born" (NASB) or "one abnormally born" (NIV).

Arndt and Gingrich define *ektrōma* as meaning "untimely birth, miscarriage." They go on to say: "So Paul calls himself, perhaps taking up an insult hurled at him by his opponents" (p. 246).

Wyclif translated the word as "a dead-born child." Marvin Vincent writes: "Paul means that when Christ appeared to him and called him, he was—as compared to the disciples who had known and followed Him from the first, and whom he had been persecuting—no better than an unperfected foetus among living men. The comparison emphasizes his condition at the time of his call" (3:274).

## Meet or Fit? (15:9)

More than 800 words in the KJV have changed their

meaning in the last 350 years. "Meet" is one of them. The Greek adjective is *hikanos,* one of whose meanings is "fit, appropriate, competent, qualified . . . worthy" (AG, p. 375). The simplest translation is "fit." In the light of his previous persecution of the "church of God," Paul felt that he was not fit to be called an apostle. However, he adds the significant assertion: "But by the grace of God I am what I am" (v. 10).

## Laboured More Abundantly (15:10)

This translation is accurate, but hardly contemporary. The verb is *kopiaō,* which means "work hard, toil" (AG, p. 444). "More abundantly" is the word *perissoteron,* which Arndt and Gingrich translate as "even more." Today we would say, "I worked harder" (Phillips, NIV).

## Rose or Was Raised? (15:12-17)

The verb *egeirō* occurs nine times in these six consecutive verses. In the NT it is found 141 times. Of these, 73, or slightly more than half, refer to the resurrection of the dead. Of these 73, again, some 48, or about two-thirds, refer to the resurrection of Jesus. There are other references in the NT to the resurrection of Jesus, but about 50 places use this word.

The verb occurs many times in each of the four Gospels. But there are less references to the resurrection from the dead and comparatively few to the resurrection of Jesus. That is easily understood, because most of the material of the Gospels relates to Jesus' ministry before His death and resurrection.

When we come to Acts, the picture changes abruptly. Seven of the 14 occurrences of this word refer to resurrection, and all but one to the resurrection of Jesus. In Romans we find the word 10 times, 9 of which refer to the resurrection of Jesus.

But it is in the great Resurrection Chapter (1 Corinthians 15) that we find it most frequently (19 times). In every instance it refers to resurrection from the dead, nine times to the resurrection of Jesus.

We have already noted (on v. 4) that the best translation here is not "rose," but "has been raised" (NASB, NIV). God raised Christ from the dead (v. 15): that is Pauline theology.

## No Resurrection? (15:12)

After the introductory section on the resurrection of Christ (vv. 1-11), Paul deals in this chapter with two basic matters: (1) The fact of the resurrection (vv. 12-34), and (2) The nature of the resurrection (vv. 35-58). These are the two main divisions of this chapter. The first topic is introduced with the question: "How say some among you that there is no resurrection of the dead?" (v. 12). The second is triggered by the twofold question: "How are the dead raised? With what kind of body will they come?" (v. 35, NIV).

The word for "resurrection" here is *anastasis,* which occurs 38 times in the NT. Nine of these times it refers to the resurrection of Jesus. Literally it means "a standing up." Over half of its occurrences are in the Gospels (16 times) and Acts (11 times).

In the Greek inscriptions around the time of Christ *anastasis* is used for the "erection" of a monument or the "setting up" of a statue. But the idea of a resurrection from the dead was foreign to Greek thinking, as Paul's experience at Athens shows. Oepke says that for the Greeks "Resurrection is impossible" (TDNT, 1:369).

The noun *anastasis* comes from the verb *anistēmi,*

which means "raise up." It is used some 23 times for the resurrection of Jesus. The noun *egersis* (from the verb *egeiro*) is found only once in the NT (Matt. 27:53). The same is true of *exanastasis,* literally "a standing up out of," found only in Phil. 3:11. Putting all these words together, we find that there are over 80 definite references in the NT to the resurrection of Jesus. It is a striking fact that the word "resurrection" does not occur in the OT.

How may we be certain that we shall share in the "resurrection of life" (John 5:29)? The answer is plain. If we have experienced an inner, spiritual resurrection, we have abundant assurance of our final resurrection.

## Of, About, or Against? (15:15)

Paul says, "We have testified of God that he raised up Christ" (KJV). The NASB reads "against God" and the NIV "about God." Which is right?

The Greek preposition is *kata,* the root meaning of which is "down." It sometimes does have the meaning "down upon" and so "against." Arndt and Gingrich devote six columns to defining this small word. They give as one meaning "with respect to" (p. 408). In their volume in the ICC series, Robertson and Plummer say: "The meaning 'respecting' or 'about' is fairly common in classical Greek, although not in the NT, and is perhaps to be preferred here" (pp. 348-49). We agree.

## Miserable or to Be Pitied? (15:19)

The word is *eleeinoteroi,* the comparative of the adjective *eleeinos* (only here and in Rev. 3:17). The comparative in Greek often signifies the superlative. It comes from the noun *eleos,* "mercy" or "pity," and the verb *eleeō,* "have pity or mercy on." So it means "most pitiable" or "most to be pitied" (NASB, NIV).

## Communications or Company? (15:33)

The noun *homilia* (only here in NT) means "company, association" (A-S, p. 316). Later on it came to be used for a sermon given in a church, and so we have "homily" and "homiletics." But here Arndt and Gingrich (p. 568) say that the adjective and noun mean "bad company" (NASB, NIV).

## Manners or Morals? (15:33)

The Greek word *ethos* (only here in NT) is used in the sense of "custom" or "manner." But Robertson and Plummer (ICC) translate this old Greek proverb: "Evil companionships mar good morals" or "Bad company spoils noble characters" (p. 363). The NASB has "morals," the NIV "character."

## Fool or Foolish? (15:36)

Four different Greek words in the NT are translated "fool" in the KJV. *Anoētos* (6 times) and *asophos* (only in Eph. 5:15) are mild terms. The first means "thoughtless," the second "unwise." A third word, *mōros* (accusative, *mōron*) sometimes has moral connotations. It occurs 13 times in the NT.

But the word here is *aphrōn* (11 times in the NT). It literally means "mindless" or "senseless." Arndt and Gingrich define it as "foolish, ignorant" (p. 127). Bertram writes: "In 1 Cor. 15:36, Paul is not pronouncing a definitive judgement with his *aphrōn*. It is a rhetorical appeal for true understanding. To cling to the negative view is to adopt the position of the *aphrōn* which is close to that of ungodliness" (TDNT, 9:231).

In view of all this, "Thou fool" (KJV) or "You fool!" (NASB) seems a bit too harsh. A better rendering would seem to be "you foolish man!" (RSV) or "How foolish!" (NIV).

## Quickened or Come to Life? (15:36)

The verb is *zōopoieō,* from *poieō,* "make," and *zōos* "alive." So it means "come to life" (RSV, NASB, NIV). Of the 12 times this verb occurs in the NT, it is translated "quicken" 9 times (see v. 45). But that is obsolete terminology.

## Corruption or Perishable? (15:42, 50)

The Greek word *phthora* does mean "corruption" or "destruction." But Arndt and Gingrich note that in the world of nature (including the human body, as here), it signifies "perishable." Here it means the "state of being perishable" and in verse 50 "that which is perishable" (p. 865). Today the word "perishable" (RSV, NASB, NIV) conveys the sense better than "corruption."

## Natural (15:44)

This verse is the crucial one in answering the second question of verse 35: "With what kind of body will they come?" (NIV). Here Paul says: "It is sown a natural body; it is raised a spiritual body."

What is meant by "natural"? The Greek word is *psychicos,* "psychical."

Abbott-Smith says that *psychicos* means "of the psychē (as the lower part of the immaterial in man), EV, *natural"* (p. 489). Arndt and Gingrich write: *"pertaining to the soul* or *life,* in our literature always denoting the life of the natural world and whatever belongs to it, in contrast to the supernatural world, which is characterized by *pneuma"* (p. 902). They translate here "a physical body" (cf. RSV). They also suggest "physical" in verse 46.

Schweizer writes: "The psychical is neither sinful as such nor does it incline to the *pneuma.* But it is corruptible and finds no access into God's kingdom, v. 50" (TDNT, 9:662).

Commenting on verses 42-44, Robertson and Plummer (ICC) say (p. 372):

> Hitherto the answer to the second question (of v. 35) has been indirect: it now becomes direct. The risen body is incorruptible, glorious, powerful, spiritual. It is quite obvious that the corpse which is "sown" is none of these things. It is in corruption before it reaches the grave. . . . It is absolutely powerless, unable to move a limb. The last epithet, *psychicon,* is less appropriate to a corpse, but it comes in naturally enough to distinguish the body which is being dissolved from the body which will be raised. The former was by nature subject to the laws and conditions of physical life *(psychē),* the latter will be controlled only by the spirit *(pneuma),* and this spirit will be in harmony with the spirit of God. In the material body the spirit has been limited and hampered in its action; in the future body it will have perfect freedom of action and consequently complete control, and man will at last be, what God created him to be, a being in which the higher self is supreme.

F. Godet, in his two-volume *Commentary on the First Epistle of St. Paul to the Corinthians,* has the best discussion of verse 44 that we have found. He translates the first half of the verse, "It is sown a psychical body, it is raised a spiritual body," and then comments (2:413):

> The terms *animated* or *animal-body* are the only ones in our language by which we can render the term reproduced in our translation by the Anglicized Greek

term. The meaning of the epithet is clear; it denotes a body, not of the same substance as the soul itself—otherwise it would not be a body—but formed by and for a soul destined to serve as an organ to that breath of life called *psychē,* which presided over its development. Neither, consequently, is the *spiritual* body a body of a spiritual nature—it would still be less than a body in that case—but a body formed by and for a principle of life, which is a spirit, and fully appropriated to its service.

Then comes a very beautiful description of the change that will take place in the resurrection (2:413-14):

The law of the beings belonging to nature is to revolve uniformly in the same circle; the privilege of spiritual being is to surmount this iron circle and to rise from the natural phase, which for it is only the means, to a higher sphere which is its end. This contrast arises from the wholly different mode of being possessed by the soul and the spirit. The soul is only a breath of life endowed with a certain measure of power, capable of taking hold of a material substance, subjecting it to itself, converting it into its agent, and using this organ for a fixed time up to the moment when it will no longer lend itself to such use. The characteristic of the spirit is that it possesses a life which is constantly being renewed. . . . In a new order of things, after extracting from the body an organ adapted to its nature, it will perpetually renew its strength and glory. Such a body will never be to the principle of its life what the earthly body so often is to the inhabiting soul, a burden and a hindrance: it will be the docile instrument of the spirit, fulfilling its wishes and thoughts with inexhaustible power of action, as we even now see the artist using his hand or his voice with marvelous freedom, and thus foreshadowing the perfect spiritualization of the body. If any one should deny the capacity of matter thus to yield to the action of the spirit, I should ask him to tell me what matter is: then, by way of showing what spiritualized matter may be, I should invite him to consider the human eye, that living mirror in which all the emotions of the soul are expressed in a way so living and powerful. These are simple foreshadowings of the glory of a resurrection body.

## Immortality (15:53-54)

The Greek word is *athanasia* (only here and in 1 Tim. 6:16, where it is applied to God). It comes from *alpha*-negative and *thanatos,* "death." So it literally means "deathlessness." Bultmann writes: "The OT has no equivalent for *athanasia,*" and adds: "In 1 Cor. 15:53 ff. the incorruptible mode of existence of the resurrected is called *athanasia* as in Hellenistic Judaism, the thought being not merely that of eternal duration but of a mode of existence different from that of *sarx* (flesh) and *haima* (blood)" (TDNT, 3:24).

## Collection (16:1-2)

The first thing we note is that "collection" (v. 1) and "gathering" (v. 2) is the same word in the Greek and obviously should be translated the same way in both places.

The Greek word is *logeia* (only here in NT). Deissmann says: "It comes from *logeuō,* 'I collect,' a verb which, like the derivate, was found for the first time comparatively recently in papyri, ostraca, and inscriptions from Egypt and elsewhere. We find it used chiefly of religious collections for a god, a temple, etc., just as St. Paul uses it of his collection of money for the 'saints' at Jerusalem" (LAE, p. 105).

In verse 2 we have a hint of Christian tithing. On the first day of the week each one was to "set aside a sum of money in keeping with his income" (NIV).

## Liberality or Gift? (16:3)

In only one other place in the KJV is the word "liberality" found (2 Cor. 8:2). There the Greek is *haplotēs,* which literally means "simplicity" or "sincerity."

But here it is a very different Greek word, *charis.* Occurring 156 times in the NT, it is translated "grace" 130 times. Here most recent versions have "gift," which is obviously the meaning in this context. But since there are other Greek words that mean "gift" in the sense of something given, the most adequate translation here would be "gracious gift."

These three verses suggest three principles governing our giving. First, it is to be *systematic*—"upon the first day of the week" (v. 2). Second, it is to be *proportionate*—as one is prospered (v. 2). Third, it is to be *voluntary*—a gracious gift, given freely (v. 3). God does not want what is given grudgingly, but what is given gladly. Paul did not want to put on the pressure when he arrived.

## Conduct or Send? (16:11)

"Conduct him forth" suggests something formal and public. The verb *propempō* has this meaning in Acts 20:38 and 21:5. But for this passage Arndt and Gingrich give: *"help on one's journey* with food, money, by arranging for companions, means of travel, etc., *send on one's way"* (p. 716). "Send him on his way" (NASB, NIV) is the simplest translation.

## Quit You like Men (16:13)

This is all one word in Greek, *andrizesthe* (only here in NT). Arndt and Gingrich define this verb as "conduct oneself in a manly or courageous way" (p. 63). Abbott-Smith has simply "play the man" (p. 35). This verb occurs in the Septuagint three times (2 Sam. 10:12; Ps. 27:14; 31:25) in combination with "be strong" *(krataiousthe),* as here. Robertson and Plummer (ICC) render the two, "Be not only manly but mighty" (p. 394).

## Charity or Love? (16:14)

The correct translation is: "Do everything in love" (NIV). That is a most significant command for all of us!

## A Good Addiction (16:15)

In these days of addiction to drugs, alcohol, and tobacco, it is refreshing to read of a family that "addicted themselves to the ministry of the saints." These first converts of Paul in Achaia (specifically Corinth) were now ministering to others.

The verb is *etaxan,* "arranged, ordered, appointed." Robertson and Plummer (ICC) comment: "They had spontaneously taken this service upon themselves. Just as the brethren appointed *(etaxan)* that Paul and Barnabas and others should go to Jerusalem about the question of circumcision (Acts 15:2), so Stephanas and his household appointed themselves *(etaxan heautous)* to the service of their fellow-Christians. It was a self-imposed duty" (p. 395).

Such spontaneous consecration to a ministry to others is an expression of true love. Probably the best translation today is "devoted themselves" (NASB, NIV).

## Anathema (16:22)

In most other places in the NT this word is translated "accursed" (see comments on Rom. 9:3 and Gal. 1:8). But here it is transliterated from the Greek. The one who does not love the Lord Jesus Christ is under a divine curse. (Paul is addressing professing Christians.) Behm says that the word means "something delivered up to divine wrath, dedicated to destruction and brought under a curse" (TDNT, 1:354).

## Maran-atha (16:22)

In the KJV there is no punctuation between Anathema and Maran-atha, though it seems there should be a period. A. T. Robertson says, "It was a curious blunder in the King James Version that connected *Maran-atha* with *Anathema*" (WP, 4:204)—a blessing or prayer, and a curse.

Also, the Bible Society Greek Text has "Maranatha" undivided. According to Edgar J. Goodspeed, the first edition of the KJV (1611) also read, "Let him be Anathema Maranatha," with no separation in the last word (*Problems of NT Translation*, p. 166).

Arndt and Gingrich say that *Maran-atha* means "(our) Lord has come." But they immediately add "better separated *marana-tha* . . . (our) *Lord, come!* an Aramaic formula which, according to *Didache* 10:6, was used in the early Christian liturgy of the Lord's Supper" (p. 492).

The *Didache* comes from the second century. The passage cited is a part of the Thanksgiving that was to be repeated aloud at the close of the Communion service. The people were to say: "Hosannah to the God of David. If any man be holy, let him come! If man be not, let him repent: Maranatha, Amen" (*The Apostolic Fathers* ["Loeb Classical Library"], 1:325). A footnote in this Loeb edition reads: "A transliteration of Aramaic words meaning 'Our Lord! Come!'"

This Didache passage reminds us of the closing promise and prayer of the NT (Rev. 22:20): "'Yes, I am coming quickly.' Amen. Come, Lord Jesus" (NASB).

Robertson and Plummer (ICC) call attention to a

slight problem. They write: "Why St. Paul gives this warning in Aramaic rather than Greek writing to Corinth is unknown. The most probable conjecture is that in this language it had become a sort of motto or password among Christians, and familiar in that shape, like 'Alleluia' with ourselves" (p. 401). The Didache seems to give some support to this view.

It is our privilege and responsibility to live in constant expectation of our Lord's return. This attitude is one of the strongest safeguards against carelessness in conduct, and it also is a powerful incentive to devoted service for our Master.

# 2 CORINTHIANS

❧⊙❦⊙❧

## Consolation or Comfort? (1:3-7)

In the KJV we find the noun "comfort" twice in verses 3 and 4, and "consolation" four times in verses 5-7. The Greek has the same word, *paraklēsis,* throughout. Helpfully and consistently the NASB and NIV have "comfort" in all six places.

We note also that the verb "comfort" *(parakaleō)* occurs three times in verse 4 and once in verse 6. "The God of all comfort" comforts us in all our affliction. By retaining "comfort" for both the noun and the verb we get the full force of the original.

Paul is fond of these words. *Parakaleō* occurs 103 times in the NT, 54 of these in Paul's Epistles. *Paraklēsis* is found 29 times, almost always in Paul (20 times). John and James do not use them at all.

Schmitz calls 2 Corinthians 1 "the great chapter of comfort in the NT" (TDNT, 5:797-98). He goes on to say, "Thus the fellowship of suffering between the apostle and the church becomes a fellowship of comfort, and both in rich measure, 2 C. 1:5-7" (p. 798). Schmitz concludes his discussion of these words by saying:

> The meaning "to comfort," "comfort," "consolation," which is rare in both the Greek world and Hellenistic Judaism, but the more common in the translation Greek of the LXX, is influenced by the OT, and especially by Is. (and the Ps.) when the reference is to salvation history (cf. the "consolation of Israel" in later Judaism). It expresses the divine aid which is already lavishly granted to the members of the suffering community of Jesus by present exhortation and encouraging events, and which will reach its goal when the NT people of God is delivered out of all its tribulations (TDNT, 5:799).

Verse 4 shows why Christians, and especially ministers, must suffer. It is that they may comfort others by the comfort they have themselves received.

## Tribulation or Affliction? (1:4)

The basic meaning of *thlipsis* is "pressure" (see notes on Rom. 2:9). It is the pressures of life that tend to crush us, so that we need the sustaining grace of God.

Both "tribulation" and "trouble" in this verse are *thlipsis* in the Greek. So the translation should be the same in both cases—either "affliction" (NASB) or "trouble" (NIV).

## Pressed or Burdened? (1:8)

The verb *bareō* comes from the noun *baros,* which means "weight" or "burden." This passage suggests the words, "with burdens too heavy to bear." The NASB translates the verb, "we were burdened."

## Out of Measure (1:8)

In the Greek this is *kath' hyperbolēn,* which is more

accurately translated "beyond measure" (Gal. 1:13). In Rom. 7:13 the KJV has "exceeding," and in 1 Cor. 12:31 it reads "more excellent." Aside from these three passages, *hyperbolē* is found only in 2 Corinthians (four times).

The word is compounded of *hyper,* "above" or "beyond," and *ballō,* "throw." So it literally means "a throwing beyond." In the NT it is used metaphorically in the sense of "excellence" or "excess" (as here). So the NASB translates the phrase, "excessively."

## Despaired (1:8)

The verb *exaporeō* (only here and in 4:8) is a strong compound, meaning "to be utterly at a loss, be in despair" (A-S, p. 159). Paul felt as if he was at the end of his rope, as far as this life was concerned.

## Sentence (1:9)

Most modern versions follow the KJV in using "sentence" here. The literal meaning of *apokrima* (only here in NT) is "answer." But Buechsel notes: "It is a technical term of official and legal speech and denotes an official resolution (on an enquiry or petition) which decides the matter" (TDNT, 3:945). He goes on to say: "By human judgment Paul could only reckon that his position was like that of a man condemned to death who had made a petition for mercy and received the answer that he must die" (p. 946).

Arndt and Gingrich agree with this and give the definition: "official report, decision." But probably "sentence of death" communicates the idea best.

## Helping Together (1:11)

Paul is fond of compounds beginning with *syn;* he had

a strong sense of "togetherness." Here we have another one, *synypourgeō* (only here in NT). It means "join in helping us" (AG; cf. NASB).

## Gift or Favor? (1:11)

The word is *charisma,* which (in KJV) is translated "gift" 15 times and "free gift" twice. Found 6 times in Romans and 7 times in 1 Corinthians, it occurs only this one time in 2 Corinthians (plus 1 Tim. 4:14; 2 Tim. 1:6; 1 Pet. 4:10). It comes from *charis,* "grace," and so means "a gift (freely and graciously given), a favor bestowed" (AG, p. 887). It is obvious that "favor" (NASB) or "gracious favor" (NIV) is the preferable translation. The context indicates that it is the favor of being granted deliverance from death.

## Rejoicing or Boast? (1:12)

The noun is *kauchēsis.* In the KJV it is translated "boasting" six times and "rejoicing" four times (plus "glorying" or "glory" twice). The correct meaning is "boast" (NIV) or "proud confidence" (NASB). The same is true of the related noun *kauchēma,* translated "rejoicing" in verse 14.

## Simplicity or Holiness? (1:12)

The KJV has the former term, the NASB and NIV the latter. Why?

Here it is a matter of textual criticism. "Simplicity" translates *haplotēti,* which is found in the fifth century manuscript D and most of the Old Latin manuscripts. But Papyrus 46 (third century), our only two fourth-century manuscripts (Vaticanus and Sinaiticus), and two fifth-century manuscripts (A, C), plus many others, have *hagiotēti,* "holiness." This seems clearly to be the original word.

## Acknowledge or Understand? (1:13-14)

The verb is *epiginoskō.* Occurring 42 times in the NT, it is translated "know" 30 times. Only here (3 times) and twice in 1 Corinthians (14:37; 16:18) do we find "acknowledge." The best translation is "understand" (NASB, NIV).

## Benefit or Grace? (1:15)

Paul says that he had wanted to visit the Corinthian Christians, in order that they might have a second "benefit." The noun is *charis,* "grace." The NASB notes correctly in the margin that the literal meaning is "have a second grace," but translates in the text: "That you might twice receive a blessing." Similarly the NIV has, "That you might benefit twice." Arndt and Gingrich render it: "That you might have a second proof of my goodwill" (p. 886). Most recent versions follow these general lines. The *Modern Language Bible (New Berkeley Version)* has: "So that you might enjoy a double blessing."

## Seal and Earnest (1:22)

The two very significant Greek words here are discussed in the comments on Eph. 1:13-14. We like the NIV of this verse: "Set his seal of ownership on us, and put his Spirit in our hearts as a deposit, guaranteeing what is to come."

## Determined (2:1)

It is the aorist of the verb *krinō,* which most frequently in the NT is used in the sense of "to judge" (so translated 88 out of 114 times in NT). But its original meaning was to "divide" or "select." Buechsel writes: "The most common meaning is 'to decide' . . . 'to judge,' 'to assess' . . . Hence, though the word is most commonly found in legal terminology, it does not belong here either exclusively or by derivation" (TDNT, 3:922). The definition that fits here is the third one given by Arndt and Gingrich: "reach a decision, decide" (p. 452).

## Sorrow or Grief? (2:1-5)

In these five verses we find the noun *lypē* twice and the verb *lypeō* five times. The noun also occurs near the end of verse 7. It is translated "heaviness" in the first verse, but "sorrow" in verses 3 and 7. The verb is rendered "make sorry" in verse 2, "grieved" or "caused grief" in verse 5. The NASB consistently translates it "cause sorrow" (vv. 2, 5) or "made sorrowful" (vv. 2, 4). This is probably best—to catch the repeated emphasis.

## Anguish (2:4)

The word *synochē* (only here and Luke 21:25) comes from the verb *synechō,* "hold together" or "press on every side," and so "oppress." Koester says of this passage: "Paul is referring to the tribulation and affliction which he suffered through hostility at Corinth. He uses the same terms as those used by the OT Psalmist when speaking of the distress which God's enemies caused him" (TDNT, 7:887).

## Overcharge? (2:5)

Today "overcharge" means to charge too much. This is not the idea here at all. The verb is *epibareō* (only here and in 1 Thess. 2:9; 2 Thess. 3:8). It literally means "to put a burden on, be burdensome" (A-S, p. 168).

Arndt and Gingrich say that *hina mē epibarō* in this passage "seems to have the meaning 'in order not to heap up too great a burden of words' = *in order not to say too much* (cf. NASB) . . . although there are no examples of it in this meaning. Other possibilities are *exaggerate, be too severe with*" (p. 290). The NIV probably catches the correct sense: "If anyone has caused grief, he has not so much grieved me as he has grieved all of you, to some extent— not to put it too severely."

## Punishment (2:6)

The noun *epitimia* (only here in NT) comes from the verb *epitimaō,* which first meant to honor someone. Then the verb came to have the sense: "to mete out due measure," and so "to censure, rebuke" (A-S, p. 176).

Similarly, the noun first had a good meaning. But in Greek inscriptions it means "punishment." Stauffer says that here it is "a technical term in congregational discipline for the censure of the church" (TDNT, 2:627). The guilty member had been sufficiently punished by public censure.

## Devices or Schemes? (2:11)

The word *noēma* is found five times in 2 Corinthians (2:11; 3:14; 4:4; 10:5; 11:3) and only once elsewhere in the NT (Phil. 4:7). It is translated three ways in the KJV: "mind," "device," "thought."

This noun comes from the verb *noeō,* which in turn comes from *nous,* "mind." So it basically means "thought." But Arndt and Gingrich note that in classical and Hellenistic Greek it also meant: *"purpose,* in a bad sense *design, plot"* (p. 542). The NASB and NIV both have "schemes."

## Satan (2:11)

This is a Hebrew word taken over into Greek (and other modern languages). It means "adversary."

Alfred Plummer, in the ICC volume on 2 Corinthians, writes: "Of the Scriptural designations of the evil one, four are found in this Epistle: 'Satan' (here, xi. 14, xii. 7), 'the serpent' (xi. 3), 'Belial' (vi. 15), 'the god of this age' (iv. 4). Elsewhere St. Paul calls Satan 'the tempter' (1 Thess. iii. 5), 'the devil' (Eph. iv. 6, etc.), 'the evil one' (Eph. vi. 16), 'the prince of the power of the air' (Eph. ii. 2)" (p. 63).

He goes on to say:

> It is not necessary to dwell on the obvious fact that here and elsewhere he regards the evil power which opposes God and the well-being of man as a personal agent. Excepting xii. 7, *Satanas* [Greek form] always has the article in the Pauline Epistles. So also most frequently in the rest of the N.T. But, whether with or without the article, *Satanas* in N.T. is always a proper name which designates the great Adversary of God and man (pp. 63-64).

## Rest (2:13)

The Greek word is *anesin,* which has been taken bodily over into English as a trade name for a relaxant. "Rest in my spirit" is translated "peace of mind" in the NIV.

## Causeth Us to Triumph (2:14)

In the Greek this is *thriambeuonti hēmas.* The verb *thriambeuō* had a technical meaning. In the Liddell-Scott-Jones *Greek-English Lexicon,* two interesting definitions are given. The first—*"lead in triumph,* of conquered enemies"—applies to Col. 2:15. The second—*"lead in triumph,* as a general does his army"—fits here (p. 806).

Plummer thinks that the first of these definitions fits both passages. He says of the present one: "The victorious commander is God, and the Apostles are—not His subordinate generals, but His captives, whom He takes with Him and displays to all the world. St. Paul thanks God, not for 'always *causing* him to triumph' (AV), but for 'at all times *leading* him in triumph.' The Apostles were among the first to be captured and made instruments of God's glory" (p. 67).

But why not both? Delling majors on the first point, but seems to approach the second. After speaking of the prisoners of the Roman emperor being led in the triumphal procession, he says: "In 2 C. 2:14 Paul describes himself as one of these prisoners. But he regards it as a grace that in his fetters he can accompany God always and everywhere in the divine triumphant march through the world" (TDNT, 3:160).

## Savour or Fragrance? (2:14, 16)

The Greek word is *osmē.* ("Savour" in verse 15 is another word *euodia,* which we might differentiate by translating as "aroma.") The best rendering for *osmē* is "fragrance."

Plummer expresses beautifully the meaning of this in the light of the context. He writes:

> When a Roman *imperator* triumphed, clouds of incense arose along the route; and in the triumph-

train [procession] of the Gospel the incense of increased knowledge of God is ever ascending. The Apostles cause this increase of knowledge, and therefore they themselves are a fragrance to the glory of God, a fragrance that is life-giving to those that are on the road to salvation, but will prove deadly to those who are on the other road (p. 67).

In this last sentence Plummer is including the context of verses 15-16.

## Corrupt or Peddle? (2:17)

The verb *kapeleuō* (only here in NT) comes from *kapelos,* "a huckster" or "peddler." Thayer says that the verb means—with the accusative of the thing (here "the word of God")—"to make money by selling anything; to get sordid gain by dealing in anything, to do a thing for base gain" (p. 324). He goes on to say: "But as peddlers were in the habit of adulterating their commodities for the sake of gain . . . *kapeleuein ti* was also used as synonymous with *to corrupt, to adulterate*" (pp. 324-25). He favors this sense here. But "peddle" (NASB, NIV) is certainly a viable translation, and perhaps the best. Paul was not peddling the gospel to make money.

## Commendation or Recommendation? (3:1)

"Commend" is the verb *synistanein,* which is a variant of *synistēmi.* Arndt and Gingrich define it as "(re)commend someone to someone" (p. 798). (See Earle, *Word Meanings,* 3:256.)

From this comes the adjective *systatikos* (only here in NT), meaning "introducing, commendatory" (AG, p. 802). In the last part of the verse the KJV is more full than the Greek, which simply says (NASB): "letters of commendation to you or from you." But the technical term today for this is what the NIV has: "letters of recommendation to you or from you."

## Of Christ (3:3)

Is the genitive case here subjective (written by Christ), objective (telling about Christ), or possessive (belonging to Christ)? As in other cases in the New Testament, we cannot be certain. Plummer (ICC) and Bernard (EGT) prefer the first. This is well represented in the NIV, "a letter from Christ."

## Ministered by Us (3:3)

The Greek is *diaconētheisa hyph' hēmon*, literally "have been served (ministered) by us." The connection with the preceding expression is well brought out by Bernard: "the Apostle conceiving of himself as his Master's amanuensis" (EGT, 3:53). This idea is caught by Weymouth—"penned by us." Paul says that the Corinthian Christians were "the result of our ministry" (NIV). The most important result of his ministry was what was written on the hearts of his converts.

## Tables or Tablets? (3:3)

"Tables of stone" is evidently a reference to the two pieces of stone on which the Ten Commandments were written (Exod. 31:18). The Greek *plax* occurs only here (twice) and in Heb. 9:4—"the stone tablets of the covenant" (NIV). The word literally means something flat, and so here a flat stone. But the correct term today is "tablets."

Contrasted with "tablets of stone" are "tablets of human hearts" (NASB, NIV). Incidentally, "in" should be "on."

## Sufficient or Adequate? (3:5)

Paul's statement here, "But our sufficiency is of God" is an answer to his very pertinent question in 2:16—"And who is sufficient for these things?" The connection is also brought out in the NASB: "And who is adequate for these things? . . . but our adequacy is from God." The adjective is *hikanos* (frequent in NT). The noun is *hikanotēs* (only here). But the KJV of verse 6, "made us able," fails to indicate that there the verb is *hikanoō* (only here and Col. 1:12), which is derived from *hikanos*. The NASB correctly represents this: "made us adequate." Our adequacy comes from Christ.

## Testament or Covenant? (3:6)

The word *diathēkē* occurs 33 times in the NT. In the KJV it is translated "covenant" 20 times and "testament" 13 times. Most commentators agree that it should probably be rendered "covenant" except in Heb. 9:16-17, and possibly Gal. 3:15 (see comments at the latter place).

## The Letter (3:6)

*Gramma* (from which we get "grammar") first meant a letter of the alphabet. Then it came to mean what is written, and so a document (usually in the plural), an epistle, and even a book. Arndt and Gingrich feel that it is used here "of the literally correct form of the law" (p. 164).

Paul says that the letter kills, but the spirit *(pneuma)* makes alive. Plummer comments:

> But we must not be misled by the common contrast in English between "letter" and "spirit," which means the contrast between the literal sense and the spiritual or inward sense of one and the same document or authority. By *gramma* and *pneuma* St. Paul

> means two different authorities; *gramma* is the written
> code of the Law, *pneuma* is the operation of the Spirit
> in producing and promulgating the Gospel (p. 87).

Schrenk agrees with this when he writes: "Any suggestion is to be rejected which would have it that the spirit of
Scripture is here opposed to its letter, or its true or richer
sense to the somatic body" (TDNT, 1:767). The contrast
is between the written Law and the life-giving Spirit.

## Ministration or Ministry? (3:7-9)

The Greek word *diaconia* (4 times here) occurs 34
times in the NT and is translated "ministry" 16 times in
the KJV. That is clearly the correct translation here (cf.
NASB, NIV).

Incidentally, it should be noted that "engraven in
stones" (v. 7) should be "engraved in letters on stone"
(NIV). That is what the Greek text says. The reference, of
course, is to the Ten Commandments.

## Plainness or Boldness? (3:12)

*Parrēsia* occurs 31 times in the NT and is translated
"boldness" 8 times, "confidence" 6 times, "openly" 4
times, and "plainly" 4 times. Only here is it rendered
"plainness of speech."

The word comes from *pas,* "all" and *hrēsis,* "speech."
So it basically means "freedom of speech." Abbott-Smith
says: "In LXX, Josephus, and NT, also (from the absence
of fear which accompanies freedom of speech), *confidence,*
boldness" (p. 347).

Schlier writes: "Above all, the discussion in 2 C.
3:12 ff. shows that for Paul *parrēsia* to God—the uncovered
face of Paul looking towards Him, 3:18—implies an uncovered face which men can see as Israel could not see the

covered face of Moses, 3:13. He who lifts up his face un-covered to God also turns uncovered to men" (TDNT, 5:883).

So we have here the ideas of openness and boldness. The latter is perhaps not only "in *our* speech" (NASB), but in general (NIV).

## Veil (3:13-16)

The noun *kalymma* is found once each in these four verses, and nowhere else in the NT. It comes from the verb *kalyptō,* "cover," and so means "a covering."

## Abolished or Fading Away? (3:13)

While the verb *katargeō* does have "abolish" as one of its meanings, "fading away" (NASB, NIV) fits much better here. It was the glory on Moses' face that faded away after a while.

The reference is to Exod. 34:33, where the KJV reads: "Till Moses had done speaking with them he put a veil on his face." Plummer says:

> This is erroneous. The correct translation is, "*When* Moses had done speaking with them he put a veil on his face" (cf. NASB). He knew that the brightness was caused by converse with Jehovah, and would fade away when he was absent from the divine presence. He did not wish the people to see the disappearance of the brightness, and therefore, when he had delivered his message, he covered his face, until he returned to the presence of the Lord (pp. 96-97).

## Open or Unveiled? (3:18)

The Greek for "open" is *anakekalymmenō,* the perfect passive participle of *anakalyptō.* This verb is found only

here and in verse 14, where it is translated "taken away."
It literally means "to unveil" (A-S, p. 30), and so the correct translation here is "unveiled" (NASB, NIV).

## Glass or Mirror? (3:18)

"Beholding as in a glass" is all one word in Greek—
*katoptrizomenoi*, the present middle participle of *katoptrizō* (only here in NT). In the middle it means "to reflect as a mirror" (A-S, p. 242). Since they did not have glass mirrors (only bronze) in Paul's day, "glass" is incorrect.

## Changed or Transformed? (3:18)

The verb is *metamorphoō*, which is rendered "transformed" in Rom. 12:2 (see comments there). This is the literal meaning of the verb and the correct translation here.

## Faint or Lose Heart? (4:1)

Today the verb "faint" is used as a synonym for "swoon"—becoming dizzy and falling down. But the verb *enkakeō* means "become weary" or "lose heart" (AG, p. 214). Achilles comments: "Weariness here is not physical but spiritual" (DNTT, 1:563). The correct translation is "lose heart" (RSV, NASB, NIV).

## Dishonesty or Shame? (4:2)

It is difficult to see where the translators got the word "dishonesty" here. The Greek simply says, "the hidden things of shame."

But what does this mean? Arndt and Gingrich suggest, "What one conceals from a feeling of shame" (p. 24).

This idea is taken over in the NASB: "The things hidden because of shame." The NIV puts it a little more generally: "Secret and shameful ways."

## Craftiness (4:2)

In the Septuagint *panourgia* means "cleverness," in a good or neutral sense. But in classical Greek and the NT it is used in a bad sense—"craftiness" or "deception" (NIV).

## Handling Deceitfully (4:2)

In the Greek this is the present participle of the verb *doloō,* which comes from the noun *dolos,* a "bait" or "snare." So the verb literally means "ensnare." But both noun and verb are used metaphorically in the sense of "deceit" or "treachery." Arndt and Gingrich say that the verb means "falsify, adulterate" (p. 202)—it was used in secular Greek for adulterating wine. One could deduce the idea here: "Don't water down the Word of God!"

## Hid or Veiled? (4:3)

The Greek word here is not related to the one translated "hidden things" in verse 2. There it was the adjective *cryptos,* from which we get "cryptic." Here it is the verb *calyptō,* "to cover or veil." So the best translation here is "veiled" (RSV, NASB, NIV).

## Lost or Perishing? (4:3)

Evangelical Christians are familiar with the thought that the unsaved are "lost." But does this word communicate the truth accurately and adequately to an outsider?

The verb *apollymi* in the active voice means "destroy"

(cf. 1 Cor. 1:19). In the middle voice, as here, it means "perish." So it seems that the best translation is "those who are perishing" (NASB, NIV). It is the same verb that is translated "perish" in John 3:16. The main argument for using "lost" here would be a connection with the three parables of the lost in Luke 15, where this verb is rendered "lose" or "lost" (seven times). But we also find the prodigal son saying, "I perish *(apollymai)* with hunger" (v. 17).

We should not discontinue using the term "lost" to describe the condition referred to here. But the other concept is also important. Oepke says that *apollymi* indicates "definitive destruction, not merely in the sense of the extinction of physical existence, but rather of an eternal plunge into Hades and a hopeless destiny of death" (TDNT, 1:396).

## The Lord or As Lord? (4:5)

Paul declared, "We preach not ourselves, but Christ Jesus the Lord" (KJV). In the Greek there is no article before "Lord." So the correct translation is "as Lord." Alfred Plummer comments: "To 'preach Christ as Lord' is to preach Him as crucified, risen, and glorified, the Lord to whom 'all authority in heaven and earth has been given'" (p. 118).

The alert reader may have noted that NASB has "Christ Jesus as Lord," whereas NIV has "Jesus Christ as Lord." Which is right? The answer is, "We cannot be sure." Our two oldest Greek manuscripts of the NT (as a whole) come from the fourth century. Of these two, Vaticanus has *Christon Iesoun* and Sinaiticus has *Iesoun Christon*. All three fifth-century manuscripts have the latter. That is probably why this reading was adopted in the United Bible Society Greek Testament, now considered the best in print. It may be noted that the correct reading at the end of v. 6 is "Christ" (NASB, NIV), not "Jesus Christ." In this case the Greek is very clear.

## Earthen or Of Clay? (4:7)

The adjective *ostracinos* is found only here and in 2 Tim. 2:20. Arndt and Gingrich say that here it is used "as a symbol, denoting breakableness" (p. 591).

This adjective is the basis of the archaeological term "ostraca," used for broken pieces of pottery that often have ancient writing inscribed on them.

## Vessels or Jars? (4:7)

The word *skeuos* is rendered "vessel" in the KJV 19 out of the 23 times it occurs in the NT. Most of the time it refers to what we today would call "jars" or "containers." "Vessel" is now used more for a ship. Here "jars of clay" (NIV) is more contemporary than "earthen vessels" (RSV, NASB).

What is meant? Gen. 2:7 suggests that God made man's body from clay. So some have thought that the reference here is to the physical body. But Plummer writes: "It was in the man as a whole, and not in his body in particular, that the Divine treasure which was to enrich the world was placed to be dispensed to others" (p. 127). He notes that this metaphor is common in the OT (Isa. 29:16; 30:14; 45:9; 64:8; Jer. 18:6).

The figure used here emphasizes the frailty of our humanity. This is in contrast to the greatness of God's power and glory.

## Troubled or Hard Pressed? (4:8)

The Greek word is the present passive participle of

*thlibō,* the verb meaning "to press." Occurring 10 times in the NT, it is translated "troubled" 4 times and "afflicted" 3 times. But since the basic meaning is "press," it seems that "hard pressed" (NIV) is best here. Plummer declares: "Here the radical signification of 'pressure' (Mk. iii. 9) must be retained, because of *stenochōroumenoi*" (p. 128).

## Distressed or Crushed? (4:8)

The verb *stenochōreomai* is found in the NT only here and in 6:12 (twice), where the KJV has "straitened." This catches better the distinctive meaning of the word. It comes from *stenos,* "narrow," and *chōros,* "space." So it means "to compress." This idea is caught by "crushed" (NASB, NIV).

## A Play on Words (4:8)

"Perplexed but not in despair." The Greek has *"apo-roumenoi* [but not] *exaporoumenoi." Ex (ek)* is a prepositional prefix meaning "out of." It acts here, as often, in the sense of a strong intensive of the simple verb. Plummer suggests: "in despondency, yet not in despair" (p. 129).

The first verb, *aporeō,* occurs four times in the NT. It means "be at a loss, in doubt, uncertain" (AG, p. 97). *Exaporeō* is found only here and in 1:8. It has the force of being "utterly at a loss," and so "in despair."

## Cast Down or Struck Down? (4:9)

The latter is preferred for *kataballomenoi* by the NASB and NIV, as being more contemporary. Phillips puts it very vividly: "We may be knocked down, but we are never knocked out!"

## By or With? (4:14)

The KJV says "by Jesus" and "with you." The Greek has the same preposition in both places—*syn,* which means "(together) with."

## Redound or Abound? (4:15)

"Redound" is an archaic word. The verb is *perisseuō,* which occurs 39 times in the NT. In the KJV it is translated "abound" 17 times and "redound" only here. The former gives the correct sense.

## Far More Exceeding (4:17)

This represents another play on words in the Greek: *kath' hyperbolēn eis hyperbolēn.* Arndt and Gingrich define the first part of this as "beyond measure." To get the full force of the double expression they suggest "beyond all measure and proportion" (p. 848). The NASB has "far beyond all comparison," the NIV "that far outweighs them all."

## Tabernacle or Tent? (5:1, 4)

The feminine noun *skēnē* (skaynay) occurs 20 times in the NT and is translated "tabernacle" all but once ("habitation," Luke 16:9) in the KJV. It often refers to the Tabernacle in the Wilderness. But here (alone) we have *skēnos* (neuter).

Today "tabernacle" suggests a large plain building, seating big crowds. So "tent" is a better translation in this place. Paul thinks of the human body as a tent pitched here in this world. It is only our temporary home. In heaven our glorified bodies will be our eternal "house."

## Dissolved or Destroyed? (5:1)

The verb *katalyō* means "destroy, cast down" (A-S, p. 236). "Dissolved" carries a somewhat different connotation today. The best translation is "torn down" (NASB) or "destroyed" (NIV).

## House or Dwelling? (5:2)

The most common word for "house" in the NT is *oikos* (114 times). *Oikia* (95 times) is the term used twice in the first verse here. Abbott-Smith distinguishes these two words thus:

> *oikos,* which in Attic law denoted the whole *estate,* *oikia,* the *dwelling* only. In classical poets *oikos* has also the latter sense, but not in prose, except in metaphorical usage, where it signifies both *property* and *household.* The foregoing distinction is not, however, consistently maintained in late Greek (p. 312).

Michel agrees. He says: "Originally Greek distinguished between *oikos* and *oikia.* . . . *Oikos* had then a broader range than *oikia,* being the whole of a deceased person's possessions . . . whereas *oikia* is simply his residence" (TDNT, 5:131). But in the NT the two are used interchangeably.

In verse 2, however, we have *oikētērion* (only here and Jude 6). It comes from *oikētēr,* "an inhabitant," and so means "habitation." Today we would say "dwelling" (NASB, NIV).

## Mortality or What Is Mortal? (5:4)

The Greek is *to thnēton.* An adjective, *thnētos* means "mortal" (see 4:11), that is, "subject to death." With the definite article *to* (neuter) it means "what is mortal" (RSV, NASB, NIV), not the abstract idea of "mortality."

## Earnest or Deposit? (5:5)

For this term see the comments on Eph. 1:14.

## At Home . . . Absent (5:6, 8, 9)

There is an interesting play on words in the Greek: *Endēmountes . . . ekdēmoumen*. The first verb means "to be at home," the second "to be away from home." They both occur only here (three times each).

## Terror or Fear? (5:11)

Out of its 47 occurrences in the NT, the noun *phobos* is translated as "fear" 41 times. Only 3 times is it rendered "terror" (Rom. 13:3; here; and in 1 Pet. 3:14). "Terror" seems too strong a translation.

## Constraineth or Compels? (5:14)

The verb is *synechō*, literally "hold together," which occurs only twice in Paul's Epistles (here and Phil. 1:23). Koester says that in these two passages it means "to be claimed, totally controlled." Commenting on verses 14-15 he says: "It is the love of Christ which 'completely dominates' Paul . . . so that on the basis of Christ's death the only natural decision for him, as for all other believers, is no longer to live for self but to live for Christ" (TDNT, 7:883).

In the David Livingstone Memorial in Blantyre, Scotland (just outside Glasgow), one can see on the wall of the last room a cross. To the left are the words: "The love of Christ constraineth us—St. Paul." To the right: "The love of Christ compels me—David Livingstone." The NIV has "compels" here (v. 14).

Is the genitive "of love" subjective, objective, or possessive? Since we cannot be sure which, we can use all three for a sermon outline:

1. Christ's love for me compels me to crucial commitment.
2. My love for Christ compels me to complete consecration.
3. Christ's love in me compels me to compassionate service.

## After the Flesh (5:16)

The phrase (twice here) is *kata sarka*—literally, "according to flesh." Plummer says that it means "according to external distinctions," "by what he is in the flesh" (p. 176).

What did Paul mean when he said that he knew Christ *kata sarka?* Plummer writes: "Almost certainly he is alluding to some time *previous* to his conversion. . . . At that time he knew Christ as an heretical and turbulent teacher, who was justly condemned by the Sanhedrin and crucified by the Romans" (p. 177). But now he knows Him in a new way.

## Know Him or Know Him So? (5:16)

The KJV says, "Yet now henceforth know we *him* no more." Taken in its absolute sense, that statement of course is not true.

The Greek simply says, "But now no longer we know" *(alla nun ouketi ginōskomen)*. The KJV added "him" in italics, to try to make the meaning clearer. Most translators have felt it necessary to add something for better sense in English, such as "thus" (NASB) or "so" (NIV).

## Creature or Creation? (5:17)

Which is better here? The NASB (as KJV) has "creature," whereas the NIV has "creation."

The noun *ktisis* first means "the act of creating." Then it came to mean "what has been created." Arndt and Gingrich write: "The Christian is described by Paul as *kainē ktisis a new creature* 2 Cor. 5:17, and the state of being in the new faith by the same words as *a new creation* Gal. 6:15" (p. 457). Some prefer to translate this second clause of the verse: "there is a new creation" (NASB margin).

## Passed Away . . . Become (5:17)

The KJV reads: "Old things are passed away; behold, all things are become new." But this fails to represent the difference in tenses. "Are passed away" is the aorist tense *(parēlthen),* which indicates a crisis experience. "Are become new" is the perfect tense *(gegonen),* indicating a continuing state. "The old things passed away; behold, new things have come" (NASB).

## Reconciliation (5:18-20)

The two greatest passages on reconciliation in the NT are this one and Rom. 5:10-11 (see comments there). The noun *katallagē* occurs twice here (vv. 18, 19) and twice in Romans (5:11; 11:15), and nowhere else in the NT. The verb *katallassō* is found three times here (vv. 18, 19, 20) and once in Rom. 5:10. In the only other place where it occurs in the NT (1 Cor. 7:11) it is used of an estranged wife being reconciled to her husband.

Buechsel says of Paul's ministry of reconciliation *(katallagē):* "It brings before men the action by which God

takes them up again into fellowship with Himself"
(TDNT, 1:258). Of the verb he writes: *"katallassein*
denotes a transformation or renewal of the state between
God and man, and therewith of man's own state. . . . By
reconciliation our sinful self-seeking is overcome and the
fellowship with God is created in which it is replaced by
living for Christ" (TDNT, 1:255).

## Fellow Workers (6:1)

"As workers together with him" is all one word in
Greek, *synergountes*. Literally it means "working together
(with)"—from *syn*, "together," and *ergon*, "work." The
NIV has "as God's fellow workers."

We have already noted that Paul's strong sense of
"togetherness" is shown by his fondness for compound
words with a *syn* prefix. A quick check discovered over 50
of these.

## Succoured or Helped? (6:2)

The verb is *boētheō*. It comes from *boē*, "a cry," and
*theō*, "run." So it literally means to "run at a cry for help"
—that is, "hurry to help someone who is in need." That is
what God does for us. The noun *boē* occurs only in James
5:4, where it represents "the cry of the oppressed" (DNTT,
1:411).

## Offence or Stumbling Block? (6:3)

The noun *proskopē* is found only here in the NT. It
comes from the verb *proskoptō*, which is used for striking
one's foot against a stone or other obstacle in the path, and
so means "to stumble." Thayer suggests that the entire
phrase here means "to do something which causes others
to stumble, i.e. leads them into error or sin" (p. 547).

The NASB, "giving no cause for offense in anything," is accurate. But the NIV, "We put no stumbling block in anyone's path," communicates the idea more clearly.

## Blamed or Discredited? (6:3)

The verb *mōmaomai* is found only here and in 8:20. The minister is to conduct himself in such a blameless way that his ministry will not be "discredited" (NASB, NIV).

## Patience or Endurance? (6:4)

Again the word is *hypomonē* (see comments on Rom. 2:7; 5:3). The correct translation is "endurance" (NASB, NIV).

Plummer notes that following "endurance" (KJV, "patience") in verse 4 we have three triplets that, taken together, illustrate the full meaning of endurance. Of the first of these (v. 4) he says: "This triplet consists of troubles which may be independent of human agency, and it is probably intended to form a climax: 'afflictions' . . . which might be avoided; 'necessities' . . . which cannot be avoided; 'straits' . . . out of which there is no way of escape" (p. 194).

He suggests that the second triplet (v. 5) "consists of troubles inflicted by men." Then he observes: "It is doubtful whether there is any climax; but St. Paul might think 'stripes' . . . less serious than 'imprisonments' . . . which stopped his work for a time, and imprisonments less serious than 'tumults,' which might force him to abandon work altogether in the place in which the tumult occurred" (p. 194).

Plummer says that the third triplet (v. 5) "consists of those troubles which he took upon himself in the prosecution of his mission." He goes on to say: "There is order in this triplet also, and perhaps one may call it a climax: *kopoi* disturb the day, *agrypniai* the night, and *nēsteiai* both" (p. 195).

## Necessities or Hardships? (6:4)

The KJV represents the original, literal meaning of *anangkē*—"necessity." But for this passage (and 12:10; Luke 21:23; 1 Cor. 7:26; 1 Thess. 3:7) Thayer says: "In a sense rare in the classics (Diod. 4, 43), but very common in Hellenistic writers . . . *calamity, distress*" (p. 36). Moulton and Milligan cite evidence of this usage as early as the third century B.C. (VGT, p. 31). Grundmann says that here the word indicates "such afflictions as those experienced by the apostle Paul, or afflictions which derive from the tension between the new creation in Christ and the old cosmos" (TDNT, 1:346). It is thus related closely to the preceding word "afflictions" and the following word "distresses." It may be rendered "hardships" (NASB, NIV).

## Stripes or Beatings? (6:5)

In the KJV *plēgē* is translated "plague" 12 times in Revelation and "wound" 4 times (plus once in Luke 10:30). Elsewhere in the NT (5 times) it is rendered "stripe" (Luke 12:48; Acts 16:23, 33; 2 Cor. 6:5; 11:23). The correct translation here is "beatings" (NASB, NIV). That is what Paul had suffered often (11:23).

## Tumults or Riots? (6:5)

*Akatastasia* (5 times in NT) basically means "disturbance" (AG). Oepke says that in this passage it signifies "personal unrest" (TDNT, 3:446). But Plummer feels that here it means "tumults," as in Luke 21:9. He comments: "Popular tumults against St. Paul are frequent in Acts" (p. 194). The contemporary term for this is "riots" (NIV).

## Labors or Hard Work? (6:5)

*Kopos* means "labor." But today we would probably say "hard work" (NIV).

## Watchings or Sleepless Nights? (6:5)

The noun *agrypnia* is found only here and in 11:27. Basically it means "sleeplessness." But Plummer writes:

> The word covers more than sleeplessness; it includes all that prevents one from sleeping. At Troas Paul preached until midnight and yet longer (Acts xx. 7, 9). In LXX the word is almost confined to Ecclesiasticus, where it is frequent and commonly means forgoing sleep in order to work. The Apostle no doubt often taught, and travelled, and worked with his hands to maintain himself by night (p. 195).

The word should be translated here either as "sleeplessness" (NASB) or, perhaps better, as "sleepless nights" (NIV).

## Fastings or Hunger? (6:5)

The word *nēsteia* is used in the same way here and in 11:27. Aside from these two places, the best Greek text has it only in Luke 2:37 and Acts 14:23; 27:9. In the first two of these three it is connected with prayer and so has a religious connotation. Acts 27:9 borders on this. But what does it mean here? Plummer says: "Not 'fasts' in the religious sense; but, just as *agrypnia* is voluntary forgoing of sleep in order to get more work done, so *nēsteia* is voluntary forgoing of food for the same reason." He adds: "We infer from xi. 27 that *nēsteiai* are *voluntary* abstentions from food, for there they are distinguished from involuntary hunger and thirst" (p. 195).

## Pureness or Purity? (6:6)

Following a dramatic list of nine hardships endured by Paul (vv. 4-5), we find a striking contrast in the nine virtues named in verses 6-7. The first virtue is *hagnotēs* (only here and 11:3). It comes from the adjective *hagnos,* "pure" (nine times in NT). The noun is rare, not occurring at all in classical Greek or in the Septuagint. Hauck defines it as "moral purity and blamelessness" (TDNT, 1:124). Rather than "pureness," today we would say "purity" (NASB, NIV).

## Unfeigned or Sincere? (6:6)

"Unfeigned" precisely represents the Greek adjective *anypocritos,* "unhypocritical" (found once each in Romans, 2 Corinthians, 1 & 2 Timothy, James, 1 Peter). But the term is outdated; "sincere" (NIV) says it today.

## Armour or Weapons? (6:7)

The Greek has the plural of *hoplon,* which originally meant a "tool" or "instrument." It is used that way in Rom. 6:13. Always plural in the NT, it often means "weapons"—literally in John 18:3, figuratively in Rom. 13:12; 2 Cor. 6:7; 10:4).

"On" (KJV) should be "in" (NIV) or "for" (NASB), indicating where the weapons are held.

## Honour or Glory? (6:8)

In the KJV *doxa* is translated "glory" 145 times and "glorious" 10 times in its 168 occurrences in the NT. It should be "glory" here.

## Evil Report and Good Report (6:8)

In the Greek this is *dysphēmia* and *euphēmia* (both only here in NT). The first means "slander."

## Bowels or Affection? (6:12)

This verse is difficult to understand in the KJV. It means, "We are not withholding our affection from you, but you are withholding yours from us" (NIV).

## Recompence or Exchange? (6:13)

*Antimisthian* is found only in Rom. 1:27, in a bad sense, and here, in a good sense—and nowhere in secular Greek literature. Arndt and Gingrich translate the clause here: "Widen your hearts in the same way in exchange" (p. 74).

## Unequally Yoked Together (6:14)

The Greek verb *heterozygeō* (only here in NT) literally means "to come under an unequal or different yoke." Here it is used metaphorically in the sense "to have fellowship with one who is not an equal" (Thayer, p. 254).

## Infidel or Unbeliever? (6:15)

This is the same word, *apistos,* which is translated

"unbeliever" in verse 14. "Infidel" now has a technical connotation that does not fit here.

## Agreement (6:16)

The word is *synkatathesis* (only here in NT). It is compounded of the verb meaning "place" or "put" (stem *the*), *kata,* meaning "down," and *syn,* "together." It was used for a joint deposit of votes (Thayer, p. 592), and so means "assent" or "agreement."

## Filthiness or Defilement? (7:1)

The noun *molysmos* (only here in NT) comes from the verb *molynō,* which means "to stain, soil, defile" (A-S, p. 296). So it means "defilement." Arndt and Gingrich translate and interpret the passage this way: *"from all defilement of body and spirit,* i.e. outwardly and inwardly" (p. 528). J. J. Packer says that it signifies "the moral and spiritual defilement that comes from embracing the pagan life-style" (DNTT, 1:449).

## Perfecting (7:1)

The verb *epiteleō* comes from *telos,* "end." The prefix *epi* is a preposition meaning "upon," but here probably has the intensive function—"bring fully to completion." In 8:6 it means "complete" (NASB) or "bring to completion" (NIV). Delling notes that one meaning of *telos* is "'completion' as a state, 'perfection'" (TDNT, 8:49). "Perfecting" seems to be the best translation here.

## Holiness (7:1)

The word *hagiōsyne* occurs only three times in the NT

(Rom. 1:4; here; and 1 Thess. 3:13) and its cognate *hagiotēs* only once (Heb. 12:10).

But the adjective *hagios,* "holy," from which these are derived, is found 229 times. The verb *hagiazō,* "sanctify," occurs 29 times, and the noun *hagiasmos,* "sanctification" 10 times. So there is a great deal of emphasis on holiness in the NT.

In Kittel's *Theological Dictionary of the New Testament* 27 pages are devoted to *hagios* and its derivatives. Procksch says that *hagiōsyne* "means 'sanctification' or 'holiness' rather than sanctifying, but as a quality rather than a state" (TDNT, 1:114). It is the quality of being holy. The sanctified Christian needs to have his whole inner being and outward life so permeated by the Holy Spirit that it all becomes holy.

## Receive or Make Room? (7:2)

At least 18 Greek verbs in the NT are translated as "receive" in the KJV. In most cases it is either *lambanō* (133 times), *dechomai* (52 times), or one of the numerous compounds of these verbs (e.g., *paralambanō* 15 times).

In contrast to these, the verb here is *chōreō* (9 times in NT), which is translated "receive" only here and in Matt. 19:11. It comes from the noun *chōros,* which means "place" or "space." Thayer says that here the verb means "make room for one in one's heart" (p. 674). So both NASB and NIV have: "Make room for us in your hearts"—a very meaningful translation.

## Defrauded or Exploited? (7:2)

The verb *pleonekteō* is found mainly in 2 Corinthians (2:11; 7:2; 12:17, 18)—elsewhere only in 1 Thess. 4:6. Its basic meaning is that of taking advantage of someone (cf.

NASB). The proper word for that today is "exploit" (NIV), which the *American Heritage Dictionary* defines as "1. To employ to the greatest possible advantage. . . . 2. To make use of selfishly or unethically" (p. 463). "Defraud" (KJV) means "to take by fraud," which is not the exact point here.

## Boldness of Speech or Confidence? (7:4)

This is one word in Greek, *parrēsia* (see comments on 3:12). Paul is not here talking about "boldness of speech" but "confidence" (NASB, NIV).

## Glorying or Boasting? (7:4)

"Boasting" (NASB) is the better translation of *kauchēsis* (see on 1:12). It may be rendered "take pride" (NIV).

## Troubled or Harassed? (7:5)

"Troubled" seems too weak a translation for *thlibō* (see comments at 4:8). "Afflicted" (NASB) is used today mostly for physical ailments. So probably "harassed" (NIV) is better.

## Fightings or Conflicts? (7:5)

The noun *machē* (related to *machaira*, "sword") literally means "a fight." But in the NT (2 Cor. 7:5; 2 Tim. 2:23; Titus 3:9; Jas. 4:1) it is "only in plural and only of battles fought without actual weapons" (AG, p. 497). So it means "a strife, contention, quarrel" (A-S, p. 280). "Conflicts" (NASB, NIV) expresses it well.

Bauernfeind notes that as early as Homer's *Iliad* the word was used "in the general sense of conflict, for battles of words." But he adds the observation: "It is not clear whether the *machai* to which Paul was exposed in 2 C. 7:5 embraced physical threats" (TDNT, 4:527-28).

## Earnest Desire or Longing? (7:7)

For *epipothēsis* all the standard lexicons give "longing." In the NT it occurs only here and in verse 11, where it is rendered "vehement desire."

Schoenweiss observes: "When Paul speaks of desire and longing in a good sense, he uses *epipotheō* . . . *epipothesis* . . . and *epipothia*"—the last found only in Rom. 15:23. He adds: "This word-group is used 13 times in the NT, 11 of them being in the Pauline writings and always in a good sense" (DNTT, 1:458). Paul was a man of strong feelings and he uses strong terms.

## Fervent Mind or Zeal? (7:7)

The Greek word here, *zēlos,* is used more frequently (five times) in 2 Corinthians than in any other book of the NT. In this Epistle the apostle is expressing strong emotions, more than in any other of his letters.

Our word "zeal" comes from this word, and it is translated that way most often (six times) in the KJV. But it is also translated "envying" five times and "envy" once. Only here is it rendered "fervent mind." In 2 Corinthians it carries a good sense always except in 12:20 ("envyings"). In 11:2 it is translated "jealousy," but in a good sense.

## Repent or Regret? (7:8)

The more common Greek verb for "repent" in the NT (34 times) is *metanoeō,* which is always translated "repent" in the KJV. The word here (twice) is *metamelomai*

(6 times), also rendered "repent" always. Each of these two words, interestingly, occurs in only one passage in Paul's Epistles (*metanoeō* in 12:21). Aside from that *metanoeō* is found exclusively in the Synoptic Gospels, Acts, and Revelation. However, the noun *metanoia*, "repentance," occurs 4 times in Paul (see comments on Rom. 2:4). It is found here in verses 9 and 10.

After emphasizing the fact that the two verbs seem to be used somewhat interchangeably in Greek literature, Thayer concludes: "But that *metanoeō* is the fuller and nobler term, expressive of moral actions and issues, is indicated not only by its derivation, but by the greater frequency of its use, by the fact that it is often employed in the imperative (*metamelomai* never), and by its construction with *apo, ek*" (p. 405). He also notes that *metamelomai* properly means, "it is a care to one afterwards," whereas *metanoeō* means "change one's mind."

Trench, in his *Synonyms*, says that in both sacred and secular writers there is "a very distinct preference for *metanoia* as the expression of the nobler repentance." He adds: "He who has *changed his mind* about the past is in the way to change everything; he who has an *after care* may have little or nothing more than a selfish dread of the consequences of what he had done" (pp. 260-61).

Michel has an excellent treatment of the words in their context in this passage. He writes:

> In 2 C. 7:8-10 there is again a plain distinction between *metamelesthai* and *metanoein*. Paul is not sorry that he sent a severe letter (*ou metamelomai*, 7:8). Even if it caused pain, this was according to God's will. . . . It is now clear to him that the pain was necessary to bring the Corinthians to a change of heart (. . . *eis metanoian*, 7:9). Suffering which corresponds to God's will brings about a change of heart which is to salvation and which will not be rued (. . . *metanoia ametamelētos*, 7:10) (TDNT, 4:628-29).

The adjective *ametamelētos* (only v. 10 and Rom. 11:29) is properly translated "without regret" (NASB). And of course the verb *metamelomai* in verse 8 should be rendered "regret" (NASB, NIV).

## Carefulness or Earnestness? (7:11)

*Spoudē* literally means "haste" (as in Mark 6:25; Luke 1:39). Then it came to mean "eagerness, earnestness" (AG, p. 771). "Earnestness" is the best translation here (NASB, NIV).

## Clear or Innocent? (7:11)

The adjective *hagnos* literally means "pure," as in 11:2. But for this passage Arndt and Gingrich suggest "innocent" (p. 11), as does Hauck (TDNT, 1:122). That fits very well (NASB, NIV).

## Have Confidence (7:16)

The verb *tharreō* is almost confined to 2 Corinthians in the NT (5:6, 8; 7:16; 10:1, 2). Elsewhere it is found only in Heb. 13:6. Its heavy use in 2 Corinthians reflects the fact that Paul was overjoyed that his confidence in the Corinthian Christians had been restored.

## We Do You to Wit (8:1)

Obviously this communicates little to the modern reader. The Greek simply says, *gnōrizomen hymin,* "we make known to you."

The verb *gnōrizō* occurs 24 times in the NT and in the KJV is translated "make known" 16 times. Only here is it rendered "do to wit," and in Phil. 1:22 "wot." Both terms are obsolete.

## Liberality or Generosity? (8:2)

The word *haplotēs* occurs eight times in the NT. Three times it is translated "simplicity"—1:12; 11:3; Rom. 12:8 (see comments there). Here it is "liberality," in 9:11 "bountifulness," and in 9:13 "liberal." In Eph. 6:5 and Col. 3:22 it is "singleness." (These two passages are closely parallel to each other.)

"Liberality" fits very well here. Perhaps "generosity" (NIV) is slightly more contemporary.

## Gift or Favor? (8:4)

In the KJV the noun *charis* is translated "grace" 130 out of the 156 times it occurs in the NT. The next most frequent translation is "favor" (6 times), which fits best here (NASB). Only in this one passage is it translated "gift."

## Grace or Gracious Work? (8:6, 7)

In these two verses "grace" (KJV) is *charis* in the Greek. Since Paul here is talking about taking up an offering for "the poor saints in Jerusalem" (Rom. 15:26), "gracious work" (NASB) is a little more specific.

This passage emphasizes the important fact that giving is a grace. This is brought out beautifully in the NIV of verse 7: "See that you also excel in this grace of giving."

"The Grace of Giving" would make an excellent sermon subject. The thought is elaborated further in verses 9 and 19.

## Forward or Desire? (8:10)

The Greek is *thelein*, which means "to be willing" or

"desire" (NASB, NIV). It is correctly translated "to will" in verse 11. The second half of verse 10 is rendered very helpfully in the NIV: "Last year you were the first not only to give but also to have the desire to do so."

## Perform or Finish? (8:11)

"Perform" and "performance" (KJV) are more accurately rendered "finish" and "completion" (NASB, NIV). The verb is *epiteleō,* which is correctly translated "finish" in verse 6. "Performance" is the articular aorist infinitive of the same verb (*to epitelēsai,* "to have completed").

## First or Present? (8:12)

Instead of "there be first," the NASB has "is present" (cf. NIV). The verb *prokeimai* means "lie before, be present" (AG, p. 714).

## Readiness or Willingness? (8:11, 12, 19)

The Greek word *prothymia* occurs five times in the NT and is translated five different ways in the KJV. It is found four times in the immediate context: in this chapter "readiness" (v. 11), "willing mind" (v. 12), "ready mind" (v. 19), and in 9:2 "forwardness of mind." In Acts 17:11 it is "readiness of mind."

The noun means "eagerness, willingness, readiness" (A-S, p. 381). The NIV uses "eagerness" in Acts and in 11:19; 9:2, but "willingness" in 8:11, 12. The NASB has "eagerness" in Acts and "readiness" in 2 Corinthians. Rengstorf suggests "cheerful resolution" for the passages in 2 Corinthians (TDNT, 6:700).

## Exhortation or Appeal? (8:17)

Arndt and Gingrich give three basic meanings for *paraclēsis:* (1) "exhortation," (2) "appeal," (3) "comfort." They comment: "2 Cor. 8:17 could stand under 1, but probably may better be classed with 2" (p. 623). In keeping with this we favor "appeal" (RSV, NASB, NIV). It seems to fit better here.

## Of His Own Accord (8:17)

The Greek adjective *authairetos* is found (in NT) only here and in verse 3 ("of themselves"). It is compounded of *autos,* "self," and the verb *haireomai,* "choose." So it basically means "self-chosen." The NIV has here, "on his own initiative."

## Chosen (8:19)

The verb *cheirotoneō* is found only here and in Acts 14:23 "ordained"; better "appointed" (RSV, NASB, NIV). It comes from *cheir,* "hand," and *teinō,* "stretch." It originally meant "to vote by stretching out the hand" in the Athenian assembly. Then it came to mean simply "appoint." Lohse says that the sense here is "to select" (TDNT, 9:437).

## Providing or Taking Pains? (8:21)

The verb *pronoeō* (only here, Rom. 12:17; 1 Tim. 5:8) literally means "think of beforehand," and so "take care, care for, provide" (AG, p. 715). Behm says that here and in Rom. 12:17 (closely parallel passages) "the meaning is 'to have regard for' what is noble and praiseworthy" (TDNT, 4:1011). "Honest things" (KJV) as the object of this verb is too narrow for *kala*, which means "good, noble" or "honorable" (RSV, NASB).

## Fellowhelper or Fellow Worker? (8:23)

The Greek word *synergos* is compounded of *syn*, "together," and *ergon*, "work." So it clearly means "fellow worker" (NASB, NIV).

## Messengers or Representatives? (8:23)

*Apostolos* occurs 81 times in the NT and is translated "apostle" 78 times in the KJV. Only here and in Phil. 2:25 is it rendered "messenger." In John 13:16 it is "he that is sent." The word literally means "one sent on an errand or with a commission." Here it refers to the appointed "representatives" (NIV) from the various churches, who traveled with the offering to Jerusalem.

## Shew . . . Proof (8:24)

There is a play on words here in the Greek *(endeiknymi . . . endeixis)* that doesn't show up in English translations. The verb "show" is *endeiknymi*, which in the middle (as here) means "to show forth, prove" (A-S, p. 152). "Proof" is the noun *endeixis*, which comes from this verb. It means a proof in the sense of something that is clearly shown to be.

## Provoke or Stir? (9:2)

The verb *erethizo* is found only twice in the NT. In Col. 3:21 it has the bad sense, "provoke" or "irritate." But here it is used in the good sense of "stir" or "stimulate." Since "provoke" usually carries a bad connotation today, "stir" is more satisfactory here.

## In Vain or Made Empty? (9:3)

The verb is *kenoō,* which comes from the adjective *kenos,* "empty." So it means "made empty" (NASB).

## Make Up Beforehand (9:5)

This is one word in Greek, the verb *prokatartizō* (only here in NT). The idea is: "finish the arrangements" (NIV).

## Bounty or Generous Gift? (9:5)

The noun *eulogia* occurs twice in this verse and twice in verse 6 ("bountifully"). Its regular meaning is "blessing," and that is the way it is translated 11 out of its 16 occurrences in the NT. (In Rom. 16:18 it is rendered "fair speech," its etymological sense.)

Arndt and Gingrich point out the transition to its meaning in these two verses. They write: "Since the concept of blessing carries with it the idea of bounty, *eulogia* gains the meaning *bountiful gift, bounty"* (p. 323).

Beyer finds a connection with the verb "bless" *(eulogeō)* in Matt. 5:44—"Bless them which curse you." He writes: "Because it springs from such unconditional love, *eulogia* can also be used . . . for the gift which Paul seeks as a collection for Jerusalem" (TDNT, 2:763). "Generous gift" (NIV) is perhaps slightly more contemporary than "bountiful gift" (NASB).

## Whereof Ye Had Notice Before (9:5)

This is all one word in Greek, *proepēngelmenēn.* The verb *propangellō* is found only here and in Rom. 1:2, where it is translated "promised afore." That is probably the correct meaning here. In the active the verb means "to announce before." But in the middle, as in both these references, it means "to promise before" (A-S, p. 380). Arndt and Gingrich give only the second meaning and translate the passage "the bountiful gift which was (previously) promised" (p. 712).

Surprisingly, Plummer writes (ICC): "It is not quite clear that the participle means 'promised long before' by the Corinthians. It might mean 'announced long before' by St. Paul" (p. 255). But almost all recent versions and commentaries adopt the first meaning.

## Cheerful Giving (9:7)

The Greek word for "cheerful" is *hilaros* (only here in NT), from which comes "hilarious." God loves a hilarious giver! It is a simple fact that when people give "generously" (v. 6, NIV), the Lord's blessing descends.

## Always . . . All (9:8)

This is one of the most striking verses in the NT—"all . . . always . . . all . . . all . . . every." And it is just as forceful in the Greek: *"pasan . . . panti pantote pasan . . . pan."* Only Paul could have written such a passage; it exactly reflects his enthusiastic personality.

## Minister or Supply? (9:10)

The verb is *chorēgeō* (only here and 1 Pet. 4:11), which comes from *choros,* "chorus," and *hēgeomai,* "lead." So it meant: "1. to lead a *choros.* 2. to defray the cost of a *choros,"* and then in late writers metaphorically, "to supply, furnish abundantly" (A-S, p. 482). So the proper translation here is "supply." The verb "ministereth" ("supplies") is the intensive compound *epichorēgeō* (five times in NT).

"Minister" (KJV) should be "will supply." The verb is future and expresses not a wish but a promise.

## Fruits or Harvest? (9:10)

"Seed" and "bread" indicate that grain is meant, not "fruits." The Greek word is *genēma* (only here in Paul). It comes from the verb *ginomai,* which means "come into being." The correct translation here is "harvest" (NASB, NIV).

## Service (9:12)

For a discussion of *leitourgia* see the comments on Phil. 2:17.

## Experiment or Proof? (9:13)

The correct meaning of *dokimē* is not "experiment" but "proof" (NASB). This noun comes from the verb *dokimazō,* which meant (1) "test," (2) "prove by testing," (3) "approve as the result of testing." Plummer (ICC) comments here: "Affliction tested the reality of the Macedonians' Christianity (viii. 2), benevolence will be a proof in the case of the Corinthians" (p. 266). *Dokimē* is translated "trial" in 8:2, but "proof" in 2:9; 13:3, and Phil. 2:22. That is what it should be here.

## Unspeakable or Indescribable? (9:15)

*Anekdiēgētos* (only here in NT) contains four elements: *a*-negative; *ek,* "out"; *dia,* "through"; and *hēgeomai,* "lead." The verb *diēgeomai* means "to set out in detail, describe" (A-S, p. 115). So *anekdiēgētos* means "inexpressible" (A-S, p. 35), or "indescribable" (NASB, NIV).

## Base or Timid? (10:1)

The adjective *tapeinos* originally meant "low." Then it came to mean "poor, lowly, undistinguished," and in a bad sense "subservient, abject" (AG, p. 811). It is in the last sense that it was used here by Paul's opponents in Corinth. This is brought out in the NIV by putting "timid" and "bold" in quotation marks, to indicate that these were terms applied to Paul by his critics. By using "meek" here, the NASB confuses it with "meekness" (first clause), which is an entirely different term in Greek.

## Bold or Courageous? (10:1-2)

In the last part of verse 1 and the first part of verse 2 "bold" is the verb *tharreō,* which means "be bold or courageous." But in the middle of verse 2 "bold" is the verb *tolmaō,* which has much the same meaning. Thayer differentiates them in this way: *"Tharreō* denotes confidence in one's own strength or capacity, *tolmaō* boldness or daring in undertaking" (p. 628). To distinguish the two words, the NASB helpfully uses "courageous" for *tolmaō.*

## Strong Holds or Fortresses? (10:4)

The word *ochyrōma* (only here in NT) means a "stronghold" or "fortress," and then metaphorically "anything on which one relies." Thayer goes on to say that here the word is used metaphorically for "the arguments and reasonings by which a disputant endeavors to fortify his opinion and defend it against his opponent" (p. 471).

## Imaginations or Arguments? (10:5)

In and of itself *logismos* simply means "a reasoning, thought" (A-S, p. 270), and it is usually translated in

Rom. 2:15 (the only other place it occurs in the NT) as "thoughts." But here it is used in a bad sense for "the thoughts of a reason which in its self-vaunting shuts itself off from God" (Heidland, TDNT, 4:287).

## Outward Appearance (10:7)

The Greek has one word, *prosōpon,* which means "face." Both the Hebrew and Greek words for "face" are used in a variety of ways.

"After the outward appearance" is *kata prosōpon.* In verse 1 the same expression is translated "in presence" (NASB and NIV have "face to face with"). But here it means "on the surface of things" (NIV).

In the KJV the first sentence of this verse is a question. But most versions today treat it as an affirmation, which is better. In the early Greek manuscripts there are no punctuation marks, and the Greek uses the same order of words for a question as for a statement—instead of reversing the order as we do in English. Since in the second person plural of the present tense the same form is used for the imperative as for the indicative, this sentence can be taken as a command: "Look at what is before your eyes" (RSV). All three possible ways of taking it are meaningful.

## Destruction or Pulling Down? (10:8)

The noun *kathairesis* comes from the verb *kathaireō,* which means "to put down by force, pull down, destroy" (A-S, p. 222). So it literally means "a pulling down."

The verb is found in verse 5, where it is translated in the KJV "casting down." The noun is rendered "pulling down" in verse 4, but "destruction" here and in 13:10 (the only three places where it occurs in NT). Since the Greek word for "edification" *(oikodomē)* means "building up," the NIV is especially good here: "the authority the Lord gave us for building you up rather than pulling you down."

## Terrify or Frighten? (10:9)

The verb *ekphobeō* (only here in NT) means "frighten, terrify" (AG, p. 246)—from *phobos*, "fear." But "frighten" (NIV) seems to fit better here. Letters are more likely to frighten people than to terrify them.

## Absent . . . Present (10:11)

These two contrasting words in English come from the Latin. But they are also somewhat parallel to the Greek words here: *apontes*, "being away," and *parontes*, "being beside."

## Make . . . of the Number (10:12)

This is one word in the Greek, the infinitive of the verb *engkrinō* (only here in NT). *Krinō* means "judge" and *en* "among" (with the plural). So this compound verb means *"to reckon among, judge among . . . to judge one worthy of being admitted to* a certain class" (Thayer, p. 167). This is well expressed by "class" (NASB) or "classify" (NIV).

"Classify or compare" (NIV) is in the Greek *engkrinai . . . synkrinai*. Paul is fond of such play on words.

## Rule (10:13)

The word *canōn* is found three times in this chapter. In verses 13 and 15 it is translated "rule" and in verse 16 "line." It is also translated "rule" in the only other place (in NT) where it occurs (Gal. 6:16).

Thayer defines *canōn* as follows: "Properly a rod or

straight piece of rounded wood to which anything is fastened to keep it straight . . . a measuring rod, rule; a carpenter's line or measuring tape," and so in 2 Cor. 10: "a definitely bounded or fixed space within the limits of which one's power or influence is confined; the province assigned to one; one's sphere of activity" (p. 324). But in Gal. 6:16 it is used in the sense of a rule or standard *(ibid.)*.

Beyer takes exception to this. He would apply the second sense to 2 Cor. 10:13-16, which he calls "a linguistically difficult passage." He says of Paul: "He thus has a canon or standard for his work and for the associated claim to apostolic authority which he has not conferred on himself but received from God." He concludes: "The measure given to Paul is not, then, a sphere marked out in space in which he alone is to work. It is the orientation laid upon him, the *charis* granted to him . . . and the blessing which God has caused to rest on his missionary activity" (TDNT, 3:599).

After discussing the idea of "sphere" (cf. NASB), Plummer comments: "But *kanōn* is generally used of *length,* and *to metron* [measure] *tou canonos* would mean 'the length of one's tether,' the length of the radius from one's centre. In this case it would mean the distance which God told the Apostle to go in his missionary work" (p. 287).

This seems to fit the passage well. But perhaps we should accept both concepts: "sphere" and "rule" or "standard."

## Glory or Boast? (10:17)

As in other places where we have met the verb *kauchaomai,* we would note that the more accurate translation today is "boast." The word occurs 5 times each in Romans and 1 Corinthians, and 21 times in 2 Corinthians. Outside of Paul's Epistles the term is used only by James (1:19; 4:16).

## Would to God (11:1)

This phrase translates one word in the Greek, *ophelon* —"2 aor. of *opheilō,* without the augment . . . used to express a fruitless wish . . . *would that"* (A-S, p. 330). This is an example of the fondness of the KJV translators for the expression, "Would to God" even though it is not in the Greek (cf. also "God forbid," 15 times). The correct translation is simply "I wish" (RSV, NASB), or "I hope" (NIV).

## Foolishness or Folly? (11:1)

Aside from Mark 7:22, the Greek word *aphrosynē* is found only in this chapter (vv. 1, 17, 21). It comes from *aphrōn,* which means "senseless, foolish." Probably "foolishness" is more contemporary than "folly." In Mark the NIV uses "folly" because a bad moral connotation is clearly suggested by the context.

## Imperative or Indicative? (11:1)

The last clause of this verse is in the form of an imperative in the KJV and RSV, but of an indicative in the NASB and NIV. Once more we have a second person plural *(anechesthe),* which can be taken either way. It is difficult here to decide between the two.

## Espoused or Betrothed? (11:2)

The verb is *harmozō* (only here in NT). It comes from *harmos,* "a joining," the origin of our word "harmony." Today we espouse a cause, not a wife. So "betroth"

(NASB) is better. The idea here is that of joining one person to another in marriage.

## Simplicity and Purity (11:3)

The KJV has only "simplicity," but the NASB adds "and purity" (cf. RSV, NIV). Why?

The answer is that the added words are found in the oldest Greek manuscripts—Papyrus 46 (third century), Vaticanus and Sinaiticus (fourth century), and Bezae (fifth century)—as well as in the best minuscule manuscripts of the Middle Ages (33, 81, 88).

## Might? (11:4)

The KJV has: "Ye might . . . bear with." But the Greek is *anechesthe* again, probably better translated as a statement, "you bear" (NASB, cf. RSV, NIV).

## Very Chiefest or Super? (11:5)

Paul takes his stand as not being a whit behind the "very chiefest" apostles. The Greek adverb *hyperlian* is found only here and in 12:11, in a parallel context. It is compounded of *hyper,* "above," and *lian,* "very, exceedingly." So it means "over much; pre-eminently" (Thayer, p. 641). Arndt and Gingrich suggest the translation, "super-apostles" for the combination expression here, and this was adopted in the NIV.

To whom is Paul referring? Arndt and Gingrich write: "These are either the original apostles . . . or, perhaps with more probability, the opponents of Paul in Corinth" (p. 849).

Plummer agrees with this. He says: "It is improbable that St. Paul would use such an expression as *hoi hyperlian apostoloi* of any of the Twelve." He adds that "there is little doubt that the phrase . . . is a sarcastic description of the Judaizing leaders, who claimed to be acting with the authority of the Twelve against one who had no such authority" (p. 298).

### Rude or Unskilled? (11:6)

The noun *idiōtēs* (only here and in Acts 4:13; 1 Cor. 14:16, 23, 24) comes from the adjective *idios*, "one's own" —that is, what is private and personal. So the noun means first "a private person" and then "one without professional knowledge, unskilled" (A-S, p. 213). The last definition fits well (cf. NASB). The NIV has here: "I may not be a trained speaker, but I do have knowledge." The current use of "rude" does not fit.

### Offence or Sin? (11:7)

The Greek word here is *hamartia*, which simply means "sin" and is translated that way 173 out of the 174 times it occurs in the NT. Why the translators chose to render it "offence" in just this one place is a mystery.

### Freely or Free of Charge? (11:7)

*Dōrean* is the accusative of *dōrea*, "a gift," used as an adverb. So it means "as a gift, without payment, gratis" (AG, p. 209). "Free of charge" (NIV) communicates this more accurately than "freely." Today preaching "freely" means speaking "with freedom."

### Chargeable or a Burden? (11:9)

*Katanarkaō* is a rare verb in Greek literature, but is found here and in 12:13, 14, where it is translated "be burdensome." That is probably the meaning here. Literally it means "to grow numb," and so metaphorically "to be inactive, be burdensome" (A-S, p. 236). Etymologically it is unrelated to the adjective *abarēs* (only here in NT), which in the last part of this verse is translated "kept from being burdensome." The NASB and NIV have in the first instance, "I was not a burden to anyone," and in the second place, "I (have) kept myself from being a burden to you."

## False Apostle (11:13)

This is one word in Greek, *pseudapostolos* (only here in NT). Paul first calls his opponents in Corinth "super-apostles" (v. 5). Then he becomes more specific and calls them "false apostles," because they were not sent by Christ, as they claimed to be.

## Transform or Masquerade? (11:13, 14, 15)

Elsewhere in the KJV "transform" is found only once —Rom. 12:2, where it is the translation of the verb *metamorphoō,* which means "change form." But the verb here is *metaschēmatizō,* which means "change appearance." This is conveyed better by "disguise" (NASB) or "masquerade" (NIV).

## Fool (11:16, 19)

Besides half a dozen other places, the adjective *aphrōn* is found twice in verse 16 and once in 19, plus 12:6, 11. It is usually treated as a substantive, "fool." Hart says that the term expresses "want of mental sanity and sobriety, a reckless and inconsiderate habit of mind" (quoted in A-S, p. 72).

Bertram writes (TDNT, 9:231):

In 2 C. 11 and 12 *aphrōn* and *aphrosynē* are used in self-criticism. The apostle's *aphrosynē* is that in the difficult conflicts with the church or congregation he apparently or provisionally sets himself on the carnal plane of self-boasting rather than on the spiritual plane. This is what Paul has in view when he speaks of his *aphrosynē* in 2 C. 11:1. In the situation at Corinth foolish boasting . . . before God and men has become necessary for him, 11:16 f.

## Suffer or Put Up With? (11:19, 20)

This is again the verb *anechō* (see vv. 1 and 4, where it is three times correctly translated "bear with," as in NASB). In verse 20, "suffer" can be very misleading, suggesting that the readers are undergoing pain. This is not the idea. The NIV helpfully has "put up with" in all four verses. That is the way we would say it today.

## Fool (11:23)

In parentheses we have the statement: "I speak as a fool." This is not *aphrōn,* but *paraphronōn,* participial form of the compound verb *paraphroneō* (only here in NT), which means "to be beside oneself, be deranged" (A-S, p. 343). The sentence may be translated "I speak as if insane" (NASB), or "I am out of my mind to talk like this" (NIV).

## Peril or Danger? (11:26)

The word *kindynos* occurs only in Rom. 8:35 (once) and 8 times in this verse. It means "danger" or "risk" (AG, p. 433).

## Painfulness or Hardship? (11:27)

*Mochthos* (found also in 1 Thess. 2:9; 2 Thess. 3:8)

means "toil, labour, hardship, distress" (A-S, p. 297). Comparing *kopos* ("weariness") with this, Thayer says that *kopos* gives prominence to the fatigue and *mochthos* to the hardship (p. 355).

## Watchings or Sleeplessness? (11:27)

*Agrypnia* occurs only here and in 6:5 (see discussion there). Its primary meaning is sleeplessness (cf. NASB, NIV).

## Fasting or Without Food? (11:27)

*Nēsteia,* usually indicating fasting, probably means lack of available food here and in 6:5 (see comments there). It is properly translated "without food" (NASB, NIV).

## Basket (11:33)

*Sagarnē* literally means "a plaited rope," and so a basket made of ropes. The word is found only here in the NT.

## Expedient or Profitable? (12:1)

*Sympheron* means "profitable" or "advantageous." The word "expedient" hardly communicates that today. The first part of the verse may rather literally be rendered: "Boasting is necessary, though it is not profitable" (NASB). The whole verse is well expressed: "I must go on boasting. Although there is nothing to be gained, I will go on to visions and revelations from the Lord" (NIV).

## Paradise (12:4)

This comes directly from the Greek *paradeisos* (here, Luke 23:43; Rev. 2:7), which is thought to be of Persian origin. Among the Greeks it was first used by the historian Xenophon in reference to the parks of Persian kings and nobles (A-S, p. 338). He describes it as shady and well watered. And so it came to mean "a garden, pleasure-ground; grove, park." Here it is used for "an upper region in the heavens" (Thayer, p. 480).

Joachim Jeremias devotes eight pages to a discussion of this word. He asserts that it is "a loan word from old Persian" (TDNT, 5:765), and adds: "Already by the 3rd. cent. B.C. it can then be used generally for a 'park'" (p. 766). The Persian term was adopted into Hebrew and Aramaic, but only in a secular sense. It was used for the Garden of Eden in Genesis 2.

Jeremias agrees with other writers (e.g., Plummer) in saying that we cannot be sure whether Paul equates "the third heaven" (v. 2) with Paradise (v. 4). It seems to us that he does.

## Thorn (12:7)

The word *skolops* (only here in NT) means "something pointed." In classical Greek it meant "a stake." But in the Septuagint it clearly is used, for the first time, in the sense of "splinter" or "thorn"—never for stake (TDNT, 7:410-11). And this is unquestionably its meaning in the papyri (VGT, pp. 578-79). "In the flesh" suggests it was a physical affliction, probably chronic malaria or poor eyesight. The idea of pain seems suggested by the context.

## Buffet (12:7)

The verb *kolaphizō* comes from the noun *kolaphos*,

"the knuckles, the closed fist." So it literally meant "to strike with the fist" (A-S, p. 252). Since thorns do not buffet a person, it seems that "torment" (NIV) is justified here.

## Reproaches or Insults? (12:10)

The word *hybris* occurs here and in Acts 27:10 (of physical disaster). Thayer says that it means "insolence, impudence, pride," and then "a wrong springing from insolence, an injury, affront, insult." He adds this comment: "in Greek usage the mental injury and wantonness of its infliction being prominent" (p. 633). It seems that "insult" conveys this better than "reproach."

## Four Things, or Three? (12:12)

The KJV of this verse sounds as if the signs of an apostle were wrought by Paul in four ways: patience, signs, wonders, and mighty deeds. But the Greek clearly names only three. The correct translation is found in the NASB: "The signs of a true apostle were performed among you with all perseverance, by signs and wonders and miracles." *Hypomonē,* usually translated "patience" in the KJV, actually means "perseverance."

## Miracles (12:12)

Three words are here used for miracles, as in the Synoptic Gospels. The first is *semeiois,* "signs." The second is *terasin,* "wonders." The third is *dynamesin*—literally, "powers," or "powerful works." *Dynamesin* is the term usually translated "miracles" in the Synoptic Gospels and Acts, as here in the NASB and NIV.

The miracles of Christ and His apostles were "powerful works." But they were also "signs," signifying a spiritual truth. And they were called "wonders" because they excited wonder in those who saw them.

## Crafty (12:16)

The adjective *panourgos* (only here in NT) literally means "ready to do anything." In classical Greek it was used mainly in a bad sense. But in the Septuagint it is used frequently in the Book of Proverbs in a good sense— "clever" or "prudent."

What does Paul mean by his use of it here? Arndt and Gingrich (p. 613) suggest a logical explanation: "Paul says, taking up an expression used by his opponents . . . crafty fellow that I am" (see NASB, NIV).

## Eight Sins (12:20)

The KJV has "debates, envyings, wraths, strifes, backbitings, whisperings, swellings, tumults." Most of these do not convey correct meanings today.

The first is *eris,* which basically means "strife" (NASB) or "quarreling" (NIV). The second, *zelos,* means "jealousy." The third, *thymoi,* suggests a boiling over. It is better rendered as "angry tempers" (NASB) or "outbursts of anger" (NIV). The fourth, *eritheiai,* suggests "factions" or "disputes." The fifth, *katalaliai,* literally means acts of speaking against. It may be translated "slanders" (NASB). The sixth, *psithyrismoi* (only here in NT) does literally mean "whisperings," but today we would call this "gossip" (NASB, NIV). The seventh, *physiōseis* (only here in NT), in the singular means "a puffing up," and so, *"swelling* with pride" (A-S, p. 476). Perhaps "arrogance" (NASB, NIV) best expresses it today. The last, *akatastasiai,* literally means "disorders" (cf. NIV) or "disturbances" (NASB).

Paul feared that he would meet these things when he returned to Corinth. No wonder he dreaded to go.

## Mouth or Testimony? (13:1)

The second sentence of this verse is a free quotation from Deut. 19:15. Probably the meaning is clear enough. Today, however, we would say "by the testimony" (NASB, NIV).

## Word or Matter? (13:1)

Abbott-Smith notes that *hrēma* is used "properly, of that which is said or spoken," and so "a word." Then it was extended to mean "a saying, statement." Parallel to the Hebrew *davar*, it finally came to be used, as here, for "a thing, matter," as "that which is the subject of speech" (p. 397). In the KJV "matter" is used in Deut. 19:15, where the Septuagint has *hrēma*. What is stated or reported has to be confirmed by two or three witnesses.

## Still Sinning (13:2)

The verb *proamartanō* is found only here and in 12:21 (the immediate context). Properly it means "to sin before" (A-S, p. 378)—from *pro*, "before," and *hamartanō*, "sin." In 12:21 it is translated "have sinned already," and in 13:2 "heretofore have sinned."

In both cases, however, it is the perfect active participle, which not only indicates completed action but also emphasizes a continuing state. So these incorrigible opponents of Paul at Corinth were still sinning.

The first part of the verse in the KJV is a literal translation of the Greek; but it makes rather awkward English and can be misunderstood. It is given more clearly in the

NIV: "I already gave you a warning when I was with you the second time. I now repeat it while absent. . . ."

## Mighty or Powerful? (13:3)

At the end of verse 3 we find the verb *dynamai* translated "is mighty," whereas in verse 4 the noun *dynamis* is twice rendered "power." By using "is powerful" in verse 3 the NIV points up the connection.

## Examine . . . Prove (13:5)

The two verbs are *peirazō* and *dokimazō*. Thayer defines the first as *"to try, make trial of, test:* (someone), for the purpose of ascertaining his quality" (p. 498). The second, he says, means *"to test, examine, prove, scrutinize* (to see whether a thing be genuine or not), as metals" (p. 154).

While these two terms seem to be used rather interchangeably in the NT, Trench warns us that "they are not perfectly synonymous." He goes on to say: "As employed in the N.T. *dokimazein* almost always implies that the proof is victoriously surmounted, the *proved* is also *approved* . . . just as in English we speak of *tried* men . . . meaning not merely those who have been tested, but who have stood the test" (*Synonyms,* p. 278).

On the other hand, *peirazō* "means properly no more than to make experience of . . . to pierce or search into." Trench continues: "It came next to signify the trying intentionally, and with the purpose of discovering what of good or evil, of power or weakness, was in a person or thing . . . or . . . revealing the same to the tried themselves; as when St. Paul addresses the Corinthians . . . 'examine yourselves'" (p. 280).

The two verbs may be translated "examine . . . prove"

(KJV), "test . . . examine" (NASB), or "examine . . . test" (RSV, NIV). They have much the same meaning here.

## Reprobates (13:5, 6, 7)

The word is *adokimoi.* It means "rejected after testing" (see *Word Meanings,* 3:38-39). The term "reprobates" does not convey that meaning today. We would now probably say "fail the test" (NASB, NIV). Paul affirms that he has not failed the test, and he hopes that his readers will not.

In the middle of verse 7 we have "approved" and at the end "reprobates." The Greek had *"dokimoi . . . adokimoi."* The NASB expresses this play on words by using "approved . . . unapproved." On the other hand, the NIV preserves the continuity of the three occurrences of *adokimoi* by having in verse 7: "stood the test . . . may seem to have failed."

## Wish or Pray? (13:9)

The verb is *euchomai,* which is correctly translated "pray" in verse 7. That is the only meaning that Abbott-Smith's *Lexicon* gives for this word, though others allow "wish." But we would agree with Greeven when he writes: "In 2 C. 13:7 Paul expressly mentions God, to whom he prays that the Corinthians may do no evil. We should understand v. 9 also of intercessory prayer rather than as a mere wish" (TDNT, 2:776).

The verb *euchomai* occurs only 7 times in the NT. Already the compound *proseuchomai* had begun to supplant the simple verb in the Septuagint, and in the NT it became dominant (87 times).

## Perfection (13:9, 11)

In verse 11 it is the verb *katartizō* (see WM, 3:196). In verse 9 it is the derivative noun *katartisis* (only here in NT). On the latter Delling writes: "Similarly *katartisis* denotes inner strength, whether of the community *(oikodomē)* in its organic relationship, or of the character of its members, i.e., their maturity as Christians (2 C. 13:9)" (TDNT, 1:476). Both "perfection" (KJV, NIV) and "completion" (NASB) fit well here. But the verb in verse 11 must be translated consistently with this.

## Sharpness (13:10)

It is the adverb *apotomōs* (only here and Titus 1:13). Abbott-Smith says it means: "abruptly, curtly," and so "sharply, severely" (p. 55). Plummer says of Paul: "He writes sharply, that he may not have to act sharply" (p. 378).

## Edification . . . Destruction (13:10)

The first noun is *oikodomē,* which literally means "building up." The second is *kathairesis* (see comments on 10:4, 8), which means "pulling down." So the correct translation here is: "for building up and not for tearing down" (NASB; cf. NIV).

# GALATIANS

∾≀⊚⋔⊚⨾∾

Paul's Epistle to the Galatians ranks only second to Romans in its theological importance. But it served a very unique and invaluable purpose in pointing Martin Luther to the truth which he embodied in the Protestant Reformation. He himself said of it: "The Epistle to the Galatians is my epistle. To it I am as it were in wedlock."

The case of John Bunyan is also striking. Seeking desperately for deliverance from his awful sense of sin, he found an old copy of Martin Luther's *Commentary on Galatians.* Here is what he says about that experience:

> When I had but a little way perused, I found my condition in his experience so largely and profoundly handled, as if his book had been written out of my heart. I prefer this book of Martin Luther on the Galatians (excepting the Holy Bible) before all the books that ever I have seen, as most fit for a wounded conscience.

Paul wrote to free the Galatian Christians from the bonds of Judaistic legalism in his day. Martin Luther wrote to free the people of his generation from the yoke of Roman Catholicism, with its religion of works-righteousness. The message of the epistle is still very pertinent. The purpose of these studies is to open some word windows for glimpsing that message more clearly.

## Apostle (1:1)

Our English word is a transliteration of the Greek *apostolos,* which comes from the verb *apostellō,* "send away, send on an errand, send with a commission." The earliest use of *apostolos* was for a fleet, an expedition. Herodotus used it for a messenger, or one sent on a mission. That was its common meaning in New Testament times.

Though used rarely in classical Greek, it occurs some 80 times in the NT. Eight of these occurrences are in the Synoptic Gospels. Cremer comments: "Perhaps it was just the rare occurrence of the word in profane Greek that made it all the more appropriate as the distinctive appellation of 'the Twelve' whom Christ chose to be His witnesses" (p. 530). In the Synoptic Gospels (mostly Luke) it regularly carries the technical sense of one of the Twelve. (In John's Gospel it is found only in 13:16, where it is translated "he that is sent.")

In the first part of the Book of Acts this usage continues. But in connection with the Gentile mission we find a broadening of the term. In Acts 14:14 we read of "the apostles Barnabas, and Paul." Since these were the two great missionaries sent out by the church at Antioch, we find here a suggestion of the modern application of the term. Today an apostle is a missionary, commissioned and sent forth. In a very real sense every preacher is an apostle. In a still more definite sense every true missionary of Christ is an apostle.

But that does not exhaust the meaning of the term. It has been suggested that the best translation for *apostolos* is "envoy." In the volume on Galatians in the *New International Commentary on the New Testament,* Ridderbos has this to say: "An *apostle* is a minister plenipotentiary" (p. 40). In connection with Gal. 1:1 he comments: "Paul is God's own and special ambassador" (p. 41).

No wonder Paul asserts his apostolic authority in opposing the heretical teachers in the churches of Galatia. He did not wear a badge pinned on him by some earthly potentate or pope. He carried in his heart the consciousness of a divine call and commission to be Christ's ambassador to men. What greater authority could one ask?

## Church (1:2)

The Greek word for church is *ekklēsia.* This comes from the verb *ekkaleō (ek,* "out"; *kaleō,* "call"), "call out." It has therefore often been emphasized that the Church is a body of "called out ones."

But the first question that should be asked is: What was the common meaning of the term in Paul's day? Because usage, rather than etymology, is the main factor in determining the meaning of a word at any given period or in any particular place.

*Ekklēsia* was the name applied to the assembly of free citizens in a Greek city. We find the term used in exactly that way in Acts 19:32, 39, 41 (particularly as in v. 39 of a "lawful assembly"; that is, one regularly convened). This would be the usage most familiar to the Gentile readers of Paul's epistles.

But there is another important background. The Septuagint (Greek translation of the OT, made 200 years before Christ) uses *ekklēsia* for the "congregation" or "assembly" of Israel. This usage is reflected in the NT, in Acts 7:38.

In the time of Christ the Jewish gathering for worship

was called the synagogue. Perhaps it was partly because of the severe persecutions from the Jews that the Christians chose *ekklēsia* rather than *synagogē* as the designation for their place of worship and for the congregation gathered there.

In the NT we find a distinct, twofold use of *ekklēsia:* "(I) The entire congregation of all who are called by and to Christ, who are in the fellowship of His salvation—the Church. (II) The N.T. churches as confined to particular places" (Cremer, pp. 334-35). The latter sense is obviously the one in which the word is used in this passage.

## Grace (1:3)

The Greek *charis* is one of the most beautiful and meaningful words in the NT. Abbott-Smith's *Manual Greek Lexicon of the New Testament* gives an excellent summary of its varied meanings, which we quote in part:

> 1. Objectively, that which causes favourable regard, *gracefulness, grace, loveliness* of form, *graciousness* of speech. 2. Subjectively, (a) on the part of the giver, *grace, graciousness, kindness, goodwill, favour;* esp. in N.T. of the divine *favour, grace,* with emphasis on its freeness and universality; (b) on the part of the receiver, a sense of favour received, *thanks, gratitude* (p. 479).

A rapid check of Moulton and Geden's *Concordance to the Greek Testament* shows that *charis* occurs in all the NT books except Matthew, Mark, and 1 John. Paul uses it dozens of times in his Epistles.

The first emphasis of this word was on physical gracefulness. But as usual, the NT gives largest place to the highest meaning. Cremer writes: "*Charis* has been distinctively appropriated in the N.T. to designate the relation and conduct of God towards sinful man as revealed in and through Christ, especially as an act of *spontaneous favour*" (p. 574).

It would be impossible to compass the tremendous scope of this term or even to delineate its particular theological signification. Here we must content ourselves with two brief observations.

First, we fear that too many conservatives glory in the orthodoxy of their emphasis on the wonderful grace of God shown in the forgiveness of our sins—the unmerited favor of God in pardoning our guilt and accepting us as His children—without facing all the implications of this beautiful term. It is not enough to thank God for His grace. We must ask, Does that grace make us more gracious? We read in the OT that God is "gracious." When Jesus spoke, the people wondered at the "gracious words" that proceeded from His mouth (Luke 4:22). Has our preaching ever produced that reaction? But, more importantly, do we rightly represent God by being gracious in all our relations with our fellowmen? To be boorish in our personal relations in life shows a tragic lack of the "grace" of God, however orthodox we may be and whatever experience we may profess.

The other observation is that this term is used for "the grace of giving." In 2 Cor. 8:7 Paul urges his readers to "abound in this grace also." In 1 Cor. 16:3 the word "liberality"—meaning an offering—is *charis* in the original. Since God has so freely given to us, we should be liberal in giving to the work of His kingdom. The greatest incentive to giving perhaps lies in this word "grace."

## Peace (1:3)

The word "peace" *(eirēnē)* means more than freedom from outward strife. It means essentially an inner harmony, something that can be brought about only by the grace of God.

Someone has defined grace as meaning "the divine adequacy." We would like to suggest that peace means "the consciousness of the divine adequacy." As Christians we have adequate resources at our disposal, in the grace of an infinite God, to meet all the emergencies of life. But we only feel peaceful as we are conscious of that adequacy.

Paul, of course, had in mind the Hebrew word for peace, *shalom,* which meant "total well-being for time and eternity" (IB, 10:447). That was the kind of "peace" that he wished for his readers. And he knew full well that that kind of peace could come to them only from "God our father and the Lord Jesus Christ." The "God of peace" is the only source of true peace.

## Sins (1:4)

The Greek word here for sin *(hamartia)* means "missing the mark." It is derived from the verb *hamartanō,* which is used in Homer some hundred times of a warrior hurling his spear but missing his foe. In classical Greek the verb came to be used for missing the right, going wrong, sinning. The noun was used in the sense of "guilt, sin," though more frequently for "fault, failure." In the NT it always has the theological connotation. Stahlin says that the NT "uses *hamartia* to denote the determination of human nature in hostility to God" (TDNT, 1:295).

Cremer has some pertinent comments. He says that *hamartia* "would seem to denote primarily, *not sin considered as an action, but sin considered as the quality of action,* that is, *sin generically* . . . Sin is not merely the quality of an action, but a principle manifesting itself in the conduct of the subject" (pp. 100-101). Paul prefers to use other words for sinful acts, reserving *hamartia* largely for the generic idea of sin as a principle, what we call the carnal nature. However, in the plural, as here, it may denote sinful acts as such.

## World (1:4)

The word translated "world" in the KJV is *aiōn,* which properly means "age" and is so rendered in most recent translations.

Originally *aiōn* meant "lifetime," the duration of a human life. Then it came to be used for a "generation," which is a life span. Finally it was expanded to mean unlimited duration, eternity.

In verse 4 it is used for "the present evil age," which is under the domination of "the prince of this world" (John 12:31; 14:30; 16:11). In John it is *cosmos,* this world-system. But here it is the time element which is indicated. It is the period of evil rule.

In verse 5 the expression "for ever and ever" is literally "to the ages of the ages." This is the fullest phrase in the NT to indicate eternity. What a glorious thought that for the saints eternity will be a never ending succession of age after age of bliss and blessing. Certainly we ought to put up with this "light affliction which is but for a moment" (2 Cor. 4:17), while living in this present evil age, with our hopes set steadfastly on that blessed life that shall never end.

## Another Gospel? (1:6-7)

The language of these verses seems strange. Paul writes: "I marvel that ye are so soon removed (lit., removing) from him that called you into the grace of Christ unto another gospel: which is not another." What does he mean by saying that it is "another" and "not another"?

Two different Greek words are used in verses 6 and 7. The KJV translates them both by "another." Recent versions more correctly read "different" in verse 6 and "another" in verse 7. The first is *heteros*, the second *allos*. The distinction between these two words is well pointed out by Trench in his *Synonyms of the New Testament*. He writes: "*Allos*, identical with the Latin 'alius,' is the numerically distinct. . . . But *heteros*, equivalent to the Latin 'alter' . . . superadds the notion of qualitative difference. One is 'divers,' the other 'diverse'" (p. 357).

When Jesus promised another Comforter (John 14:16) the word *allos* is used. The Holy Spirit would be a distinct Personality; but He would not be a different *(heteros)* kind of Paraclete. Rather, He would be another of the same kind *(allos)*.

Now the language of Paul is clear. He bemoans the fact that the Galatian Christians are turning to a "different" gospel, which is really "not another" gospel. What they were now following was not the glad, good news that men can be saved through faith in Christ but the very depressing idea that one must work for his salvation. Legalistic Judaism did not present another way of salvation. It was heterodoxy, "different opinion"; not orthodoxy, "straight opinion." There is only one true gospel, Paul would say, only one way of salvation. That is not to be found in the law, but in Christ.

## Gospel (1:6)

Our English word comes from the old Anglo-Saxon *godspell*, "good tidings." The Greek word is *euangelion*. A cognate noun is *euangelistēs*, which we have taken over into English as "evangelist."

The word *euangelion* was first used in classical Greek for "a reward for good tidings," or "sacrifice for good tidings." Later Greek writers use it for the good news itself. In the NT it carries the specialized sense of "the good tidings of the kingdom of God and of salvation through Christ."

In his excellent article on *euangelion* in the *Theological Dictionary of the New Testament* Gerhard Friedrich writes: "For Paul the heart of the good news is the story of Jesus and His suffering, death and resurrection" (2:730). He also declares: "The Gospel does not merely bear witness to salvation history; it is itself salvation history. It breaks into the life of man, refashions it and creates communities" (2:731).

The verb *euangelizō,* which gives us "evangelize," occurs many times in the NT. Usually it is translated "preach" or "preach the gospel," whichever fits more smoothly into the context.

But there are two passages that illustrate the original meaning of the word: "bring glad tidings." One is Luke 1:19. The angel Gabriel said to Zacharias: "I . . . am sent . . . to *shew* thee these *glad tidings.*" The other is 1 Thess. 3:6. Here Paul says that Timothy came from Thessalonica "and *brought* us *good tidings* of your faith and charity." Aside from these two passages the word usually has the technical meaning of publishing the good tidings of the gospel.

## Deserters and Perverters (1:6-7)

There are two interesting Greek words in verses 6 and 7. The first is *metatithesthe;* the second, *metastrepsai.* In the RSV the former is translated "you are deserting"; the second, "to pervert." The KJV also has "pervert" for the second, but "ye are removed" for the first. The RSV translation suggests that the Galatians were deserters, and their teachers perverters.

The first word, *metatithēmi,* means "transfer to another place, change." Vincent notes that in classical Greek it is used "of altering a treaty, changing an opinion, deserting an army" (4:85). It is this last usage which has suggested the striking translation of the RSV.

The other word, *metastrephō,* means "turn about, change, reverse"; and in an evil sense, "pervert, corrupt." Vine (3:180) says the word means "to transform into something of an opposite character." As an illustration of its meaning here we might cite Acts 2:20, "the sun shall be turned into darkness." That is what the false teachers in Galatia were doing: turning the glorious sunlight of God's truth into the darkness of error. They were transforming the gospel of Christ into something that was not a gospel at all. That is the keynote of verses 6-10. These Galatian Christians were being duped and deceived by this erroneous teaching and were deserting Christ and His free gospel of salvation.

## Angel (1:8)

Paul goes so far as to say that even if "an angel from heaven" should preach to them a gospel contrary to what he had preached, "let him be accursed." It is difficult to imagine what stronger language he could have used to assert the utter uniqueness of the gospel he preached.

The word "angel" is taken directly from the Greek *angelos,* which means "messenger." It occurs about 200 times in the NT. More than one-third of these instances (some 76) are found in the Book of Revelation. Luke also refers frequently to angels in his Gospel and Acts.

In practically all instances the word is transliterated as "angel." But the literal translation "messenger" occurs in seven places in the NT. Three of them are in the quotation of Mal. 3:1 in Matthew, Mark, and Luke. A fourth case is found in 2 Cor. 12:7, where Paul refers to his thorn in the flesh as "the messenger of Satan."

The other three occurrences are clear examples of the simple meaning "messenger." In Luke 7:24 we read of the messengers *(angeloi)* whom John the Baptist sent to interrogate Jesus. In Luke 9:52 we are told that Jesus sent messengers on ahead to make arrangements for the night's lodging. And in James 2:25 mention is made of the messengers sent by Joshua.

What then is an angel? The answer is found in Heb. 1:14—"Are they not all ministering spirits, sent forth to minister for them who shall be heirs of salvation?" The angels are God's messengers, running errands and carrying messages for Him.

Yet Paul declares that even if one of these heavenly messengers should preach a different gospel from what he preached, he should be accursed. Either Paul was a bigoted egotist, a fanatical fool, or else he had a valid and overwhelming consciousness of a divine inspiration that certified the infallible source of his message. Nineteen centuries of Christian history have proved that the latter was the case. The authority of Paul's gospel is authenticated by the transformation it has wrought in millions of men and women who have heard and obeyed it.

## Accursed (1:8)

The Greek noun *anathema* occurs only seven times in the NT, and the verb *anathematizō* four times.

The noun is found in the Septuagint as the translation of the Hebrew *cherem*. This word had two distinct meanings. It is translated "accursed," "accursed thing," etc. But it is also translated "devoted," "devoted thing." The cognate verb *charam* is rendered in the KJV at least 12 ways: "consecrate, destroy, devote, make accursed, utterly destroy (40 times), utterly slay, be devoted, be forfeited, be utterly destroyed," etc. The essential idea of the noun is *"devoted to destruction,* something given up to death on account of God" (Cremer, p. 547).

That is the regular meaning of *anathema* in the NT. Some have tried to weaken its force in one or two places to the sense of excommunication. But Cremer objects to this. He holds that the word "denotes not punishment intended as discipline, but *a being given over,* or *devotion to divine condemnation"* (p. 548). In other words, it always in the NT has the idea of a curse attached to it, as it did in the secular Greek of that time.

Paul says here, If we as ministers of the Word preach any other gospel than that clearly revealed in the NT we place ourselves under the awful curse of God. Better never to have entered the ministry than to stand in the pulpit and preach some substitute for the gospel. Those who reject the atonement of Christ are teaching basically the same heterodox human opinions that were being circulated in Galatia in the first century, namely, that one is saved through his own work-righteousness rather than through the divine righteousness provided in Christ. A Christless gospel is no gospel at all. Salvation by works either presents man with a ladder he can never climb or else it lulls him to sleep in the false security of self-righteousness.

## Revelation (1:12)

Paul declares that his gospel is not human, for neither did he receive it from man nor was he taught it, but it came to him by direct divine revelation. Oepke says that the mystery hidden from the ages became known to Paul "through the self-revelation of Jesus Christ. . . . This is how Paul received his Gospel (Gal. 1:12, 16). . . . God used revelation to convince him of the resurrection of the Crucified. This altered at a stroke his whole attitude to what he already knew of Jesus. The lying message became the message of salvation, and Paul's task was now to pass it on" (TDNT, 3:584).

The Greek word for "revelation" is *apocalypsis,* which we have taken over into English as "apocalypse," the name often given to the Book of Revelation in the NT.

The noun comes from the verb *apocalyptō,* which means "uncover, disclose." It "refers primarily to the removal of what conceals, an uncovering, and in some cases the choice of the word seems to be due to the thought of a previous concealment" (Burton, p. 433). Consequently *apocalypsis* means "an uncovering, disclosing, laying bare."

Burton (ICC) gives a good outline of the NT usage of *apocalypsis:*

> 1. An appearance or manifestation of a person, a coming, or coming to view; used of the coming of Christ.
> 2. A disclosure of a person or thing such that its true character can be perceived.
> 3. A divine revelation or disclosure of a person in his true character, of truth, or of the divine will, made to a particular individual, and as such necessarily involving the perception of that which is revealed (p. 434).

Cremer says of *apocalyptō:* "The word serves especially in the N.T. to denote the act of divine revelation" (p. 342). He notes that *apocalypsis* is rare in secular Greek. Then he adds: "In the N.T. it is applied exclusively to disclosures and communications proceeding from God or Christ, of objects of Christian faith, knowledge, and hope, that are in and by themselves hidden, unknown, and unrecognized" (p. 343).

It has long been a conviction of the writer that we do not have a firm faith in the deity of Jesus unless and until there is a revelation of the divine Christ to our own hearts. No amount of instruction can produce that sense of certainty that takes the crook out of question marks and thereby turns them into exclamation points. We may be logically persuaded as to the reasonableness and scripturalness of the doctrine of the deity of Jesus. But we need more than that if we are going to preach with the conviction that produces convictions.

Preaching opinions learned from others will never carry authority. The people were astonished because Jesus taught them with authority, and not as the scribes (Matt. 7:29). What was the difference? The scribes discussed and debated the traditions of the elders. Jesus spoke with a sense of inner certainty that gripped His hearers. We today can have a revelation of Jesus Christ to our own hearts by the Holy Spirit that will carry complete conviction of the truth of His deity. No man has the right to stand in the pulpit to preach unless he is dead sure of the deity of Jesus Christ. That is the *sine qua non* of the ministry.

## Conversation or Conduct? (1:13)

There are three different Greek words which are translated "conversation" in the KJV of the NT. But none of them has to do with "conversation" as we use that term today.

The first is *politeuma*, found only in Phil. 3:20. It comes from *politeuō*, "be a citizen, live as a citizen." That verb comes from *politēs*, "citizen," which, in turn, comes from *polis*, "city" (cf. Indianapolis, Minneapolis, etc.). So the meaning of *politeuma* is "citizenship," as correctly rendered in the ASV (1901).

The second word translated "conversation" in the KJV is *tropos*, which means "way or manner." The third, found here, is *anastrophē*, which literally means "a turning down or back, a wheeling about." But in later writers, as in the NT, it is used in the sense of "manner of life, behavior, conduct." One could well cross out "conversation" wherever it occurs in the KJV of the NT (Gal. 1:13; Eph. 4:22; 1 Tim. 4:12; Heb. 13:5, 7; Jas. 3:13; 1 Pet. 1:15, 18; 2:12; 3:1, 2, 16; 2 Pet. 2:7; 3:11) and write "conduct" above it as a more correct rendering. The trouble is that our English word "conversation" has greatly narrowed its meaning in the last 300 years, so that it no longer refers to all of one's conduct, but only to "talk." But the Greek words mean much more than that. The one exception is Phil. 3:20, where it should be translated "citizenship" or "commonwealth."

The two occurrences of "conversation" in the OT (Ps. 37:14; 50:23) should be changed to "way."

## Wasted or Destroyed? (1:13)

In verses 13 and 23 of this chapter we find the verb *portheō*. In the KJV it is rendered "wasted" in verse 13 and "destroyed" in verse 23 (as also in Acts 9:21, its only other occurrence in the NT). In the earliest Greek writers, such as Homer, *portheō* is a military term. It was used of destroying or ravaging cities. It regularly conveyed the idea of violent destruction. In the NT it is used only to describe Paul's activities. The imperfect tense would suggest that Paul "was ravaging" the Church and trying to destroy it, but that he did not completely succeed.

## Profit or Advance? (1:14)

We read that Paul "profited" in the Jews' religion (Gk., Judaism). The word is *prokoptō*, literally meaning "cut before," and so "advance." The figure is that of a runner in a race cutting ahead of others. Paul was away out in front, already a leader as a young man.

## Equals (1:14)

Paul says that he advanced beyond "many my equals." What does he mean? The word in the original is *sunēlikiōtēs,* which occurs only here. Its meaning is "one of the same age, an equal in age." Even as a young man in Judaism Paul was forging away ahead of his "contemporaries." The glorious thing is that as a Christian he did exactly the same thing again.

## See or Visit? (1:18)

After his conversion Paul went into Arabia—probably the quiet countryside near Damascus—to meditate and think through the implications of his newfound faith in Jesus, the Messiah. After some few weeks or months he returned to Damascus. "Then after three years" he went up to Jerusalem (vv. 17-18).

What was the purpose of Paul's journey to Jerusalem? The KJV says that he went up to "see" Peter. But the term thus translated is not one of the five common Greek words for "see," which together occur hundreds of times in the NT. This is a more rare term, found only here in the NT. It is *historeō,* from which we get our word "history." Originally it meant "inquire into, learn by inquiry," and then "narrate, record"—suggesting "history." However, in late writers it came to mean "visit, become acquainted with." This is its meaning here.

Paul is emphasizing the fact that he did not go up to Jerusalem to take a course of theological instruction under the apostles. Rather he went to get acquainted with Peter, and he paid him a brief visit of only two weeks. That would not have given him time to be "taught" (v. 12) the gospel, which instead he received by divine revelation.

## Reputation (2:2)

Paul states that he went up to Jerusalem and "communicated unto them that gospel which I preach among the Gentiles, but privately *to them which were of reputation.*" These last six words are only two in the Greek, *tois dokousin.* This is the definite article with the present participle of *dokeō.* The same combination occurs twice again in verse 6 and once in verse 9. In verse 6 it is translated "who seemed" and "who seemed to be somewhat." In verse 9 it is translated "who seemed." The RSV translates: "those who were of repute" (v. 2), "those who were reputed," and "those who were of repute" (v. 6), "who were reputed" (v. 9). It could be rendered "those in esteem."

The verb *dokeō* means "be of opinion, think, suppose." It also means "seem, be reputed." It occurs 63 times in the NT. In the KJV it is translated "think" 33 times, "seem" 13 times, "suppose" 7 times, "seem good" 3 times, "please" and "acount" twice each, and once each it is rendered "trow," "be of reputation," "pleasure."

What does Paul mean by these men who were "of reputation"? Some have thought he was ironical. But the majority of the best scholars are agreed that he was not. For instance, Trench says of *dokeō:* "There is ever a predominant reference to the public opinion and estimate, rather than to the actual being; however the former may be a faithful echo of the latter. Thus, while there is no touch of irony, no shadow of depreciation, in St. Paul's use of *hoi dokountes* at Gal. 2:2 (and 6) and while manifestly there could be no slight intended, seeing that he so characterizes the chief of his fellow Apostles, the words for all this express rather the reputation in which these were held in the Church than the worth which in themselves they had, however that reputation of theirs was itself the true measure of this worth" (pp. 305-06).

The other side of the picture, however, is found in Galatians 6:3—"For if a man think himself to be something, when he is nothing, he deceiveth himself." Here *dokeō* ("think") obviously refers to an opinion of oneself which is sadly distorted. But in Galatians 2, it is the opinion of others which is indicated; that is, one's reputation. One's opinion of himself may be much farther from the truth than the reputation which he has.

We should be concerned as to what men think of us, more concerned as to what we think of ourselves, but most concerned as to what God thinks of us. And always we should strive to make sure that what we *seem* to be is what we actually are.

## Privily or Secretly? (2:4)

Paul speaks of "false brethren unawares brought in, who came in privily to spy out our liberty which we have in Christ Jesus." The expression "unawares brought in" is all one word in Greek, the adjective *pareisaktous.* "Came in privily" is likewise one word, the verb *pareisēlthon.* Both are double compounds, with the two prepositional prefixes *para* (beside) and *eis* (in). The rest of the adjective is from *agō,* "lead, bring," and the simple verb is the second aorist of *erchomai,* "go, come." The adjective is correctly translated "brought in secretly." The verb means "came in secretly."

"Privily" is the obsolete term for "privately." But the real meaning here is "secretly." These false brethren sneaked in underhandedly "to spy out" the liberty which the Gentile Christians were enjoying. Lightfoot comments: "The metaphor is that of spies or traitors introducing themselves by stealth into the enemy's camp" (p. 106).

## Person (2:6)

"God accepteth no man's person." The Greek here is *prosōpon*, which means "face." This literal translation is usually found in the KJV. Other renderings, however, are: "presence," "countenance," "appearance," "before," and "fashion."

Here the Greek literally says, "God does not receive a man's face." One is reminded of the words of the Pharisees and Herodians—quoted in all three Synoptic Gospels (Matt. 22:16; Mark 12:14; Luke 20:21)—"Thou regardest not the person of men" (lit., "look not on men's faces"). The idea goes back to the OT, where "face" often means "presence." The meaning here is clearly indicated by the RSV, "God shows no partiality," or by the NIV, "God does not judge by external appearance."

## Wrought or Mighty? (2:8)

Here we find the same Greek word translated by two rather different expressions. "Wrought effectually" and "was mighty" are both translations of *energeō*, from which we get "energy" and "energize." It means, "be at work, be in action, operate." Moulton and Milligan state that the verb "seems always to have the idea of effective working" (VGT, p. 214). They prefer the translation "by Peter" rather than "in Peter" (KJV) or "for Peter" (ASV). The RSV renders v. 8 "for he who worked through Peter for the mission to the circumcised worked through me also for the Gentiles."

One can hardly refrain from commenting that if ever there was an "energetic" individual that one was the apostle Paul. His counterpart in modern times was John Wesley. No one can visit John Wesley's home in London, kneel in his prayer room, and stand in his pulpit in City Road Chapel, without being tremendously impressed with the almost measureless "energy" of this small but mighty man whose incomparable life spanned the eighteenth century. One comes away with the cry in his heart: "O Lord, make me more like John Wesley, and the apostle Paul, but especially like the Christ who inspired them both."

## Fellowship (2:9)

The word is *koinonia*, from *koinos*, "common." Thayer defines it as "fellowship, association, community, communion, joint participation . . . the share which one has in anything" (p. 352). The word is translated "fellowship" in almost all English versions. In KJV it is rendered "fellowship" 12 times, "communion" 4 times, "contribution," "communication," "to communicate," and "distribution" once each.

Moulton and Milligan show that in the papyri (contemporary with NT times) the word was clearly used in the sense of "partnership." Hauck calls attention to "partners" in Luke 5:10, where the same root *(koinonoi)* is used (TDNT, 3:804).

This adds a beautiful thought here. Not only were James, Peter, and John displaying a good spirit of Christian fellowship towards Paul and Barnabas, but they were shaking hands as partners in a business enterprise. Wisely they decided on a distribution of labor. The first three were to minister to Jews; the latter two were to go to the Gentiles.

## Blamed or Condemned? (2:11)

The verb *kataginōskō* means "blame, condemn." But in the only other two occurrences of the word in the NT (1 John 3:20, 21) the KJV uses "condemn"—"If our heart condemn us," "if our heart condemn us not." Clearly that is the right translation there. Should it be translated the same way here?

The answer of practically all good scholars and commentators is, "Yes." Lightfoot says: "Not 'reprehensible', but 'condemned'. His conduct carried its own condemnation with it" (p. 111). Burton affirms that this is "evidently much more appropriate in a clause in which Paul gives the reason for resisting Peter" (p. 103). Huxtable, in the *Pulpit Commentary,* says: "The rendering *to be blamed,* correct so far as it reaches, is inadequate in expressing the sense which St. Paul had of the *gravity* of St. Peter's offense" (p. 80).

## Dissimulation (2:13)

The verb translated "dissemble with" is *synypokrinomai,* which occurs only here in the NT. The noun "dissimulation" is *hypokrisis,* which gives us our English word "hypocrisy." ("Hypocrite" is also from the Greek *hypokritēs.*)

The verb *hypokrinomai*—to which *syn* ("with") is added here—means literally "answer from under"; that is, from under a mask as an actor would do when playing his part. Vine (1:242) writes: "It was a custom for Greek and Roman actors to speak in large masks with mechanical devices for augmenting the force of the voice." So the verb here, *synypokrinomai,* means "join in acting the hypocrite, in pretending to act from one motive, whereas another motive really inspires the act" (Vine, 1:324). Probably the best translation of this verb is "play the hypocrite." And "dissimulation" should be changed to "hypocrisy," as in most of the recent versions.

How could their conduct be thus labeled? Vincent says: "Their act was *hypocrisy,* because it was a concealment of their own more liberal conviction, and an open

profession of still adhering to the narrow Pharisaic view."
Peter and Barnabas had both associated freely with Gen-
tile Christians. In his present attitude Peter was repudiat-
ing the light he had received at Joppa on the housetop
(Acts 10). Paul saw clearly the serious consequences for the
Church in dividing it into Jewish and Gentile branches.
That is why he dealt so firmly with the situation.

Wilckens points out the fact that in distinction from
classical Greek, the Septuagint uses these words in a bad
sense (TDNT, 8:563). This negative sense is also found in
Philo and Josephus, as well as in the literature of Disper-
sion Judaism in general (p. 565). Of our present passage
Wilckens writes: "Paul's charge is not that they deceived
the envoys from Jerusalem by their sudden change of
practice. Their *hypocrisis* was not culpable tactical hypocrisy. . . . The real point was that by breaking off table
fellowship between Jews and Gentiles in the one Church
they were not walking straight according to the truth of the
gospel, Gal. 2:14" (p. 569). Cremer writes: "The hypocrite
seeks to appear before men as he ought to be but is not
before God" (p. 380).

## Walk Uprightly (2:14)

The verb is *orthopodeō*, found here for the first time in
Greek literature. It comes from *orthos* ("straight") and
*pous* ("foot"). The expression means "make a straight
path, pursue a straight course." Vine says that it is "used
metaphorically in Gal. 2:14, signifying a course of conduct
by which one leaves a straight track for others to follow"
(4:195). The implication is that Peter and Barnabas had
swerved aside from the path of truly Christian conduct.
Burton writes: "The present word is apparently not simply
a general ethical term for doing right, but, as the context
implies, denotes straightforward, unwavering, and sincere

conduct in contrast with the pursuing of a crooked, waver-
ing, and more or less insincere course, such as Paul had
just attributed to Peter and those who followed him" (p.
110). Williams (CGT) agrees with Vine in holding that the
word "suggests not only a crooked walk but the crooked
track thereby made, likely to lead others astray." Perhaps
the best translation is, "They were not walking straight."

## Justified (2:16-17)

The verb *dikaioō* occurs three times in v. 16 and once
in v. 17. It is uniformly translated "justify" in most English versions. However, Goodspeed has "made upright"
and Young has "declare righteous." Verkuyl inconsistent-
ly has "made righteous" the first two times and "justify"
the last two times. Williams employs the rather lengthy
circumlocution "Come into right standing with God."

What does *dikaioō* really mean? The difficulty is
shown somewhat by the fact that Cremer devotes 16 pages
in his *Lexicon* to *dikaios* and its cognate terms.

He defines the adjective *dikaios* as meaning "what is
right, conformable to right, pertaining to right—just." He
then goes on to say (p. 184): "Righteousness in the biblical
sense is a condition of rightness the standard of which is
God, which is estimated according to the divine standard,
which shows itself in behaviour conformable to God, and
has to do above all things with its relation to God, and
with the walk before him." He further notes that it designates "the normal relation of men and their acts, etc., to
God."

Under *dikaiosyne* (righteousness) Cremer comes
closer to our problem, when he writes: "The Pauline conception of righteousness denotes the state of the believing
man called forth by the divine acquittal" (p. 193).

The verb *dikaioō* occurs rarely in classical Greek. But

in the NT it is found 39 times (27 in Paul), while its cognate terms occur about 200 times. Unquestionably it is one of the central ideas of the NT.

Cremer gives as its fundamental meaning in the NT, "to recognize, to set forth, as righteous, to justify" (p. 195). He also says that with Paul it "denotes nothing else than the *judicial act* of God, whereby man is pronounced free from guilt and punishment" (p. 197).

Abbott-Smith defines righteousness as "conformity to the Divine will in purpose, thought and action." He gives the meaning of the verb in the NT as "show to be righteous." Thayer agrees with this. He says that negatively it means to "declare guiltless," positively to "declare acceptable."

Burton (ICC) has 15 pages on *dikaios* and its cognate terms. He notes that *dikaios* in classical Greek was "fundamentally a forensic or court term" (p. 460). But in Hebrew usage the corresponding words are "prevailingly moral as well as forensic" (p. 466). In the NT "righteousness" means "conduct and character which satisfy the ethical requirements of God, and so render one acceptable to him." It also means, in a more forensic sense, "acceptance with God" (p. 469). It includes forgiveness. "Since, according to Paul, 'all have sinned and are destitute of the divine approval,' forgiveness is included in righteousness, either distinctly and explicitly, or by implication" *(ibid.)*.

But is this all that the term implies? Vincent objects strongly to that conclusion. He says: "The meaning *to declare* or *pronounce righteous* cannot be consistently carried through Paul's writings in the interest of a theological fiction of imputed righteousness." He calls attention to passages that speak of justification by works of law, and then observes: "If one is justified by the works of the law, his righteousness is a real righteousness, founded upon his conformity to the law. Why is the righteousness of faith any less a real righteousness?" (4:104).

In connection with Rom. 3:20, Vincent gives an extended discussion of *dikaioō*. After recognizing the fact that the main emphasis in classical Greek is judicial, he defines its NT meaning as indicating "the act or process by which a man is brought into a right state as related to God." He further emphasizes the idea of a right state by saying: "Justification aims directly at *character*. It contemplates making *the man himself* right" (3:39). He concludes with this significant statement: "Justification which does not *actually remove* the wrong condition in man which is at the root of his enmity to God, is no justification. In the absence of this, a legal *declaration* that a man is right is a fiction" (3:40).

So although, as many commentators note, the philological background of *dikaioō* suggests primarily the judicial sense, yet the strong moral emphasis of the NT demands that God shall *make* righteous those whom He *declares* righteous.

## Foolish (3:1)

Paul's strong emotions while writing this letter are revealed in the opening words of chapter 3: "O foolish Galatians." The word is *anoētos,* which Young, Ballantine, and Verkuyl render "thoughtless." Moffatt, Goodspeed, and Williams translate it "senseless." It is a combination of *nous* (mind) and *alpha*-privative, which negates the meaning of a word to which it is attached (e.g., amoral means non-moral). So the fundamental meaning of this adjective is "not thinking."

But the translation "thoughtless" seems too weak to convey the force of the expression here. Vincent notes that *"nous* is used by Paul mainly with an ethical reference, as *the faculty of moral judgment."* Hence his deduction: *"Anoētos* therefore indicates a folly which is the outgrowth of a moral defect" (4:110). If we take "foolish," not as a half-playful expression, but as a serious, earnest accusation of moral and mental failure, then perhaps it is a better rendering than either "thoughtless" or "senseless," both of which may seem to stress the mental aspect more than the moral.

## Bewitched (3:1)

*Baskainō* (only here in NT) originally meant "slander, speak ill of one." Then it came to have the meaning "blight by the evil eye, fascinate, bewitch." Vincent says: "Paul's metaphor here is: *who hath cast an evil spell upon you?"* (4:111). Concerning the use of this word in the papyri, Moulton and Milligan write: "The popular belief in the power of the evil eye, underlying the Pauline metaphor in Gal. 3:1, is well illustrated by the common formulas in closing greetings" (VGT, p. 106). As an example they cite these words from a papyrus letter of about A.D. 25: "But above all I pray that you may be in health unharmed by the evil eye and faring prosperously." The entire phrase "unharmed by the evil eye" is one word in Greek, *abaskantos.*

This does not mean, of course, that Paul believed in magic, although the masses of his contemporaries apparently did. Paul is simply saying: "You folk are acting as though someone has bewitched you. You seem charmed by these false teachers who are leading you astray."

How often we feel that way today about vacillating Christians or prospects who suddenly turn away! The only adequate explanation seems to be the influence of some satanic power that diverts them from God.

## Placarded or Portrayed (3:1)

Paul declares that, before the very eyes of the Galatians, Jesus Christ "hath been evidently set forth." The phrase is one word in the Greek, *proegraphē*. The ASV translates it "openly set forth." Moffatt renders it "placarded" and the bulk of the best commentators favor this translation. Weymouth has "portrayed" and the RSV "publicly portrayed."

The verb *prographō* literally means "write beforehand," and that is its use in Rom. 15:4. But it very early took on the meaning, "write up in public, placard." Lightfoot says: "It is the common word to describe all public notices or proclamations." And he makes the pertinent observation: "This placard ought to have kept their eyes from wandering, and so to have acted as a charm against all Judaic sorceries" (p. 134). Vincent puts it well: "Who could have succeeded in bringing you under the spell of an evil eye, when directly before your own eyes stood revealed the crucified Christ?" (4:112).

The homiletical hint here is obvious. We need to warn people to keep their eyes on Jesus in order that they may not become "fascinated" (Latin for casting a spell) by the worldly allurements around. When our eyes are filled with the bright shining of the Light of the World, we shall not be captivated by the dazzling neon signs of the world's pleasures. When we are following *the* Light, other little flashes may annoy us, but they will not divert us from the narrow way that leads to life and light eternal.

## Spirit or spirit? (3:3)

The perplexing question confronts the translator: Should "spirit" be spelled with a capital or a small *s?* He must ask, "Is the reference here to the human spirit or the

Holy Spirit?" Almost all English translators have taken it in the latter sense and so have written "Spirit." One exception is Ballantine *(Riverside New Testament),* who uses a small *s.* Weymouth paraphrases the question: "Having begun by the spiritual, are you now going to reach perfection by the external?" That wording is true to the Greek, and gives clear meaning to the passage.

Of course the Greek manuscripts give us no help here, since the oldest copies have large, square "uncial" letters and the later copies have a running ("cursive") script. In each case the letters are all the same.

The Greek word is *pneuma,* from which we get "pneumonia," "pneumatic," etc. It originally meant "a movement of air, wind, breath." But when a person's breath leaves his body, he is dead; that is, his spirit is gone. So the word for "breath" was also used for "spirit."

Vine writes:

> In Gal. 3:3, in the phrase "having begun in the Spirit," it is difficult to say whether the reference is to the Holy Spirit or to the quickened spirit of the believer; that it possibly refers to the latter is not to be determined by the absence of the article, but by the contrast with "the flesh"; on the other hand, the contrast may be between the Holy Spirit who in the believer sets His seal on the perfect work of Christ, and the flesh which seeks to better itself by works of its own (*Expository Dictionary,* 4:63-64).

Obviously, this is an open question, where dogmatism is out of place. But the meaning is much the same whichever way we take it. It is the Holy Spirit who gives us spiritual life. The main emphasis is on keeping the spiritual, rather than the material, supreme. Probably we should follow the majority of translators in capitalizing "Spirit" here.

## Minister or Supply? (3:5)

The Greek word *epichorēgōn* is translated "ministereth" in KJV and "supplies" in RSV. The verb *chorēgeō*
comes from *choros* (chorus, choir) and *hēgeomai* (lead).
So the word originally meant "lead a chorus"; then, "supply a chorus"; that is, defray the expense of providing a
chorus at a public feast. In later Greek it means simply
"furnish, supply." But it also carries the added idea of
supplying lavishly or abundantly. Probably the prepositional prefix *epi* in the compound verb here emphasizes
still further the idea of abundance (so Lightfoot, Burton).

The form here is the present participle, which would
suggest continuous action—"the one supplying to you the
Spirit." While there is a crisis moment in which the Holy
Spirit comes into the believer's heart, yet there is also a
sense in which the Spirit is being supplied richly to us as
we walk in the light.

## Accounted (3:6)

Abraham's believing "was accounted to him for righteousness." The RSV has "was reckoned to him as righteousness" and the NIV "credited." As is frequently the
case, all these translations are entirely correct.

The verb is *logizomai*. It is a favorite word with Paul,
"being used (exclusive of quotations) some 27 times in his
Epp., and only four times in the rest of the N.T." (Thayer,
p. 379). Its original usage was mathematical: "reckon,
count, compute, calculate." There is probably an example
of this in Luke 22:37, in a quotation from the Septuagint:
"He was reckoned among the transgressors." Then the
word came to be used metaphorically in the sense "reckon,
take into account." That is the meaning here, where the
statement is quoted from the Septuagint of Gen. 15:6.

Cremer exhibits a strange and strong Calvinistic bias in his treatment of *logizomai* in relation to this verse and similar passages in Romans. He stresses the ideas of imputation and substitution. For instance, we find this statement, all in italics: "That is transferred to the subject in question, and imputed to him, which in and for itself does not belong to him" (p. 399). Again he says: "But faith is now put in the place of righteousness" *(ibid.).* He seems to imply that though a man is not actually righteous he is reckoned so in God's sight. We hold that God could not "reckon" a man as righteous unless and until He had made him righteous. Faith is put to one's account as the grounds of making righteous, not as a substitute for righteousness.

## Faithful or Believing? (3:9)

Those who come to God by the faith route are blessed with "faithful" Abraham. The Greek word has two distinct meanings: (1) "faithful, trustworthy"; (2) "believing, trusting." That the second is the proper meaning here is clear from the context. It does not mean here "faithful to God" but "full of faith." The KJV translates it correctly in John 20:27—"Be not faithless, but *believing."* It should be so translated here—"believing Abraham."

Heidland writes: "Faith is reckoned for righteousness because this is pleasing to the will of Yahweh, not because faith has this value intrinsically" (TDNT, 4:289).

## Tree or Wood? (3:13)

At the end of this verse we find a quotation from the Septuagint of Deut. 21:23, which reads: "Cursed is every one who hangs upon a tree."

The last word is *xylon,* which is found 20 times in the NT (including Rev. 22:19, which reads "book of life" instead of "tree of life" in the KJV). Exactly half of these times it is translated "tree." In it first five occurrences— all connected with the arrest of Jesus in Gethsemane—it is rendered "staves," in the dual phrase "with swords and staves." We would say "clubs" today.

Three times *xylon* is translated "wood" and once "the stocks" (Acts 16:24). In the latter case the meaning is that they were wooden stocks which held the feet of Paul and Silas in the Philippian jail. One of the references where it is translated "wood" is 1 Cor. 3:12, where we find the combination "wood, hay, stubble."

The basic meaning of *xylon* is "wood." Liddell and Scott give "wood, cut and ready for use; firewood, timber" as the earliest usage. Then comes "piece of wood, log, beam, peg or lever." A further development is represented in "cudgel, club, gallows, stake, stocks," which we have found illustrated in the NT. Finally the word came to be used for "live wood, a tree," as 10 times in the NT. It is used 4 times in the last chapter of the Bible (Revelation 22) for the tree of life.

The typical Greek word for "tree" is *dendron,* which is also our biological term for tree. It is so translated in all 26 of its occurrences in the NT.

While in later Greek *xylon* was used for a live tree, yet modern Greek has gone back to its original meaning, "wood." In the papyri, which come from the Hellenistic period in which the NT was written, the word has both meanings. Moulton and Milligan cite passages for "tree" and also those which use it in the sense of "beam, staves, log." Always the idea of "wood" is dominant.

Three times in Acts we find *xylon* used for the cross of Christ (Acts 5:30; 10:39; 13:29). It is translated "tree," as in our passage in Galatians, for lack of a better word to express the exact idea.

The only trouble with this translation is that when we

read of a person "hanging on a tree" we form a mental picture of a person strangled with a rope around his neck, dangling from the limb of a tree, as was done with horse thieves in the frontier days. But that, of course, is not the correct picture when applied to Christ.

Actually crucifixion was not a Jewish, but a Roman, method of punishment. The typical Jewish method of capital punishment was stoning, as illustrated in the case of Stephen. That was what was ordained in the Law of Moses for Sabbath-breakers, blasphemers, etc. After the person had been stoned, sometimes his body was hung from a tree until sundown, as a warning example to others (Deut. 21:22). This was considered to be a particularly disgraceful fate. That apparently is the background of the statement quoted from Deuteronomy: "Cursed is every one who hangs upon a tree." So "tree" is best here.

## Covenant or Testament? (3:15)

In both vv. 15 and 17 we find the word "covenant." The first is in a general statement of principle. The second relates to the covenant made with Abraham. There is practically no question about the meaning of the word in v. 17, although Moffatt uses "will" there. But there is considerable debate as to whether the word should be "covenant" or "will" (testament) in v. 15. Several translations (including the RSV) give the latter rendering.

The Greek word is *diathēkē,* which occurs some 33 times in the NT. In the KJV it is rendered "covenant" 20 times and "testament" 13 times. It is obvious that the word carries both meanings. But which should we adopt in Gal. 3:15?

Burton gives a full treatment of the subject in his commentary on Galatians (pp. 496-505). He notes first of all that in classical Greek *diathēkē* normally meant a will or testament. However, it sometimes was used for "an arrangement or agreement between two parties in which one accepts what the other proposes or stipulates" (p. 496). This, of course, is close to the idea of a covenant. It also has been shown that such an agreement could be revoked only by mutual consent of both parties.

The word *diathēkē* occurs over 300 times in the Septuagint. There it is normally the translation of the Hebrew word *berith,* which uniformly means "covenant" or "compact." It is most commonly used for "a covenant between God and men in which case the initiative being thought of as wholly with God, the compact assumes in general the form of a gracious promise on God's part to do certain things, accompanied by the imposition of certain conditions and obligations upon men" (Burton, p. 497).

The ordinary Greek word for a compact was *synthēkē.* But this term was avoided by the Septuagint translators because it suggested the equal rank of the two parties, whereas the OT *berith* is used for "a relationship between God and man graciously created by God, and only accepted by man" (p. 498).

In the Greek papyri *diathēkē* always means "a will." Since many of these are dated in the first century it is clear that such a will would be the main sense of the term among the Greeks when the NT was written. On the other hand, the Jewish usage at this time was still "covenant." Burton states clearly the difference in the two ideas: "The essential distinction between the two meanings is that in a testament the testator expresses his will as to what shall be done after his death, esp. in respect to his property; the covenant is an agreement between living persons as to what shall be done by them while living" (p. 500).

The question then remains: Is Paul using *diathēkē* in the Greek sense or the Hebrew sense? Behm says, "The many legal terms in the passage make it clear that he is here using the word *diathēkē* in the sense of Hellenistic law" (TDNT, 2:129). Sir William Ramsay also argues for this in Gal. 3:15. He feels that the context clearly indicates it, especially the mention of "inheritance" in verse 18 and the discussion of "heir" in chapter 4 (pp. 349-70). But Burton presents convincing answers to these arguments.

In his commentary on Hebrews, B. F. Westcott has a lengthy note likewise on *diathēkē* (pp. 298-302). He feels that its meaning in the New Testament should be determined first of all by its use in the Septuagint. We have already noted that that is definitely "covenant." Westcott says: "There is not the least trace of the meaning 'testament' in the Greek Old Scriptures, and the idea of a 'testament' was indeed foreign to the Jews till the time of the Herods" (p. 299).

But what about its use in the NT? Westcott is positive on this point: "In the N.T. the sense of 'covenant' is unquestionable, except in two passages: Gal. 3:15; Heb. 9:15 f."

How are we to translate *diathēkē,* then, in Gal. 3:15? We incline toward Meyer, Alford, Ellicott, Lightfoot, and Burton—the most scholarly commentators on Galatians—that the best translation here is "covenant." That accords best with the regular usage of the NT, and specifically of Paul, and seems to fit the context better here. It would seem best to make Heb. 9:15 ff. the only exception to this translation in the NT.

## Make Idle or Destroy? (3:17)

The expression "make of none effect" is all a translation of *katargēsai,* the aorist infinitive of *katargeō.* Exactly what does this word mean?

It occurs 27 times in the NT. In the first of these (Luke

13:7) it has its weakest meaning, "make idle." The KJV translates it "cumbereth."

*Katargeō* is a peculiarly Pauline term in the NT. Aside from Luke 13:7, it occurs outside of Paul's Epistles in only one passage, Heb. 2:14, where it is translated correctly in the KJV as "destroyed."

The meaning of this word is a bit flexible. (It is translated 15 different ways in the KJV in its 27 occurrences in the NT.) Frankly, it must be admitted that in the papyri it usually has the weaker sense of "hinder." But does this define its Pauline usage? Cremer says that with Paul "it clearly signifies more than hindering, or cessation from outward activity" (p. 260). Then he goes on to make this very significant assertion: "With him it always denotes a complete, not a temporary or partial ceasing. Elsewhere it signifies a putting out of activity, out of power or effect; but with St. Paul it is—to *annihilate, to put an end to, to bring to nought*" (p. 261, italics his).

We need make no apology, then, for retaining the word "destroy" in Rom. 6:6—"that the body of sin might be destroyed." Godet, the outstanding conservative French commentator, supports that rendering. Cremer says it means "annihilate."

Even in Gal. 3:17 "destroy" makes good sense. The promise would be destroyed if the law superseded it.

## Law . . . Promise (3:18-21)

In this section of the Epistle, Paul asks a very pertinent question, one which might well occur to the reader: "Why then the law?" It would seem from his previous discussion that there was no need for the law at all.

The apostle answers the question by saying that the law was added (to promise) on account of transgressions. It was a temporary arrangement in God's dealing with man, to produce a consciousness of sin and compel men to seek salvation.

## Concluded or Shut Up? (3:22-23)

"Concluded" in v. 22 and "shut up" in v. 23 are translations of the same verb, *synkleiō*. It means "shut in on all sides, shut up completely."

The prepositional prefix *syn* normally means "with" or "together." Hence some give the meaning of *synkleiō* as "shut together, enclose." It is clearly used in that sense in Luke 5:6—"they inclosed a great multitude of fishes." In Rom. 11:32 (the only other place where it occurs in NT) it is translated "hath concluded," as in Gal. 3:22.

While "shut together" fits the passage in Luke, the majority of scholars would rule it out in Romans and Galatians. In the papyri it is used of being "shut up" in prison. And it is used of only *one* person being confined. So it seems better to take the *syn* as intensive, and render it "shut up." This is obviously its meaning in the Septuagint of Josh. 6:1—"Jericho was *straitly shut up.*"

The figure in Galatians and Romans is that of being confined in prison. In Romans it says that God has shut them all up in unbelief. In Galatians it says that "the scripture" has shut up all under sin.

In Gal. 3:22 sin is the jailer that holds people in prison. In v. 23 it is the law that acts as jailer.

## Schoolmaster or Attendant? (3:24-25)

The Greek term in question occurs in only one other passage in the NT (1 Cor. 4:15). There it is translated "instructor."

The word is *paidagōgos*. Alford says of it: "The *paidagōgos* was a faithful slave, entrusted with the care of the boy from his tender years till puberty, to keep him from evil physical and moral, and accompany him to his amusements and studies" (3:36). Lenski translates the word "slave-guardian." Literally it means "child-leader," from *pais* ("child") and *agō* ("lead"). Young renders it "child-conductor." Weymouth gives it as "tutor." The RSV has "custodian." Actually there is no word in English which exactly represents the meaning of this Greek word. Goodspeed and Williams use "attendant" which seems best.

But does it mean "schoolmaster"? Scholars answer with almost one voice, "No!" Vine writes: "In this and allied words the idea is that of training, discipline, and not impartation of knowledge. The *paidagōgos* was not the instructor of the child; he exercised a general supervision over him and was responsible for his moral and physical well-being" (2:265).

Lightfoot agrees. He says: "Thus his office was quite distinct from that of the *didaskalos* (teacher), so that the English rendering, 'schoolmaster,' conveys a wrong idea" (p. 148).

What we need is an English word to represent the masculine counterpart to "governess." The *Pulpit Commentary* ("Galatians," p. 142) gives a very interesting passage from Plato, showing that the attendant took the child to the teacher's house. Socrates is questioning a young man. "'But as to this, who has the ruling of you?' 'This man here,' he said, 'a *tutor.*' 'Being a slave, eh?' 'But what of that?' said he. 'Yes, only a slave of our own.' 'An awfully strange thing this,' I said, 'that you, freeman that you are, should be under the ruling of a slave. But further, what does this tutor of yours, as your ruler, do with you?' 'He takes me,' said he, 'to a teacher's house, of course.'"

Because of this clear meaning of the word, some have held that the law is pictured as a slave taking the Jews to Christ, the Schoolmaster. But the context does not support this latter idea. Lightfoot says: "The tempting explanation of *paidagōgos eis Christon,* 'one to conduct us to the school of Christ,' ought probably to be abandoned. . . . There is no reference here to our Lord as a *teacher"* (p. 149). The best commentators are in agreement on this point.

## Put On or Clothe Yourselves? (3:27)

The Greek verb is *endyo.* It is used most naturally of putting on clothing. This meaning occurs in the papyri. In modern Greek a similar verb form means "dress." Paul says that the believers "have put on Christ." Probably a better translation would be, "You clothed yourselves with Christ" (aorist middle indicative).

Rendall gives the background for understanding Paul's statement. He writes:

> At a certain age the Roman youth exchanged the *toga praetexta* for the *toga virilis* and passed into the rank of citizens. . . . Here the author evidently has in mind the change of dress which marked the transition from boyhood to manhood. Greeks and Romans made much of this occasion and celebrated the investment of a youth with man's dress by family gatherings and religious rites. The youth hitherto subject to domestic rule, was then admitted to the rights and responsibilities of a citizen, and took his place beside his father in the councils of the family (EGT, 3:174).

This interpretation fits well with the context. In v. 26 Paul writes: "You are all sons of God through faith in Christ Jesus" (Weymouth). Under the law they were minors, as he notes in the next chapter. But now they have come into the glorious liberty of being sons of God. No longer are they under a *paidagōgos.*

## Infant or Minor? (4:1)

Paul reminds his readers that as long as the heir is a

*nēpios* ("child") he has no more authority than a servant, though he will finally be lord of all his father's estate.

Etymologically, *nēpios* is equivalent to the Latin *infans*. Both literally mean not-speaking (*nē*, "not"; *epos*, "word"). That is, *nēpios* refers most strictly to an infant without the power of speech, not yet able to talk. That is its sense in Matt. 21:16—"Out of the mouths of babes and sucklings thou hast perfected praise."

But then it came to be used in a more general sense. Six times in the KJV it is translated "babe." Seven times it is translated "child" and once "childish." It occurs four times in 1 Cor. 3:11. Always it has as its dominant emphasis the idea of immaturity. This is especially evident in 1 Cor. 3:1 and Heb. 5:13.

But what is its meaning here? Vine says it is used "of the Jews, who, while the law was in force, were in a state corresponding to that of childhood, or minority, just as the word 'infant' is used of a minor, in English law" (1:93).

*Nēpios* does not appear to have been used in a technical, legal sense in Greek circles of Paul's day. Lightfoot says: *"Nēpios* seems to be here 'a minor' in any state of minority." Rendall (EGT) agrees with this when he writes: *"Nēpios* is not a legal term, but an appropriate description for a child of tender years, naturally subject to the control of guardians."

## Guardians and Stewards (4:2)

Paul says that this "minor" is under "tutors and governors" (KJV) until he becomes of age. The Greek words are *epitropos* and *oikonomos*. The former has the general meaning of "administrator, steward," and is so used in the only two other places where it occurs in the NT (Matt. 20:8; Luke 8:3). In both of those passages it is translated "stewards." It comes from the verb *epitrepō,* "commit, entrust." In the papyri it is used frequently for the guardian of a minor, as here.

The second word is from *oikos,* "house," and *nemō,* "manage." Hence it properly means the manager of a household or estate, a house steward. It is the more common word for "steward" in the NT (eight times). In Rom. 16:23 it is used for the city treasurer ("chamberlain," KJV). But it is also used four times in the Epistles for Christians as stewards "of God," "of the mysteries of God," "of the manifold grace of God."

Apparently, then, *epitropos* refers primarily to a personal "guardian," *oikonomos* to a "steward" of property. Lightfoot renders the whole expression, "controllers of his person and property" (p. 166).

Rendall gives the background for Paul's language here:

> The illustration is obviously borrowed from testamentary systems prevailing among Greeks and Romans (not among Hebrews) which enabled a father to appoint guardians for his orphan children during their minority. These testamentary powers differed considerably in different parts of the Roman world according to the municipal laws of various cities. Whereas Roman citizens became wards of the state at fourteen, so that the powers of testamentary guardians were strictly limited, the discretion of the father was allowed a wider range in Greek cities. At Athens, for instance, the guardians of Demosthenes retained control over his property till he became a full citizen after eighteen; and in Asiatic Greece the custody of property was sometimes prolonged to twenty-five, though the personal authority ceased at fourteen (EGT, 3:175).

What Paul is contending is that the rule of law was not a permanent regime. It was just a preparatory period before the coming of Christ.

## Elements or Rudiments? (4:3)

In this verse we find the phrase "elements of the world," and in v. 9 "weak and beggarly elements." In the ASV "elements" is changed to "rudiments."

The Greek word is *stoixeion,* which properly means one of a row *(stoixos)* or series. It was used for an elementary sound or letter of the alphabet. Then it was used for the elements or rudiments of knowledge. That seems to be its meaning here and in Heb. 5:12. In 2 Pet. 3:10, 12 it apparently refers to the material elements of the universe. The word was also used for the heavenly bodies. Recently scholars have held that it sometimes means demons or "tutelary spirits of nature." Deissmann holds that in this Galatian passage it means "cosmic spiritual beings" (VGT, p. 591).

This is apparently the background for the translation of the RSV, "elemental spirits." We question, however, whether this is the best rendering. It seems to us more likely that Paul is using the word *stoixeia* in the simpler sense of "elements" or "rudiments." The latter avoids the suggestion of physical "elements." The KJV uses "elements" in Gal. 4:3, 9, but "rudiments" in Col. 2:8, 20 and "principles" in Heb. 5:12. In 2 Pet. 3:10, 12 it is translated "elements" again.

The Early Church fathers usually interpreted this word as referring to the observance of days and seasons, which are regulated by the heavenly bodies. One man, Victorinus, even interpreted it as meaning the influence of the stars on the heathen before the time of Christ. Augustine held that Paul was referring to "the Gentile worship of the physical elements." (See Lightfoot, p. 167.)

Alford argues for the simpler meaning as being more natural. He would agree with Conybeare in rendering "elements of the world" as "elementary lessons of outward things." Lightfoot says that "elementary teaching" is "probably the correct interpretation." He concludes: "St. Paul seems to be dwelling still on the rudimentary character of the law, as fitted for an earlier stage in the world's history" (p. 167). Delling (TDNT, 7:684-85) supports this idea.

## Redeem or Ransom? (4:5)

Paul introduces one of his rather frequent statements on the Atonement. He says that God sent forth His Son "to redeem them that were under the law."

The word "redeem" is *exagorazō*. It is a Pauline term and is translated "redeem" in all four places where it occurs in the NT (Gal. 3:13; 4:5; Eph. 5:16; Col. 4:5).

The word literally means "buy out of." The Greek word *agora* means "marketplace." So *agorazō* means "buy" in the marketplace. *Exagorazō* has the added idea of buying "out" or "up." It may also mean "buy back."

The word was used frequently of ransoming slaves. Lightfoot says categorically that this meaning "is required here." In spite of the objection of some scholars we feel that he is correct. Christ came to ransom the Jews from their slavery under law and give them freedom as sons of God.

## Adoption Of or As? (4:5)

This verse contains another interesting word, *huiothesia,* "adoption." It is a compound of *huios,* son, and *thesis,* a placing (from *tithēmi,* "place" or "put"). So the word clearly means a placing as son.

Paul uses it in Rom. 8:15, 23; 9:4; and Eph. 1:5, besides this passage in Galatians. Older commentators state that it occurs nowhere else in Greek literature. But in recent years it has been found in a number of inscriptions. Martitz says, "The word is attested only from the 2nd cent. B.C. and means 'adoption as a child'" (TDNT, 8:397). The usage there suggests that adoptions were frequent in the Greek world of Paul's day, and so his readers would be familiar with the term (BS, p. 239). Moulton and Milligan also show that it was common in the papyri, though it is not in the LXX.

Probably "adoption as sons" (RSV) is a little clearer and more accurate than "adoption of sons" (KJV). It is our adoption by God as His sons that the apostle is talking about. What a glorious privilege is ours! Though born as aliens to God, we can by acceptance of Jesus Christ be adopted into the family of God.

## Weakness of the Flesh (4:13)

In v. 13 the apostle states that "through infirmity of the flesh" he had preached the gospel in Galatia, during his former visit there. What was this weakness of the flesh?

"Flesh" here does not mean the carnal nature. Paul is clearly talking about some bodily affliction. This passage is usually connected by Bible students with 2 Cor. 12:7, where Paul mentions his "thorn in the flesh." It seems likely that the reference in both passages is to the same physical infirmity. What was its nature?

The most common answer is that it was poor eyesight. This idea is derived from several allusions in Paul's Epistles. In 4:15 the apostle declares that the Galatian Christians would have plucked out their eyes and given them to him. This has been taken as a suggestion that these new converts felt sorry for Paul's difficulty with his poor eyesight. But this is far from being positive proof of such a condition. The apostle may simply mention the eyes as being the most precious part of the body. The Psalmist prays: "Keep me as the apple of the eye" (Ps. 17:8). The prophet Zechariah (2:8) comforts the people with this assurance from the Lord: "He that toucheth you toucheth the apple of his eye."

In Gal. 6:11 Paul says: "You see with how large letters I wrote (epistolary aorist—'I write') to you with my own hand." It is generally assumed that this suggests poor eyesight on the part of the apostle.

Then again, in Acts 23:5 Paul declares that he did not recognize the high priest when he stood trial before the Sanhedrin in Jerusalem. Perhaps the most natural explanation is that Paul could not see very well.

A second identification of the "thorn in the flesh" has been epilepsy. Sholem Asch has popularized this in his novel *The Apostle*. It has been pointed out that many great geniuses, such as Napoleon Bonaparte, were epileptics. But there is no clear indication of this in the case of Paul, and there seems no reason for accepting it.

Perhaps the best suggestion is that made by Sir William Ramsay in *St. Paul the Traveler* and in his commentary on Galatians. He holds that the apostle's particular affliction was chronic malaria.

## Through or Because of? (4:13)

The KJV reads "through infirmity of the flesh I preached the gospel." Now *dia* with the genitive means "through"; but with the accusative it means "because of, on account of." Here "infirmity" (literally, "weakness") is in the accusative. So what Paul is saying here is that it was "because of weakness of the flesh" that he preached the gospel to the Galatians.

Ramsay suggests that Paul had a severe attack of malaria in the low, swampy seacoast of Pamphylia. Hence, he informed Barnabas that he would have to move immediately to the mountains. So instead of evangelizing the province of Pamphylia, Paul and Barnabas climbed the hills to the high, interior province of Galatia.

We cannot be sure what Paul's ailment was. But we can agree with Burton's summary statement: "The language can refer only to some physical ailment hard to bear, and calculated to keep him humble and, in some measure, to repel those to whom he preached" (p. 239).

## My Temptation or Your Temptation? (4:14)

Speaking further of his affliction, Paul writes: "My temptation which was in my flesh ye despised not, nor rejected." But a majority of the oldest Greek manuscripts have, "Your temptation in my flesh." This suggests the idea that the apostle's repulsive appearance was a trial to his hearers. It may have been to them a "temptation" to reject both him and his message.

We cannot be sure that "your" is the correct reading, since the third-century Chester Beatty papyrus (our oldest manuscript) has "my." The general reference to the effect of Paul's affliction on his hearers is the same, whichever reading we adopt.

The Greek word translated "rejected" is a very strong one and occurs only here in the NT. Literally it means "spit out" *(ekptuō)*. The word is onomatopoetic; that is, the sound of it suggests the sense. Paul's hearers might have been tempted to express their disgust of him as one might spit out some objectionable thing. But instead they received him as an angel of God.

## Question or Exclamation? (4:16)

One of the problems connected with translating the NT is that the early Greek manuscripts have no punctuation marks. Furthermore, the indicative mood is used for both questions and assertions. So the only way one can decide whether a sentence is interrogative or declarative is by the context—and this is not always decisive.

Verse 16 is one such instance in the NT. In many English versions it is translated as a question. But Burton prefers to treat it as an exclamation: "So that I have become your enemy by telling you the truth!"

## Affect or Seek? (4:17-18)

The word "affect" in these verses does not fit very well. It leaves both verses, especially 17, rather obscure in meaning.

The Greek verb, which occurs three times, is *zēloō*. It first meant "be jealous," and is so used a number of times in the NT. But then it swung over nearer to our meaning "be zealous." In several passages it means "seek or desire eagerly." That is clearly its meaning here. Burton renders it: "They zealously seek you, not honestly, but wish to shut you out that ye may seek them. But it is good to be zealously sought after in a good thing, always, and not only when I am present with you."

What was it from which the Judaizers were trying to exclude the Galatian Christians? The most obvious answer is that it was Christ, or the privileges of the gospel. The Judaizers wished these new converts to submit to the law of Moses. It was necessary to separate them from Christ in order to get them to follow the Judaizers.

Another interpretation is possible. One of the best ways to cause people to want to join an organization is to make its membership exclusive. It is human nature to be indifferent to accessible territory until a fence is put up around it. Then we become eager to get in.

It may be that the Judaizers held the Galatian believers at arm's length, thus causing them to "zealously seek" admittance to the Judaistic group. Thus the latter would seek to win them away from loyalty to Paul and his gospel.

The apostle reminds them (v. 18) that he had sought after them for a good purpose when present with them. Now, far away from them, he travails over them that they may be renewed once more in Christ.

## Maiden or Maidservant? (4:22)

Five times (vv. 22, 23, 30, 31) we find the Greek word *paidiskē*. In the KJV it is translated "bondmaid" in v. 22, but "bondwoman" in the other four instances. It is the same Greek word throughout.

The original and proper meaning of *paidiskē* was "young girl, maiden." But it came to be used colloquially for a young female slave or a maidservant. Vincent says that the word in classical Greek "means also a free maiden; but in N.T. always a slave." In the Septuagint it has both meanings, though more frequently the latter. In the NT it may be translated "bondwoman," "slave woman," "bondmaid," or a number of other ways.

This illustrates the unreasonableness of insisting that a certain word has only one meaning and cannot be translated in other ways with equal accuracy and propriety. No one can devote much time to the arduous and exacting work of translating the Scriptures without feeling keenly the many distressing difficulties of the task.

## The Free Woman (4:22)

In contrast to the bondwoman, Hagar, Paul places the free woman, Sarah. The word for "free woman," is *eleuthera,* the feminine from of the adjective used as a substantive. Cremer says of this adjective that in its absolute sense it means "free, unconstrained, unfettered, independent, or one who is not dependent upon another." Of this passage he says: "The social relationship serves, in Gal. IV. 22-31, to illustrate the difference between the Old and New Test. economy" (p. 250).

How thankful we ought to be for this glorious freedom which we enjoy in Christ, "unconstrained" and "unfettered" by the minute rules and regulations of the Mosaic law! How careful it ought to make us to use our freedom for God's glory and man's good!

## Allegory or Allegorized? (4:24)

The word "allegory" is *allegoroumena,* the present participle of *allegoreō,* which is found only here in the NT. It refers to speaking or interpreting allegorically; that is, "not according to the primary sense of the word, but so that the facts stated are applied to illustrate principles" (Vine, 1:47). Allegorizing does not deny the literal, historical sense of statements in the OT, but it gives them an added spiritual application.

The present participle of the verb is used here, rather than the noun *allegoria.* It would therefore seem most natural to translate it, "Which things are being spoken allegorically." Indeed, Young in his *Literal Translation of the Holy Bible,* uses "allegorized." But Burton argues at length that the best translation is, "Which things are allegorical utterances," the participle being taken as "an adjective participle used substantively" (p. 253).

The allegorical interpretation of the Old Testament was greatly overworked by Philo, an Alexandrian Jew contemporary with Christ. It was also carried to unfortunate extremes by such Early Church fathers as Origen and Augustine. But that does not justify us in ruling it out altogether; Paul clearly uses it here. However, it should be used with restraint, because men's imaginations can contrive all sorts of foolish speculations.

## Answers to or Corresponds to? (4:25)

The verb is *systoicheō*. It is from *syn* (with) and *stoicheō* (be in a row or line). Hence it means "be in the same row with." The modern equivalent is "corresponds to."

In military connections the word meant "stand or march in the same file with." In a metaphorical sense, as used here, it carries the idea of being in the same category.

What Paul is saying is that Hagar and Ishmael correspond to the old covenant and the earthly Jerusalem, whereas Sarah and Isaac correspond to the new covenant and the heavenly Jerusalem.

This is in line with Paul's emphasis throughout this Epistle on the bondage of the law. Those who are under the law are confined in prison, or under the rule of stewards, or in the care of pedagogues. But the gospel has brought freedom from all this. Grace is the gift of God and makes us free.

## Rejoice . . . Break Forth . . . Cry (4:27)

Paul uses strong words to express the joy of the barren woman who becomes the mother of children. He says, "Rejoice!" The word means "make joyful, be delighted with." Here it is in the aorist passive and is best rendered, as in most English versions, by "rejoice." It is used in Greek literature of making merry at a feast.

The next exclamation begins with a word that means to break forth into speech. Its original meaning was "rend, break asunder." All three Synoptic Gospels use this verb in Jesus' saying about new wine bursting old wineskins (Matt. 9:17; Mark 2:22; Luke 5:37). Just as fermenting wine will burst old, already stretched wineskins, so a new-found joy must find means of expression. Thayer gives "break forth into joy" as the proper translation in v. 27.

The third verb in this quotation is *boaō*, translated in the KJV "cry." A better rendering would be "cry out." The RSV has "shout." Thayer gives as its meaning "to cry aloud, shout."

Three different Greek words in the NT may properly be translated "cry out"—*kaleō, boaō, krazō.* The first signifies crying out for a purpose, involving intelligence particularly. The third suggests a harsh cry, perhaps inarticulate. But *boao* refers to crying out as a manifestation of feeling, and so relates primarily to the sensibilities.

## Freed for Freedom (5:1)

According to the best Greek text, this verse reads: "For freedom Christ set us free; keep on standing, therefore, and do not be entangled again with a yoke of bondage."

The phrase "for freedom" has an interesting usage in the papyri. Deissmann explains this in *Light from the Ancient East* (1927 English edition, p. 322). A slave who wanted to become free could pay the price of his freedom to the temple of his god. Then the owner would bring him there, receive the money from the temple treasury, and turn his slave loose. Thereupon the slave would become the property of the god. "Against all the world, especially his former master, he is a completely free man."

Deissmann gives (p. 323) a Greek inscription from Delphi, of about 200 B.C. It states that the god Apollo "bought from Sosibius of Amphissa, *for freedom,* a female slave . . . *with a price.*" (The last expression is found in 1 Cor. 6:20 and 7:23.) The inscription ends with the repeated words *ep eleutheriai,* "for freedom," the exact phrase found in Gal. 5:13, where the KJV has "unto liberty."

There is one marked difference between this ancient pagan custom of freeing a slave and our release from the bondage of sin and the law. In preparation for the pagan rites the slave had to pay to the temple treasury the price of his freedom. Only by a threadbare fiction did the god buy him out of slavery. But in our case we could never by any means have paid the purchase price for our freedom. It was Christ himself who paid the price of His own blood to set us free. Ours should be an undying gratitude for this precious token of His love.

## Who Did Hinder You? (5:7)

The verb here is *enkoptō* which literally means "cut in or into." Paul says to the Galatians: "You were running well; who cut in on you?" The figure is that of a runner in a race who is making good progress until someone cuts into his path.

The person who has the inside lane on a circular track is at an advantage. But if another runner chooses to block him by cutting in on him he may more than lose his advantage. The Galatians had made an excellent start in the Christian race. But the Judaizers were blocking their path and hindering them from running. We find the same danger suggested in Heb. 12:1-2.

## Cut Off or Mutilated? (5:12)

The verb "cut off" is *apokoptō* (*apo*, "from"; *koptō*, "cut"). This literal meaning of the word seems clear enough in the active voice, as in John 18:10 and other passages. But here the middle voice is used, hence Abbott-Smith's *Lexicon* gives "to mutilate oneself, have oneself mutilated." Thayer's *Lexicon* agrees. He says it is incorrect to interpret this as "cut themselves off from the society of Christians."

Alford says that the verb cannot be passive, as the KJV takes it. He continues: "It can hardly mean 'would cut themselves off from your communion.'" He agrees with the Early Church fathers and "the great consensus of ancient and modern commentators" that the word here refers to physical mutilation. He concludes: "It seems to me that this sense *must be adopted,* in spite of the protests raised against it" (3:55-56).

One of those who protests against it is Ellicott. In his excellent commentary he decides in favor of the other meaning. So does Barnes. But they stand almost alone among leading commentators in this position.

Lightfoot paraphrases the thought: "Why do they stop at circumcision? Why do they not mutilate themselves, like your priests of Agbele?" He then explains what seems to be a very extreme position taken by Paul. "Circumcision under the law and to the Jews was a token of a covenant. To the Galatians under the gospel dispensation it had no such significance. It was merely a bodily mutilation, as such differing rather in degree than in kind from the terrible practices of the heathen priests" (p. 207).

Rendall (EGT) supports this interpretation. Findlay (EB) holds to the literal interpretation, but thinks that Paul was speaking sarcastically rather than seriously.

Not only did the word have this clear usage in the then pagan world, but this is also its meaning in the Septuagint. It occurs in Deut. 23:1 (v. 2 in LXX), where it is translated "whose male member is cut off" (RSV). Such a person was to be excluded from the congregation of the Lord.

Vincent calls this word "perhaps the severest expression in Paul's Epistles." He gives what seems to be a good explanatory paraphrase: "These people are disturbing you by insisting on circumcision. I would that they would make thorough work of it in their own case, and, instead of merely amputating the foreskin, would castrate themselves, as heathen priests do. Perhaps this would be even a more powerful help to salvation" (4:162).

Paul has been accused of stooping to the use of vulgar language here. But one must remember that sucn terms were common on the lips of even the best people of his day.

## Liberty or License? (5:13)

The Greek word for "liberty" is *eleutheria*. It was used especially in NT times of the freeing of slaves. Paul says that the Christian is not to use his new freedom "for an occasion to the flesh"—or, "as an opportunity for the flesh"—"but by love serve one another."

True liberty is governed by love. But too often license is dominated by lust instead of taking our freedom as an opportunity for loving service to others. It is *freedom to do right* which the Christian enjoys and which the one who is shackled by sin does not have.

## "Flesh"—Physical or Moral? (5:13)

The term "flesh" *(sarx)* has been used in a physical sense thus far in this Epistle. But here in chapter 5 it is employed with an ethical meaning, indicating that it is the part of man's nature which seduces to sin—what is often called the carnal nature. Paul uses the term in both senses frequently. One of the important problems in the exegesis of his Epistles is deciding which meaning the word *sarx* has in any particular passage. In this chapter it appears to have primary reference to the carnal self, or the sinful nature within.

In the "works of the flesh" enumerated in verses 19-21

we find not only sins related to the physical body but also wrong attitudes of the spirit. In fact, all nine mentioned in verse 20 are of the latter type. It is obvious that here "flesh" is not synonymous with "physical body," as many have contended.

## Holy Spirit or Human spirit? (5:16-18)

The problem in this passage relates to the word "spirit." In vv. 16 and 18 the Greek word *pneuma* occurs twice without the article. In v. 17 it is found twice with the article. The question is: Are we going to spell it with a capital *S* and thus refer it to the Holy Spirit, or are we going to spell it with a small *s* and refer it to the human spirit? Such distinctions are not indicated in Greek. So the problem becomes one of interpretation. We have to decide how we are going to interpret *pneuma* before we can write our translation in English.

Since the article occurs in v. 17, it is rather clear that the translation here is "the Spirit." But in vv. 16 and 18, where *pneuma* is found without the definite article, the matter is more difficult.

The division of opinion is not along theological lines. One of the most conservative commentators of our generation, Lenski, argues strongly that *pneuma* here refers to the human spirit. On the other hand, Burton, who is rather liberal, is equally emphatic in insisting that the reference is to the Holy Spirit. How are we to decide? Perhaps the answer lies partly in the fact that the human spirit is in a sense dead apart from the Holy Spirit. Hence, a spiritual life and a Spirit-led life mean the same thing. So, although the difficulty of translation here is an insoluble problem, the essential interpretation of the passage is the same whichever way we translate it. The only way to avoid fulfilling fleshly desire is to keep walking in the Spirit, or in the realm of spirit rather than in that of flesh.

The Holy Spirit comes in His fullness to cleanse our hearts from all sin. But the only way we can keep clean is to keep filled with the Spirit. The only way we can keep sanctified is to let the Holy Spirit dwell in our hearts unhindered.

## Lust or Desire? (5:16-17)

The word "lust" is found many times in the KJV. In most of the recent translations this is changed to "desire." Why?

"Lust" is usually too strong a rendering for the noun *epithumia* and the verb *epithumeō*. These words properly refer to desire of any kind, whether good or bad. That is the usage of classical Greek writers and even of the Septuagint. Not only so, but we find the same spread of meaning in the NT, where only the context can indicate whether the desire is good or evil.

Of its use in these verses Burton says: "It is clearly without moral colour in the present passage" (p. 300). It is clear that the term "lust" is not a correct translation for us today, however satisfactory it may have been 300 years ago. A better translation for our day would be "desire."

## Overtaken (6:1)

The verb *prolambanō* means "take beforehand, be beforehand, anticipate." But it also means "overtake, surprise."

Some scholars have held that the reference here speaks of a Christian being surprised in his sin by some fellow Christian who caught him in the act. But it seems much more natural to hold that it refers to the believer being himself overtaken by sin, perhaps to his own surprise. That is, it suggests the deceitfulness of sin in causing us to stumble before we realize fully the danger we are in. Burton says that it means being taken by surprise or seized unawares. The element of surprise should be emphasized.

## Fault (6:1)

The word *paraptōma,* means "a false step,·a blunder, a misdeed, a trespass" (A-S). Moulton and Milligan (VGT) say that in the papyri the word is used for "a 'slip' or 'lapse' rather than a wilful 'sin.'" Though it is one of the many Greek words for sin in the NT, it suggests the less serious type of sin, that which is not deliberate or premeditated.

This word is translated in the KJV in a variety of ways. It is rendered nine times by "trespass," seven times by "offence," three times by "sin," and twice each by "fault" and "fall."

There is a very real sense in which all of us are guilty of "trespasses" against others' rights. The proper attitude is to ask forgiveness or apologize as soon as we become aware of the offense.

But the word in this context seems to carry a somewhat stronger connotation. It refers to a lapse in Christian experience which requires a restoration. The unfortunate one, however, has been overtaken or seized suddenly and unexpectedly. That often happens, especially to the new convert.

## "Spiritual" (6:1)

We have put this word in quotation marks because the question may well be raised as to whether the term is to be taken literally or ironically. A comparison with 1 Corinthians suggests that there were in the Early Church what might be called "supersaints." They prided themselves on being more spiritual and looked down on all other church members as being less spiritual. In Corinth they were the ones who said they were "of Christ" (1 Cor. 1:12). Probably they were the most contentious ones in the whole church, speaking in tongues and putting a high premium on spiritual gifts and ecstatic experiences. In the earlier part of this Epistle, Paul has also been dealing with professed Christians whose spirit was entirely foreign to the spirit of Christ.

It may be, however, that the word here should be taken literally, rather than ironically. In that case the verse is an exhortation to the more spiritual members of the church to watch over the weaker ones with loving care and solicitous prayer.

In any case it is definitely an admonition that we should not criticize those who may lose out spiritually, but that we should seek to restore them. It is always easier to condemn than to assist, to push a person down than to lift him up. Too often Christians take the easier, selfish way in such cases.

## Restore (6:1)

The verb *katartizō* means "mend, repair." It is used in Matt. 4:21 and Mark 1:9 of the fishermen on the Lake of Galilee mending their nets. It speaks here, then, of a broken relationship that needs to be repaired.

## Burden (6:2, 5)

On the surface it would seem that these verses contradict each other. The first commands: "Bear ye one another's burdens." The second declares: "For every man shall bear his own burden." But when we examine the Greek we find two different words for "burden." The distinction in their meanings will eliminate the seeming contradiction.

The word in v. 2 is *baros*. It comes from *bareō*, which means "depress, weigh down." The verb is used in 2 Cor. 1:8 ("we were pressed out of measure") and 5:4 ("do groan, being burdened").

It obviously refers to being pressed down by a crushing weight. The adjective *barus* is translated in the KJV "heavy," "weighty," and "grievous."

The word in v. 5 is *phortion*. It comes from the verb *pherō*, which means "bear, carry." So *phortion* means "something carried."

Putting these two verses together we get the thought clearly. When any Christian has an extra heavy, crushing burden—such as unexpected illness, sudden death of a loved one, loss of home, financial pressure, or the like—other Christians should help to lift the pressing burden, lest it crush him to the ground. But that does not mean that we are to shirk our regular responsibilities in life. Verse 2 is no excuse for laziness or expecting others to do our work. We like to translate v. 5: "For every man must carry his own load." We are to shoulder our own responsibilities and not push them off on others.

## Communicate (6:6)

The word "communicate" in this passage does not mean what it does to us today. It is one of over 200 words in the KJV that have radically changed their meaning since 1611.

The Greek word is *koinōneō*. It means "to share in (something) with (someone)." Now the passage becomes clear. Those who are taught spiritual truth should share their material goods with the teacher. It is in line with Paul's regular teaching that ministers of the gospel should receive financial remuneration in order that they may devote their full time to spiritual duties.

## Letter or Letters? (6:11)

The word Paul uses is *grammasin* (dative-instrumental plural). The Greek word *gramma*—from which we get our word grammar—was used first for "that which is traced or drawn, a picture." Then it meant "that which is written." It is used primarily of letters of the alphabet. Only once in the NT is it used for an epistle (Acts 28:31).

The usual Greek word for "letter" in the sense of a document is *epistolē*, from which our word *epistle* comes. But that is not the word used here. The Greek does not say, "You see what a lengthy letter I have written." It very clearly says: "You see with how large letters I wrote to you with my own hand."

Why did Paul write with large letters? Three answers might be given. The first is that he was writing under the pressure of strong feeling. He was excited and distressed over the situation in the churches of Galatia. So he "scrawled" with large letters. Another suggestion is that he may have had poor eyesight—as hinted elsewhere—and so had to make his letters large. A third possible reason is that Paul wanted to emphasize the importance of what he was saying. The large letters would then have the force of underlining or of boldface type.

## Marks (6:17)

The Greek term is *stigma,* which has been taken over into English. It occurs only here in the NT.

Betz writes: "*Stigma,* from *stizō* 'to prick,' 'tatoo,'

'mark' with a sharp instrument . . . means basically 'prick,' 'point,' then the mark burned on the body with hot iron, then generally 'distinguishing mark'" (TDNT, 7:657). He goes on to say, "Branded marks were carried especially by domestic animals, slaves, criminals, and later soldiers" (p. 658).

Paul often speaks of himself as a slave of Christ. So we may translate here: "I bear in my body the brand-marks of the Lord Jesus."

What were these marks? Betz suggests: "The most convincing explanation is that the reference is to his wounds and scars" (p. 663).

# EPHESIANS

❦

## Saints (1:1)

The word "saints" occurs more frequently (9 times) in Ephesians than in any other book of the NT, with the exception of Revelation. It is found once in Matthew (27:52) but nowhere else in the Gospels. In Acts it occurs 4 times. It is used twice in Hebrews, twice in Jude, and 13 times in the Book of Revelation. But it is in Paul's Epistles that it is most frequently used (40 times) making a total of 62 times in the NT. It is always plural except in Phil. 4:21.

The Greek word is the adjective *hagios,* which means "holy" and is so translated 162 times in the NT. Thus its literal meaning is "holy ones," and this is the translation in Spencer's *The New Testament* (1937).

The earliest meaning of *hagios* was "devoted to the gods," and so "sacred, holy" (LSJ, p. 9). Thayer notes that it comes from the noun *hagos,* "religious awe, reverence." Hence its meanings are: "1. properly *revered, worthy of veneration* . . . 2. *set apart for God, to be, as it were, exclusively his* . . . 3. of sacrifices and offerings; *prepared for*

*God with solemn rite, pure, clean . . .* 4. in a moral sense, *pure, sinless, upright, holy"* (pp. 6-7).

Cremer notes, as most writers do, that it was used very rarely in classical Greek (p. 36). After tracing the use of *qadosh* in the OT he concludes: "God's holiness, accordingly, must manifest itself in and upon Israel, Israel must participate in it. 'Ye shall be holy, for I am holy,' is henceforward the keynote and the norm of the union subsisting between God and His people; so that the 'I am holy' is explained, 'I am holy, Jehovah, who sanctifieth you,' Lev. 21:8; Ex. 31:13" (p. 43).

Pursuing further the OT presentation, Cremer writes: "It thus appears how fully *righteousness . . .* is the necessary correlative of holiness" *(ibid.).* He continues: "Man's true relationship to God's holiness accordingly is that *blending of fear and trust* which we find in Holy Scripture throughout" (p. 46). Again he says: "Opposition to sin is the first impression which man receives of God's holiness. . . . God's holiness signifies *His opposition to sin manifesting itself in atonement and redemption or in judgment"* (pp. 46-47).

Shifting to the NT picture, Cremer notes: "As God's holiness becomes sanctification, and believers are received into the fellowship of the redeeming God . . . the predicate *hagios* is suitable of them also, seeing that it expresses the special grace which they experience who are in the fellowship and possession of the New Testament salvation" (p. 51).

It seems clear that in the NT the term "saints" is used for all Christians. Vine is correct when he says: "In the plural, as used of believers, it designates all such and is not applied merely to persons of exceptional holiness" (3:315). It designates Christians as those who are set apart to God in a saving relationship to Him through Jesus Christ. As such they partake of His nature and so are in a very real sense "holy ones."

## Blessings (1:3)

The word "blessing" (singular in the Greek) is *eulogia,* from which we get "eulogy." The verb—"who hath blessed"—is *eulogeō* ("eulogize"), which means "to speak well of, praise . . . bless, prosper, bestow blessings on" (A-S, p. 187). The first "blessed" of this verse is the adjective *eulogētos.* The *New English Bible* translates it "praise be to." Perhaps that conveys about as accurately as can be done what it means to "bless" God. It suggests offering praise to Him who deserves it preeminently.

## In Heavenly Places (1:3)

"In the heavenlies" is the literal Greek for "in heavenly places." Arndt and Gingrich say that it means simply "in heaven" (p. 306). This agrees with Thayer: *"the heavenly regions,* i.e., heaven itself, the abode of God and angels" (p. 247). Traub is in accord with this, asserting that the expression is equivalent to "in the heavens" (TDNT, 5:539). Vine says it means "heavenly, what pertains to, or is in, heaven (*epi,* in the sense of 'pertaining to,')," and so describes "the present position of believers in relationship to Christ" (2:209).

Salmond says of "spiritual": "It is best . . . to take *pneumatikē* to define the blessings in question as *spiritual* in the sense that they are blessings of grace, blessings of a Divine order, belonging to the sphere of immediate relations between God and man" (EGT, 3:246).

The phrase "in the heavenlies" occurs five times in this Epistle and nowhere else in the NT. It is the key phrase of Ephesians.

Lightfoot has a beautiful comment on the significance of this expression. He writes: "The heaven, of which the Apostle here speaks, is not some *remote locality,* some *future abode.* It is the heaven which lies within and about the true Christian" (p. 312).

This passage states a tremendous truth. God blesses us "with every spiritual blessing" (ASV) in the heavenlies in Christ. He has not promised everything *material* that we might wish. But He does offer every *spiritual* blessing. These spiritual blessings come to us in heavenly fellowship with Christ. We cannot have the blessings without Him. The greatest blessing any man can enjoy is the conscious presence of Christ in his heart.

## In Christ (1:3)

This is the key phrase of Paul's Epistles—*en Christō.* It is the heart of his theology. Of its use here Salmond says: "The phrase expresses the supreme idea that pervades the Epistle" (EGT, 3:247). The great apostle saw clearly that all the blessings we receive from God come to us "in Christ." Paul's theology is definitely Christocentric. We cannot bypass Christ and find God. Neither can we find any spiritual blessings except as we seek them in Christ. He is in every sense the Mediator between God and men (1 Tim. 2:5).

The Greek preposition *en* (in) occurs three times in the latter half of this verse. God has blessed us *in* every spiritual blessing *in* the heavenlies *in* Christ. Lightfoot notes the force of this: "We are united to God *in* Christ; so united we dwell *in* heavenly places; so dwelling we are blessed *in* all spiritual blessings" (p. 312).

The challenge that confronts every Christian is to make sure that he remains "in Christ." Here alone are safety and salvation, peace and protection. Blessing comes through abiding in Him. As long as we are in Him we are His.

## Chosen . . . in Him (1:4)

The doctrine of election bulks rather large in Ephesians. Paul here places a great deal of emphasis on the inevitable carrying out of God's eternal, sovereign purpose.

The word for "chosen" is *eklegō*. It means *"to pick out, choose. In NT always middle . . . to pick out for oneself, choose"* (A-S, p. 139). Occuring 21 times in the NT, it is regularly translated in the KJV as "choose" (choose out, make a choice). But the adjective derived from it, *eklektos*, is translated "elect" 16 times and "chosen" 7 times. Thus the idea of election is definitely involved.

On this passage Cremer makes the pertinent comment: "Ephesians 1:4 . . . cannot be taken to imply a division of mankind into two classes according to a divine plan before history began; it simply traces back the state of grace and Christian piety to the eternal and independent electing-love of God." He also points out that this verb is always used in Scripture for "God's dealings towards men in the scheme of redemption" (p. 404).

Schrenk writes: "This is the one place in the NT where we find *eklegesthai* with an accent on eternity." He goes on to say: "The purpose of election is described as responsible calling to a consecrated walk in the presence of God, in love" (TDNT, 4:175).

Alford prefers the idea of selection rather than election. He writes: "I render *selected*, in preference to *elected*, as better giving the middle sense,—'Chose for himself'— and the *eks*, that it is a choosing *out* of the world" (3:70).

On the general import of this doctrine Salmond says: "The idea of the divine election in the NT is not a philosophical idea expressing the ultimate explanation of the system of things or giving the *rationale* of the story of the human race as such, but a religious idea, a note of grace, expressing the fact that salvation is originally and wholly of God" (EGT, 3:249).

## Without Blame (1:4)

The adjective *amōmos* is used in the Septuagint in connection with animals to be sacrificed on the altar. There it means "without blemish." But it also carries the ethical connotation, "blameless." Arndt and Gingrich note that it is used in this moral and religious sense in a number of secular Greek writers (p. 47).

This is the first occurrence of the adjective in the NT. It occurs again in 5:27. In the seven places where it is found in the NT it is translated six different ways in the KJV.

Trench objects to the translation "without blame." He thinks that in later Hellenistic Greek it always means "without blemish" (p. 379). That is the way it is uniformly rendered in the English Revised Version. Vine approves this, but notes that it is used in the sense of "blamelessness in character and conduct" in the Psalms and Ezekiel (1:132).

Salmond emphasizes the fact that "blameless" is the meaning in classical Greek and the inscriptions. He concludes: "Little indeed depends on the decision between the two senses; for both terms, 'without blemish' and 'without blame,' may have *ethical* applications" (EGT, 3:249).

Concerning the two terms in this verse, "holy" and "without blame," Eadie writes: "The first is inner consecration to God, or holy principle—the positive aspect; the latter refers to its result, the life governed by such a power must be blameless and without reprehension—the negative aspect" (p. 21). He further adds: "The eternal purpose not only pardons, but also sanctifies, absolves in order to renew, and purifies in order to bestow perfection. It is the uniform teaching of Paul, that holiness is the end of our election, our calling, our pardon and acceptance" (pp. 21-22). The election here described is not that of the sinner to salvation but of the saint to sanctification.

In somewhat the same strain Alford says: "This holiness and unblamableness must not be understood of that justification by faith by which the sinner stands accepted before God: it is distinctly put forth here (see also ch. 5:27) as an ultimate *result* as regards us, and refers to that sanctification which follows on justification by faith, and which is the will of God respecting us. 1 Thess. 4:7" (3:71).

The expression "before him" is both a warning and a consolation. It is a warning because His all-seeing eye will miss nothing. One cannot harbor insincerity in his soul and get by with God. But it is also a comforting thought. One can never hope to be blameless in the eyes of men; Jesus was not. But God's eyes of love will overlook our faults and see our worthy motives. Alford expresses it beautifully thus: *"Before Him* (i.e. in the deepest verity of our being— thoroughly penetrated by the Spirit of holiness, bearing His searching eye, ch. 5:27: but at the same time implying an especial nearness to His presence and dearness to Him —and bearing a foretaste of the time when the elect shall be 'before the throne of God,' Rev. 7:15)" (3:71).

## Predestinated (1:5)

The verb "predestinate" is *proorizō*. In Acts 4:28 it is rendered "determined before." Its other five occurrences are all in Paul's Epistles. It is translated "predestinate" twice in Romans (8:29, 30) and twice in Ephesians (1:5, 11). In 1 Cor. 2:7 it is rendered "ordained," which is an inadequate translation, since the *pro-* is equivalent to *fore-* or *pre-*. The verb means "foreordain" or "predestinate";

that is, "to determine or decree beforehand" (Cremer, p. 462). Cremer also insists that the main emphasis of this verb lies on the purpose of the decree. He writes: "The matter to be considered when the word is used is not who are the subjects of this predestination, but what they are predestined to" *(ibid.)*.

Eadie has a good comment here:

> Foreknowledge, which is only another phase of electing love, no more changes the nature of a future incident, than afterknowledge can affect a historical fact. God's grace fits men for heaven, but men by unbelief prepare themselves for hell. It is not man's non-election, but his continued sin, that leads to his eternal ruin (p. 24).

## Adoption (1:5)

What is that to which God has foreordained us? The answer is: adoption. The Greek word is *huiothesia,* which occurs three times in Romans (8:15, 23; 9:4), once in Galatians (4:5), and here. It is a typically Pauline expression. Literally the term means "a placing as son."

"Adoption of children" should be "adoption as sons." We become children of God by the new birth; we become sons of God by adoption. The latter is a legal term.

Adoption was not a Jewish custom, but a Roman one (Latin, *adoptio*). After noting the informal adoption of Esther by Mordecai (Esther 2:7), Salmond states: "Adoption in the sense of the legal transference of a child to a family to which it did not belong by birth had no place in the Jewish law." He continues: "Thus among the Romans a citizen might receive a child who was not his own by birth into his family and give him his name, but he could do so only by a formal act, attested by witnesses, and the son thus adopted had in all its entirety the position of a child by birth, with all the rights and privileges pertaining to that" (EGT, 3:251-52).

This custom is reflected in the inscriptions of that period, though very rare in the literature. Deissmann writes: "The frequency with which these formulae occur permits of an inference as to the frequency of adoption, and lets us understand that Paul was availing himself of a generally intelligible figure when he utilized the term *huiothesia* in the language of religion" (BS, p. 239).

Moulton and Milligan cite an interesting example of a legal form of adoption, found on a fourth-century papyrus at Oxyrhynchus, Egypt. It reads: "We agree, Heracles and his wife Isarion on the one part, that we have given away to you, Horion, for adoption (*eis huiothesian,* same phrase as here) our son Patermouthis, aged about two years, and I, Horion, on the other part, that I have him as my own son so that the rights proceeding from succession to my inheritance shall be maintained for him" (VGT, pp. 648-49). We, as adopted sons, are heirs of God and joint heirs with Christ (Rom. 8:17).

## Accepted (1:6)

"Accepted in the beloved" is a beautiful phrase. The expression "he hath made . . . accepted" is all one word in the Greek, *echaritōsen.* Its only other occurrence in the NT is in Luke 1:28—"thou that art highly favoured." The verb *charitoō* comes from the noun *charis,* "grace." It means "to endow with *charis,*" or "to cause to find favour" (A-S, p. 480). The idea here is that God has extended His favor or grace to us in Christ.

## Redemption or Release? (1:7)

This word occurs more frequently in Ephesians (1:7,

14; 4:30) than in any other book of the NT (twice in Romans and twice in Hebrews; once each in Luke, 1 Corinthians, and Colossians). The Greek term *apolytrōsis* was formed from *lytron,* "a ransom." It was used originally for *"buying back* a slave or captive, *making* him *free* by payment of a ransom" (AG, p. 95). Buechsel says: "It means 'setting free for a ransom,' and is used of prisoners of war, slaves, and criminals condemned to death" (TDNT, 4:352). The ransom price paid is indicated by the phrase that follows: "through his blood." The NEB has "release" instead of "redemption," but the KJ translation is somewhat fuller in meaning.

## Forgiveness or Remission? (1:7)

The word *aphesis* occurs eight times in the Gospels and five times in Acts, but only twice in Paul's Epistles (here and Col. 1:14) and twice in Hebrews. In the KJV it is translated "remission" nine times, "forgiveness" six times, and once each "deliverance" and "liberty." The last two are in a quotation from the OT in Luke 4:18.

Thayer defines the word thus: "1. *release,* as from bondage, imprisonment, etc. . . . 2. *aphesis hamartiōn, forgiveness, pardon,* of sins (properly *the letting them go,* as if they had not been committed), *remission of their penalty"* (p. 88). Abbott-Smith gives first *"dismissal, release"* and then *"pardon, remission* of penalty" (p. 70). Arndt and Gingrich have: "1. *release* from captivity. . . . 2. *pardon, cancellation* of an obligation, a punishment, or guilt . . . with *hamartiōn forgiveness of sins,* i.e., cancellation of the guilt of sin" (p. 124). Cremer gives its meaning in the NT as "setting free, remission" (p. 297).

Deissmann has made an interesting study of the use of *aphesis* in the Septuagint (BS, pp. 98-101). There it is translated "brooks" (Joel 1:20) and "rivers" (Lam. 3:47).

He shows that this is probably due to the use of the term in Egypt—the Septuagint was made in that country—for the "releasing" of water by opening the sluices. Then there is the common use in the Septuagint of *aphesis* for the Year of Jubilee. It was a time of release of land. In Egypt the word was used for the "release" of land from the payment of taxes. This usage is found both on the famous Rosetta Stone (196 B.C.) and the papyri. The Septuagint also uses it for the sabbatical year (Exod. 23:11).

Moulton and Milligan carry the matter a step farther. They write: "A nearer approach to the Pauline use for 'forgiveness' is afforded by the occurrence of the word in inscriptions for remission from debt or punishment" (VGT, p. 96). Vine points out that it is never used in the Septuagint for the remission of sins (2:123).

On the other hand, says Trench, *"aphesis* is the standing word by which forgiveness, or remission of sins, is expressed in the New Testament"* (p. 114). He explains its meaning thus: "He, then, that is partaker of the *aphesis,* has his sins forgiven, so that, unless he bring them back upon himself by new and further disobedience (Matt. 18:32, 34; 2 Pet. 1:9; 2:20), they shall not be imputed to him, or mentioned against him any more" (p. 119).

Is "remission" or "forgiveness" the better translation? That is hard to answer. The former is more technically correct, but "forgiveness" is more understandable today.

## Sins or Trespasses? (1:7)

The word here is *paraptōma*. It is translated "trespass" nine times, "offence" seven times (all in Romans), "sin" three times (Ephesians and Colossians), "fall" twice (Romans) and "fault" twice. The first is accurate and probably should have been used throughout the NT, as it is, indeed, in Eph. 2:1.

The earliest meaning of the term is "a false step, blunder," and so "a misdeed, trespass" (A-S, p. 342). Literally it means "a falling beside." Trench defines it as: "an error, a mistake in judgment, a blunder" (p. 246). Eadie writes: "The word, therefore, signifies here that series and succession of individual acts with which every man is chargeable, or the actual and numerous results and manifestations of our sinful condition" (pp. 41-42).

## Prudence or Insight? (1:8)

The word *phronēsis* occurs only once elsewhere in the NT (Luke 1:17). There it is rendered "wisdom." Coming from *phrēn*, "mind," it literally signifies "way of thinking." Trench says that it means "a right use and application of the *phrēn*" (p. 284). Arndt and Gingrich give: "understanding, insight, intelligence" (p. 874).

Comparing *phronēsis* with *sophia* ("wisdom"), Eadie writes: "*Sophia* is the attribute of wisdom, and *phronēsis* is its special aspect, or the sphere of operation in which it develops itself." He goes on to say: "Intellectual action under the guidance of *sophia* is *phronēsis*—intelligence" (p. 47).

The concensus today is that "insight" is the best translation (so Moffatt, Goodspeed, Berkeley, RSV, NEB). *The Twentieth Century New Testament* and Knox have "discernment." The question as to whether "in all wisdom and prudence" modifies "abounded" or "having made known" is much debated and cannot be settled.

## Good Pleasure or Good Will? (1:9)

The word is *eudokia*. It is translated "good pleasure" here and in v. 5, as well as Phil. 2:13 and 2 Thess. 1:11. But in Luke 2:14 and Phil. 1:15 it is rendered "good will." Which is better?

Cremer says that *eudokia* denotes: *"a free will* (willingness, pleasure), *whose intent is something good"* (p. 214). Moulton and Milligan note that the term "is apparently confined to Jewish and Christian literature." After citing several instances of the word in the papyri, they say: "All these passages confirm the meaning 'good pleasure,' 'goodwill,' which *eudokia* seems to have in all its New Testament occurrences" (VGT, p. 260).

Abbott-Smith defines the meaning as: "good pleasure, good-will, satisfaction, approval" (p. 185). Arndt and Gingrich prefer "favor, good pleasure" here (p. 319). Vine says that the word "implies a gracious purpose, a good object being in view, with the idea of a resolve, shewing the willingness with which the resolve is made" (1:298). Westcott defines *eudokia* as meaning "gracious purpose" (p. 13). The *Modern Language Bible* (Berkeley) reads "kind intent." It is difficult to decide between "good pleasure" and "good will." The term seems to denote both ideas.

## Dispensation? (1:10)

The Greek word is *oikonomia*. It comes from *oikos,* "house," and *nemō,* "manage." An *oikonomos* is a house-manager or "steward," as the word is correctly translated in the NT. So *oikonomia* rightly means "the office of a steward" and is properly translated "stewardship" in Luke 16:2-4. But that does not seem to fit well here. Some modern attempts are "arrangement" (Berkeley), "plan" (RSV) and "arranging" (Goodspeed).

The difficulty here is highlighted by Alford: "After long and careful search, I am unable to find a word which will express the full meaning of *oikonomia*" (3:76). He finally settles for "economy." Salmond says the meaning here is "an *arrangement* or *administration* of things" (EGT, 3:259). Though the term "dispensation" has been abused in recent times, it is difficult to find a satisfactory substitute. The necessary thing is to hold to its original meaning of "a dispensing," which is what "stewardship" really is. Westcott writes: "The exact meaning which it conveys appears to be in each case that of a distribution of Divine treasures, which have been committed by God to chosen representatives, that they may be faithfully administered by them" (p. 13).

## Fulness of Times (1:10)

There are two Greek words for "time." Westcott differentiates them thus: "'Time' *(chronos)* expresses simply duration: 'season' *(kairos)* a space of time defined with regard to its extent and character" *(ibid.)*. *Kairos* is the term used here. The whole phrase, "the fulness of times" refers, not to the end of this age, but to "the whole duration of the Gospel times" (Alford, 3:76). It means "the filling up, completing, fulfillment, of the appointed seasons, carrying on during the Gospel dispensation . . . the giving forth of the Gospel under God's providential arrangement" *(ibid.)*.

## Gather Together in One (1:10)

The whole phrase "that . . . he might gather together in one" is a single word in Greek *(anakephalaiōsasthai)*. The term was used in classical Greek for *"repeating summarily* the points of speech." Salmond continues: "In late Greek the verb means also to present in *compendious form* or to *reproduce"* (EGT, 3:261).

The meaning is well expressed by Westcott: "The word here expresses the typical union of all things in the

Messiah, a final harmony answering to the idea of creation" (p. 14).

## Inheritance or Heritage? (1:11)

The verb *klēroō* (only here in NT) is from *klēros*, "lot." It therefore signifies properly: "(1) to cast lots. (2) to choose by lot. (3) to assign by lot, assign a portion" (A-S, p. 249). Arndt and Gingrich would translate here: "in whom our lot is cast" (p. 436). Eadie defines the verb as, "I assign an inheritance to someone"; in the passive, "I have an inheritance assigned to me"; and would render it here: "We have been brought into possession" (p. 59).

Salmond notes the connection with the assignment of territories by lot to the various tribes of Israel, and adds: "Thus the idea of *lot* or *portion* passed over into that of *inheritance.*" He prefers here to translate either "we were made a heritage" or "we were taken for God's inheritance" (EGT, 3:263). Ellicott, in his commentary on the Greek text of Ephesians, adopts: "In whom we were also chosen as His inheritance" (p. 26). Recent translations support this; e.g., "made a heritage" (Berkeley), "have been given our share in the heritage" (NEB).

## Counsel and Will (1:11)

The first word is *boulē*, the second *thelēma*. The former occurs 12 times in the NT and is rendered "counsel" 10 of these times (once "will"; once "advise"). The cognate *boulēma* is found twice and is translated "purpose" and "will." The verb *boulomai* occurs 34 times and is rendered "will" 15 times and "would" 11 times.

Abbott-Smith defines *boulē* as: "*Counsel, purpose* (in classics, especially of the gods.)" (p. 84). The meaning of *boulomai* is: "*to will, wish, desire, purpose, be minded,* implying more strongly than *thelō* the deliberate exercise of volition" *(ibid.).* Arndt and Gingrich define the noun as "resolution, decision," although they say that *boulomai* is "no longer different in meaning from *thelō*" (p. 145). Thayer thinks the former indicates deliberation, the latter inclination (p. 286).

The second word, *thelēma,* occurs 64 times in the NT. It is translated "will" all but two of these times (once "desire"; once "pleasure"). It comes from *thelō,* which is found over 200 times and is almost always rendered "will." In later Greek (including NT) it seems to be used interchangeably with *boulomai,* taking over the functions of the latter. Salmond says: "The distinction between *boulē* and *thelēma* is still much debated, scholars continuing to take precisely opposite views of it." Nevertheless he concludes:

> In a connection like the present it is natural to look for a distinction, and in such cases the idea of *intelligence* and *deliberation* seems to attach to the *boulē*. This appears to be supported by the usage which prevails in point of fact in the majority of NT passages, and particularly by such occurrences as Matt. 1:19. Here, therefore, the will of God which acts in His foreordaining purpose or decree, in being declared to have its *boulē* or "counsel," is set forth not *arbitrarily,* but *intelligently* and by deliberation, not without reason, but for reasons, hidden it may be from us, yet proper to the Highest Mind and Most Perfect Moral Nature (EGT, 3:264).

Ellicott says that the entire phrase ("counsel of his own will") "solemnly represents the Almighty Will as displaying itself in action; *thelēma* designating the *will* generally, *boulē* the more special expression of it" (p. 27).

## Trusted or Hoped? (1:12)

The verb is *proelpizō,* found only here in the NT. Since the KJV correctly translates *elpis* as "hope" 53 out of the 54 times it occurs (once "faith"), it is difficult to understand why it uses "trusted" in this passage. All modern versions have the correct rendering, "hoped." Literally the verb means "hoped before," though "first hoped" is used in recent versions (RSV, NEB; cf. NIV).

## Sealed (1:13)

By the Holy Spirit the sanctified Christian is "sealed." The verb *sphragizō* is from the noun *sphragis*, a "seal" or "signet," or the impression made by this seal. Arndt and Gingrich give as one meaning of the verb: *"mark* (with a seal) as a means of identification . . . so that the mark which denotes ownership also carries with it the protection of the owner" (p. 804).

The *Harper's Bible Dictionary* has an excellent article on the "seal." Thousands of tiny seals, many of them like small spools in shape and size, have been found in excavations in the Middle East. They were "used to affix the ancient equivalent of written signatures to documents" and also "widely used whenever security from molestation was important," as in sealing jars of wine and oil, or bales of goods (p. 657).

The dominant idea of a seal is that it was a mark of ownership. When a person surrenders himself completely to Christ, to belong wholly to Him and no longer to be his own property, then he is "sealed" with the Holy Spirit as a sign that he belongs no more to himself, but to God.

Eadie comments as follows: "The sealing followed the believing, and is not coincident with it" (p. 66). The aorist participle, "having believed," normally signifies action antecedent to that of the main verb. He also writes: "The Divine image in the possession of the Spirit is impressed on the heart, and the conscious enjoyment of it assures the believer of perfection and glory. . . . That seal unbroken remains a token of safety" *(ibid.)*.

## Earnest (1:14)

The word *arrabōn* was a "legal and commercial technical term" meaning *"first instalment, deposit, down payment, pledge,* that pays a part of the purchase price in advance, and so secures a legal claim to the article in question, or makes a contract valid. . . . In any case, *arrabōn* is a payment which obligates the contracting party to make further payments" (AG, p. 109). Behm writes: "The Spirit whom God has given them is for Christians the guarantee of their full future possession of salvation" (TDNT, 1:475). So the Holy Spirit is the Christian's down payment on his heavenly inheritance, the guarantee that he will receive the rest, as well as being a foretaste of what heaven will be like. Moulton and Milligan say: "The above vernacular usage (found in the papyri of that period) confirms the NT sense of an 'earnest,' or a part given in advance of what will be bestowed fully afterwards" (VGT, p. 79).

But they also note that in Modern Greek *arrabona* is used for "the engagement-ring" *(ibid.)*. This suggests that after the Christian has fallen in love with Christ he will someday be confronted with the challenge: "Will you be wholly mine, be my bride and belong to no other?" When a full, final Yes is given to that question, the Holy Spirit is given as an engagement ring, sealing our betrothal to Christ. Keeping this engagement ring—the Holy Spirit dwelling ungrieved in our hearts—assures us of final union with our Lord at the Marriage Supper of the Lamb (Rev. 19:7-9).

## Possession (1:14)

The word *peripoēsis* is here translated "purchased

possession." Occurring five times in the NT, it is rendered five different ways in the KJV—"to obtain" (1 Thess. 5:9); "the obtaining" (2 Thess. 2:14); "the saving" (Heb. 10:39); and "peculiar" (1 Pet. 2:9). The true sense of the term is described by Vincent: "The word originally means *a making to remain over and above; hence preservation; preservation for one's self; acquisition; the thing acquired,* or *a possession"* (3:369).

The rendering "purchased possession" is an overtranslation, found first in Tyndale (1535). The word denotes no more than "possession." It is possible that "purchased" was introduced from Wycliffe, who had "purchasynge." The Genevan version had "that we might be fully restored to liberty." The Rhemish (Catholic) version correctly says, "the redemption of acquisition."

The question is whether this is our possession in Christ or God's possession in us. Salmond favors the latter, as being more in line with the Old Testament concept of Israel as the people God acquired for himself (EGT, 3:270).

## Faith or Love? (1:15)

One of the more difficult problems of textual criticism occurs in this verse. The words *tēn agapēn* ("love") are omitted in the earliest Greek manuscripts we have. They are missing not only in the two great fourth-century manuscripts, Vaticanus and Sinaiticus, but also in the third-century Papyrus 46. These are the three oldest manuscripts of Ephesians extant. Add to this Alexandrinus of the fifth century and it makes a formidable array of evidence against the genuineness of the words.

But without "love" the passage reads awkwardly. What is meant by faith toward the saints? Salmond rightly observes: "The documentary evidence is on the side of the omission. But the difficulty is to find in that case a suitable sense." He goes on to say: "The *pistis,* in short, if it belong to both clauses, must be introduced in two different aspects, as *belief* in the first clause and as *faithfulness* in the second" (EGT, 3:271). He doubts the reasonableness of doing this.

Westcott and Hort considered the words to be an interpolation from Col. 1:4 and omitted them from their Greek Testament. For that reason, apparently, they were omitted in the English Revised Version of 1881, which Westcott and Hort helped to produce. Though their Greek text was published that same year, advance copies of it were made available to the translation committee.

On the other hand, "love" is included in the ASV (1901), the RSV (1946), and the NEB (1961). It appears in the Nestle text. The translators of RSV and NEB were instructed to make their own decisions about variant readings as they went along, rather than following any printed text.

It is impossible to solve the problem with the data now at hand. Perhaps the best course is to leave "love" in the passage, without placing undue weight on it.

## spirit or Spirit? (1:17)

This is one of many passages in the NT where it is difficult to decide whether the reference is to the human spirit or the Holy Spirit. The older English versions have the former. But Salmond argues for the latter. He writes: "It is necessary, therefore, to take *pneuma* as = the *Holy Spirit*" (EGT, 3:274). Ellicott follows this interpretation, as do Eadie and Meyer. This seems to be preferable (cf. NIV).

## Revelation (1:17)

One of the strong reasons for interpreting *pneuma* in this passage as "Spirit" rather than "spirit" is this word *revelation*. The human spirit may possess "wisdom," but not "revelation." As Salmond rightly points out, *apocalypsis* (literally, "an uncovering") "has the stated meaning not of *understanding* mysteries but of *disclosing* them . . . not a *susceptibility* for knowledge, nor a *mind open* to revelation" *(ibid.)*. Rather, *apocalypsis* is always used in the NT (18 times) for a divine disclosure. The verb *apocalyptō* is translated "reveal" in every one of its 26 occurrences. "Wisdom" may in a limited way be postulated of the human, but never "revelation." And the most important revelation is "the knowledge of him," which is beyond all merely human understanding.

## Full Knowledge (1:17)

The regular Greek word for "knowledge" is *gnōsis*. Paul uses it 23 times (out of 29 in NT). But the word here is *epignōsis*, which the apostle employs 15 out of the 20 times it occurs in the NT. Is there any difference?

Trench writes: "Of *epignōsis*, as compared with *gnōsis*, it will be sufficient to say that *epi* must be regarded as intensive, giving to the compound word a greater strength than the simple word possessed" (p. 285). Lightfoot says: "The compound *epignōsis* is an advance upon *gnōsis*, denoting a larger and more thorough knowledge" *(Colossians,* p. 138). And Salmond agrees: "It means a knowledge that is true, accurate, thorough, and so might be rendered 'full knowledge'" (EGT, 3:274).

Paul is fond of compound words. This fact seems to be a reflection of his powerful personality. He felt deeply and expressed himself strongly. His use of compounds with the intensive *epi* was but a projection of his very intense nature, which manifested itself also in a life of unsurpassed devotion to his Lord.

## Understanding or Heart? (1:18)

For "eyes of your understanding" the Greek has "eyes of your heart" *(kardia)*. The RSV is to be complimented for bringing this out in English. It is true that the Greek *kardia* (cf. cardiac), like the Hebrew *leb,* has a broader connection than is usually included in the English "heart." It is related to the intellect and will, as well as to the emotions. In the OT it is used for the physical organ, but never so used in the NT. Matthew 12:40 has the expression "the heart of the earth." But the regular use of the term in the NT is thus defined by Abbott-Smith: "In a psychological sense, the seat of man's collective energies, the focus of personal life, the seat of the rational as well as the emotional and volitional elements in human life, hence that wherein lies the moral and religious condition of the man" (p. 230).

This spread of meaning is emphasized by Thayer. He gives these definitions: "The soul or mind, as it is the fountain and seat of the thoughts, passions, desires, appetites, affections, purposes, endeavors" (p. 325). Arndt and Gingrich make the main definition, "The seat of physical, spiritual, and mental life" and especially emphasize it "as center and source of the whole inner life, with its thinking, feeling, and volition" (p. 404).

Salmond points out the reason for the phrase here: "The knowledge is a *spiritual* knowledge; hence 'the eyes of the heart,' *kardia* being the 'inner man,' the seat and centre of the mental and spiritual life" (p. 275).

## Inheritance (1:18)

The word *klēronomia* (already in v. 14) is related to the verb *klēroō* (v. 11). As noted there, the root *klēros* means "lot." But all the cognate terms gradually lost sight of the method of casting lots and came to be related only to the idea of an inheritance or an inheritor ("heir").

What is meant by "his inheritance"? Salmond sounds a word of caution: "The *klēronomia* is not the inheritance which God has in us (a sense which the word seems never to have in the NT), but the inheritance which God gives to us and which is the object of our hope" *(ibid.)*. The inheritance is "his" in that it comes from Him as its source of origin. Of the nature of this heritage Meyer comments: *"Doxa, glory,* is the essential character of the Messianic salvation to be received from God as an inheritance at the Parousia" *(Ephesians,* p. 340).

It should be noted that some very good exegetes explain "his inheritance in the saints" as meaning "the inheritance which *God* has in *His people,"* as well as "that which they have in Him" (Alford, 3:84). Perhaps a combination of these meanings is best.

## Exceeding (1:19)

The verb *hyperballō* (twice in 2 Corinthians, three times in Ephesians, nowhere else in NT) literally means "throw over or beyond" or "run beyond." In the NT it is always used metaphorically with the idea of "to exceed, surpass, transcend" (A-S, p. 458).

Vincent makes the apt observation: "Compounds with *hyper, over, beyond,* are characteristic of Paul's intensity of style, and mark the struggle of language with the immensity of the divine mystery, and the opulence of divine grace" (3:371). A glance at the *Englishman's Greek*

*Concordance* or Moulton and Geden's *Concordance to the Greek Testament* will show that of 25 compounds with *hyper* in the NT, 16 are found only in the Pauline Epistles and others are used mainly by Paul. They reflect the apostle's strong personality and his almost frustrated desire to seek to express in words the inexpressible greatness of God's grace.

This sense of the inadequacy of language to convey spiritual truths is even more prominent in the Greek text than in English translation. Paul is struggling to say what cannot be said. It is utterly impossible to put the fullness of divine reality in human language, to compress the infinite into what is finite. That is why one cannot receive the full impact of the meaning of the Word of God except as the Holy Spirit illuminates his mind to understand it. Just so, Paul struggled to express the great thoughts with the words which so weakly convey them. It is with words that we have to deal. But our goal is always to get behind those words to the meaning. Biblical interpretation is the most challenging, demanding task that anyone can undertake.

The sincere student, and especially preacher, of the Word of God will seek to use all the human tools he can get hold of—study of the original Greek and Hebrew, the best reference works available, the studies made by careful scholars. The minister who fills his shelves only with canned sermons and popular "how" books is not true to his calling. What he needs is spades with which to dig out eternal truths. Above and beyond all this he needs the Holy Spirit's help and guidance.

## Greatness (1:19)

The word *megethos* is found only here in the NT. Such Pauline *hapax legomena* (words used only once) again reflect the outreach of the great apostle's mind in seeking to describe the wonders of divine redemption. One can almost see words stretching at their seams as Paul tries to pour more meaning into them.

## Power (1:19)

The word *dynamis* occurs here for the first of five times in Ephesians. It is twice translated "might," but "power" is the best English equivalent. The terms derived from it—dynamic, dynamite, dynamo—suggest something of the thrust of this word, which is found 120 times in the NT.

## Who Believe (1:19)

"Who believe" is, in the Greek, "who are believing" (present participle of continuous action). This underscores the fact that this power is operating not in those who only once upon a time believed in Jesus Christ, but in those who are right now constantly believing in Him.

## The Working (1:19)

"Working" is *energeia.* Abbott-Smith defines it: *"Operative power* (as distinct from *dynamics, potential power)"* (p. 153). Salmond agrees with this when he writes that it denotes: "power as *efficiency, operative, energising* power" (EGT, 3:276). The term is used only by Paul—six times in the three Christological Epistles (Ephesians, Philippians, Colossians), and twice in 2 Thessalonians of Satan. In every case it is superhuman power.

## Mighty Power (1:19)

The Greek has *kratos* of His *ischus*. Vincent comments:

> The A.V. frequently impairs the force of a passage by combining into a single conception two words which represent distinct ideas; translating two nouns by an adjective and a noun. . . . The idea is thus diluted, and the peculiar force and distinction of the separate words is measurably lost (3:371-72).

Eadie agrees with this when he writes: "To suppose that the apostle uses these terms including *energeia* without distinction, and for no other purpose than to give intensity of idea by the mere accumulation of synonymns, would indeed be a slovenly exegesis" (p. 94).

He distinguishes the meaning thus:

> *Ischus* . . . is—power in possession, ability or latent power, strength which one has, but which he may or may not put forth. . . . *Kratos* . . . is that power excited into action—might. *Energeia,* as its composition implies, is power in actual operation. *Ischus,* to take a familiar illustration, is the power lodged in the arm, *kratos* is that arm stretched out or uplifted with conscious aim, while *energeia* is the same arm at actual work, accomplishing the designed result (pp. 94-95).

Salmond supports these distinctions. He writes: "*Kratos* is power as *force, mastery,* power as shown in *action: ischus* is power as *inherent,* power as possessed, but passive. The phrase, therefore, means 'the efficiency of the active power which expresses inherent might'" (EGT, 3:276).

Vincent expresses the same general ideas in somewhat different language, as follows:

> *Strength (kratous)* is used only of God, and denotes *relative* and *manifested* power. *Might (ischuos)* is *indwelling* strength. *Working (energeian)* is the active, efficient *manifestation* of these. Hence we have here God's *indwelling* power, which inheres in the

divine nature *(strength); the relative quality* or *measure* of this power *(might);* and the *efficient exertion* of the divine quality *(working)* (3:372).

The best translation of the entire phrase would probably be: "that working of the strength of his might" (ASV). The next verse gives an illustration of this in the case of the resurrection of Christ.

On the reason for the striking combination of those forceful words Eadie has this good comment:

> The use of so many terms arises from a desire to survey the power of God in all its phases; for the spectacle is so magnificent, that the apostle lingers to admire and contemplate it. . . . The mental emotion of the writer is anxious to embody itself in words, and, after all its efforts, it laments the poverty of exhausted language (p. 95).

## Principality (1:21)

Four parallel terms are used in this verse. The first, *archē,* literally means "beginning." That is the way it is translated in the first verse of Mark's and John's Gospels. It is so rendered in 40 out of the 58 times it occurs in the NT. Eight times it is "principality," as here.

For its meaning in this passage Thayer suggests: "the first place, principality, rule." He adds: "Hence the term is transferred by Paul to angels and demons holding dominions entrusted to them in the order of things" (p. 77). Arndt and Gingrich's explanation is similar: "Also of angelic and demonic powers, since they were thought of as having a politicial organization" (p. 112).

Cremer carries the discussion a point farther. He notes that *archē* used in conjunction with the other terms in this verse signifies "supramundane powers," and then writes:

> The several synonymous designations by no means indicate a relationship of the angels one to another, nor

a difference of rank . . . for the synonymousness of the designations forbids such a distinguishing. They rather bear upon the relation and conduct of angels toward mankind. . . . We have therefore no indication of, or connection whatever with, the Rabbinical or Neo-Platonic angelology, which in itself, upon closer comparison, is found to be altogether inappropriate (p. 115).

J. Massie thinks differently. He says that the four terms used here, "or their linguistic equivalents, are found among the orders of angels in Jewish-Christian books ranging over the New Testament period or its immediate neighbourhood" (HDB, 1:616). So perhaps this idea should not be ruled out altogether.

Meyer feels that the picture given here is of ranks of angels. He says that the group of terms here

> is neither to be understood . . . of the *Jewish hierarchs,* nor . . . of the various grades of *Gentile rulers,* nor . . . of *human powers in general,* nor of . . . 'any kind of glory and dignity'; but, as is shown by the immediate context . . . and the analogous passages, iii. 10, Col. i. 16, Rom. viii. 38 (comp. also I Pet. iii. 22), of the *angels* who are designated according to their *classes of rank* . . . and, in fact, of the *good* angels, since the apostle is not here speaking (as in I Cor. xv. 24) of the victory of Christ over *opposing* powers, but of His exaltation above the *existing* powers in heaven.

Meyer adds, however, that "the Rabbinical theory of classes of angels, elaborated under the influence of Platonism, yet dissimilar, is not in keeping with the designations of the apostle, and has evidently been elaborated at a later date" (pp. 342-43).

## Power (1:21)

The word is *exousia,* which is more correctly translated "authority." Abbott-Smith defines the word thus: "1. properly, *liberty* or *power* to act, freedom to exercise the inward force or faculty expressed by *dynamis*. . . . 2. Later . . . of the power of *right, authority*" (pp. 161-62). Cremer maintains this distinction between *exousia* and *dynamis* when he writes: "If the latter imply the possession of ability to make power felt, the former affirms that free movement is ensured to the ability" (pp. 236-37).

## Might (1:21)

This is *dynamis,* which is properly translated "power." Arndt and Gingrich note that while the first meaning of the word is "power, might, strength, force," it may also signify *"power* as a personal supernatural spirit or angel" (p. 207).

## Dominion (1:21)

The word *kyriotēs* is from *kyrios,* "lord." So it properly means "lordship." The King James rendering comes from the Latin word for "lord," which is *dominus.* Arndt and Gingrich indicate that while the term is used especially for "the majestic power that the *kyrios* wields," it is employed in this passage (and Col. 1:16) for "a special class of angelic powers" (p. 461).

What do these four terms taken together signify? We have already noted several opinions, but might add two or three more. Eadie connects them thus: "Whoever possesses the *archē* enjoys the displays *exousia;* and whoever is invested with the *dynamis,* wields it in his appointed *kyriotēs.*"

Alford gives a rather careful discussion of distinctions. He writes:

> The most reasonable account of the four words seems to be this: *hyp. pas. archēs* gives the highest and fullest expression of exaltation: *k. exousias* is added as filling out *archēs* in *detail: exousia* being not only gov-

ernment, but every kind of official power, primary and delegated. . . . Then in the second pair, *dynamis* is mere *might,* the raw material, so to speak, of power: *kyriotēs* is that preeminence or lordship, which *dynamis* establishes for itself. So that in the first pair we descend from the higher and concentrated, to the lower and diffused: in the second we ascend from the lower and diffused, to the higher and concentrated. The following shows that in this enumeration not only earthly, nor only heavenly authorities are to be included, but both together,—so as to make it perfectly general (3:85).

Finally we note Salmond's conclusions. He opposes all idea of a graduated scale of angelic or demonic powers. Says he: "It is true that in the non-canonical writings of the Jews . . . the idea of variety of ranks among the angels appears, and that in the later Rabbinical literature it took strange and elaborate forms." Then he adds: "But between these and the simple statements of the New Testament there is no real likeness, and there is nothing here to point either to an ascending *scale* or to a *descending"* (EGT, 3:278).

Salmond summarizes his attitude toward this passage as follows:

> We must take the terms, therefore, not as dogmatic terms either teaching or implying any doctrine or graduated ranks, differentiated functions, or organized order in the world of angels, but as rhetorical terms brought together in order to express the unique supremacy and absolute sovereignty proper to Christ, and meaning simply that whatever powers or dignities existed and by whatever names they might be designated, Christ's dominion was above them all *(ibid.).*

That seems to be a wise interpretation. Actually it does not differ radically from that of Alford. Verkuyl expresses it similarly in his *New Berkeley Version.* He translates the words: "All government and authority, power and lordship." Then he adds this in a footnote: "No classifying of spiritual orders, but a mention of the whole seen and unseen realm."

## Put in Subjection (1:22)

The word "put" is *hypotassō*. It was originally used as a military term, meaning "to place" or "rank under"; then, "to subject, put in subjection" (A-S, p. 463). "All things" *(panta)* will not only be placed under Christ's feet, but put there in a state of complete subjection to Him. Only then will there be peace among men.

The verb is in the aorist tense, indicating that this has now been done. But this might almost be called a prophetic aorist. In the mind and purpose of God everything is already in subjection under His Son. But the actual completing of this will, in action, waits for the end of this age (Heb. 2:8-10).

## Gave (1:22)

The verb is *didōmi,* which means *"to give*—in various senses, according to context—*bestow, grant, supply, deliver, commit, yield"* (A-S, p. 114). Arndt and Gingrich prefer the translation "made" (so RSV). The NEB has "apointed." But Alford objects to this rendering. He says: *"'Presented;'* keep the literal sense: not 'appointed'" (3:86). Eadie agrees when he writes, "There is no reason for changing the ordinary meaning of *edōke,* and rendering it 'appointed'" (pp. 104-5). Salmond also takes this position, against Calvin and some other earlier exegetes. He says: "The *edōken* is not to be taken in the technical sense of *appointed, installed* . . . but, as is indicated by the simple dative *tē ekklesia,* in its ordinary sense of *gave*" (EGT, 3:280).

In the Greek "him" precedes the verb. which is the

emphatic position. More than that, the pronoun—which in Greek is included in the verb—is expressed separately as well. This is done only in cases where the writer desires to give added prominence to it. So the position and separate expression of the pronoun give double emphasis to Christ. The thought is this: *Him*—the One whom God raised from the dead and exalted to His right hand (v. 20), far above every power and name (v. 21)—God has given to the Church as its Head. What a glorious thought!

## Head (1:22)

The word *kephalē* occurs 76 times in the NT and is always translated "head." But the term is used both literally (of the physical head) and figuratively. In general one can say that the word is used literally in the four Gospels, Acts, and Revelation, as well as a few times in the Epistles. The metaphorical use is confined largely to Paul—1 Cor. 11:3 (three times), Ephesians (four times), and Colossians (three times). In addition we have the expression "head of the corner" used of Christ several times (Matt. 21:42; Mark 12:10; Luke 20:17; Acts 4:11; 1 Pet. 2:7). One might also say that the figurative sense is found in Rom. 12:20 and Acts 18:6.

## Church (1:22)

The Greek word *ekklēsia* occurs 62 times in Paul's Epistles. Salmond gives a good summary of its meaning:

> Used by the Greeks to designate an *assembly of the people called for deliberation* (cf. Acts xix. 39), and by the Septuagint as the equivalent of the Hebrew *qahal, the congregation* of Israel, especially when called in religious convention (Deut. xxxi. 30, 35c.) it expresses in the New Testament the idea of the fellowship or assembly of believers meeting for worship or for admin-

istration. And it expresses this in various degrees of extension, ranging from the small company gathering for worship in one's house (. . . Rom. xvi. 5; I Cor. xvi. 19, etc.), or the single congregation of village or city (Acts v. 11; viii. 3; I Cor. iv. 17, etc.), to the larger Christian communities of provinces and countries (I Cor. xvi. 1, 19; II Cor. viii. 1; Gal. i. 2, 22) and finally to the Church universal, the Church collectively, the whole fellowship of believers throughout the world (Matt. xvi. 18; I Cor. xii. 28; Phil. iii. 6; Col. i. 18, 24, 35c.). Here and in the other occurrences in this Epistle the word has this largest extension of meaning, with the further mystical idea of a unity vitally related to Christ, incorporated in Him, and having His life in it (EGT, 3:280).

# Body (1:23)

The word *sōma* was used by Homer (ca. ninth cent. B.C.) for a *dead* body. But beginning with Hesiod (eighth cent. B.C.) it came to be employed for *living* bodies, whether of animals or men. Metaphorically it is "used of *a* (large or small) *number of men united into one society,* or *family as it were; a social, ethical, mystical body;* so in the *New Testament of the church*" (Thayer, p. 611).

This figure of the Church as the "body" of Christ is found 10 times in the NT. As would be expected, it occurs most frequently in the Christological Epistles—5 times in Ephesians (1:23; 4:12, 16; 5:23, 30) and 3 times in Colossians (1:18, 24; 2:19). It is also found once each in Romans (12:5) and 1 Corinthians (12:27). Besides this, the Church is referred to as a "body" in several other passages without specifically stating "the body of Christ" (1 Cor. 10:17; 12:13; Eph. 2:16; 4:4; Col. 3:15). The meaning of the latter phrase in 1 Cor. 10:16 may be open to debate.

Concerning the significance of the Church as the Body of Christ, Alford writes: "He is its Head; from Him comes its life; in Him, it is exalted; in it, He is lived forth and witnessed to; He possesses nothing for Himself,—neither His communion nor His glorified humanity,—but all for His Church" (3:86).

Salmond points out the implication of "body" in this way: "The relation between Christ and the Church, therefore, is not an external relation, or simply one of Superior and inferior, Sovereign and subject, but one of life and incorporation" (EGT, 3:281). The Church is "the instrument also by which He works" *(ibid.)*. The last sentence is a very solemnizing thought.

Eadie points out a bit more specifically some further implications. He says:

> There is first a connection of life: if the head be dissevered, the body dies. The life of the church springs from its union to Christ by the Spirit, and if any member or community be separated from Christ, it dies. There is also a connection of mind: the purposes of the head are wrought out by the corporeal organs—the tongue that speaks, or the foot that moves. The church should have no purpose but Christ's glory, and no work but the performance of His commands. There is at the same time a connection of power: the organs have no faculty of self-motion, but move as they are directed by the governing principle within . . . Energy to do good, to move forward in spiritual contest and victory, and to exhibit aggressive influence against evil, is all derived from union with Christ. There is, in fine, a connection of sympathy. The pain or disorder of the smallest nerve or fibre vibrates to the Head, and there it is felt. Jesus has not only cognizance of us, but He has a fellow-feeling with us in all our infirmities and trials (pp. 107-8).

The above has been quoted at length because it presents a splendid, usable outline for a sermon on this subject. Aside from a contemplation of the members of the Trinity, there are few topics more rich in blessing and helpfulness for the Christian than the relation of Christ to His Church. A sermon on this subject should serve to inspire and uplift, to challenge and comfort. The trouble with most Christians is that they live—in their conscious thoughts and feelings—too much in isolation from Christ, the Head.

## Fulness (1:23)

The word is *plērōma.* Thayer says of it: "1. etymologically it has a passive sense, *that which is* (or *has been*) *filled;* very rarely so in classical Greek." He further suggests: "In the New Testament the body of believers, as that which is filled with the presence, agency, riches of God and of Christ" (p. 158). Somewhat similarly Cremer writes that in this passage the fullness of Christ "is a name given to the church, because the church embodies and shows for all that Christ . . . is" (p. 501).

The word comes from the verb *plēroō,* which means "fill, make full, fill to the full." Abbott-Smith goes on to define *plēroma* thus: "the result of the action involved in *plēroō . . . ,* hence, 1. in passive sense, *that which has been completed, complement,* plenitude, fullness" (pp. 365-66).

Arndt and Gingrich indicate the difference of opinion as to the exact meaning of *plērōma.* Under the definition "that which makes something full or complete, supplement, complement," they say: "Figuratively, perhaps of the church which, as the body, is *to plērōma, the complement* of Christ, who is the head Eph. 1:23"; then they add: "Much more probably the Ephesian passage belongs under 2. *that which is full of something"* (p. 678).

Alford agrees with this, as he says: "Here, the simple and primary meaning is by far the best,—*'the thing filled,'* —*'the filled up receptacle'* . . . the meaning being, that the church being the Body of Christ, is dwelt in and filled by God: it is His *plērōma* in an especial manner—His fulness abides in it, and is exemplified by it" (3:87).

Eadie has a long discussion of *plērōma*. He first asserts, against Erasmus and others, that it is in apposition with *sōma* (body). That seems clearly correct. He further rejects the idea that *plērōma* means either multitude or the divine glory. Finally he sets aside the active connotation of *plērōma*—the thought that the Church complements Christ—held by Chrysostom, Calvin, and others. He comments: "The idea is a striking, but a fallacious one. It is not in accordance with the prevailing usage of *plērōma* in the New Testament, and it stretches the figure to an undue extent" (p. 112). He writes: "The word, we apprehend, is rightly taken in a passive sense—that which is filled up." And then he concludes: "So the church is named *plērōma,* or fulness, because it holds or contains the fulness of Christ" (p. 113). It is obvious that this is in agreement with Alford's interpretation.

With this consensus Salmond agrees. He says: "Hence *plērōma* is to be taken in the passive sense here, as is done by most commentators, and the idea is that the Church is not only Christ's body but that which is *filled by Him."* After comparing this usage with the similar one in Colossians, he concludes: "Here the conception is that this plenitude of the divine powers and qualities which is in Christ is imparted by Him to His Church, so that the latter is pervaded by His presence, animated by His life, filled with His gifts and energies and graces" (EGT, 3:282).

In his commentary on Colossians and Philemon, Lightfoot has an extensive special note, "On the meaning of *plērōma"* (pp. 257-73). He points out, as do all lexicons, that the verb *pleroun* has two distinct meanings—(1) "To fill," or (2) "To fulfil, complete, perfect, accomplish"—and adds: "The word occurs about a hundred times in the New Testament, and for every one instance of the former sense there are at least four of the latter" (p. 257). He differs from the majority of commentators in insisting that it is this second meaning which should be applied to the noun. He writes: "As *pleroun* is 'to complete,' so *plērōma* is 'that which is completed,' i.e. the complement, the full tale, the entire number or quantity, the plenitude, the perfection" (p. 258). He believes this agrees with "its commonest usages in classical Greek" *(ibid.)*.

After noting the use of *plērōma* in the Gospels, Lightfoot finally comes to a comparison of its meaning in Colossians and Ephesians. This is governed by the differences in aim in the two Epistles. He continues:

> While in the former the Apostle's main object is to assert the supremacy of the Person of Christ, in the latter [Ephesians] his principal theme is the life and energy of the Church, as dependent on Christ. So the *plērōma* residing in Christ is viewed from a different aspect, no longer in relation to God, so much as in relation to the Church. It is that plenitude of Divine graces and virtues which is communicated through Christ to the Church as His body. The Church, as *ideally* regarded . . . becomes in a manner identified with Him. All the Divine graces which reside in Him are imparted to her; His "fulness" is communicated to her: and thus she may be said to be His *plērōma* (p. 263).

Westcott is in essential agreement with Lightfoot. He says: "For while, on the one side, Christ gives their true being to all things by His presence . . . and Christians in a special sense reach their 'fulness,' their complete development, in Him . . . on the other side, all things are contributary to Him, and He himself finds His fulness in the sum of all that He brings into a living union with Himself" (p. 28).

It would appear that we should allow both meanings: the Church as the receptacle of divine fullness, and the Church as the completion of Christ. The second interpretation is dismissed by many commentators as being too daring. But F. W. Beare helpfully suggests that this completion of Christ is not to be referred to His divine nature, which obviously was eternally complete, but rather to "the contingent manifestation of him in his function as Messiah. . . . In this contingent sense the church is necessary to his completion" (IB, 10:637). Beare quotes Westcott (above) approvingly and adopts his interpretation of *plērōma.*

## Quickened (2:1)

This verse serves as a good example of the apparent necessity for supplying words in an English translation which have no direct support in the Greek. For this purpose the King James translators used italics, to indicate that such words were not represented in the original.

Often the added words in italics dilute the effectiveness and force of the Greek text (e.g., 1 Thess. 4:3). At other times they actually distort the true sense of the passage. For instance, "somewhat" in Rev. 2:4 is positively misleading. The Greek says clearly: "But I have against you that you neglected (or left) your first love."

But in the case of the passage before us, some addition seems necessary. Literally it reads: "You [plural] being dead in your trespasses and sins." The Greek has no main verb in the first three verses of this chapter, which seem to constitute a sentence. A Greek sentence can be complete without any verb; but that is not the case in English. Usually, though, it is only the copulative verb ("to be") which must be supplied. Here something more is needed— or so it seems.

The first printed English New Testament was by Tyndale (1525). His translation became the main basis for the KJV. He has: "And hath quickened you also that were deed in trespasse and synne." The Great Bible (1539) comes a little closer to the KJV. It reads: "And you hath he quyckened, where as ye were deed in trespasses, and synnes." The Geneva Bible (1560) introduced the use of italics for words not in the original. It has: "And you *hath he quyckened also,* that were dead in trespasses and synnes."

Weymouth (1902) varies strikingly in placing the verb at the end of verse 3—"to you God has given Life." But other private translators have usually supplied the copulative verb. *The Twentieth Century New Testament* (1901) has: "To take your own case again. Once you were, so to speak, dead because of your offences and sins." Moffatt (1913; rev. ed., 1922) reads rather similarly: "As with us, so with you. You were dead in the trespasses and sins" (continuing the sentence to the end of verse 3). Goodspeed (1923) also carries on the sentence. He has: "You also were dead because of the offences and sins in the midst of which you once lived." Charles B. Williams (1937) follows this same line: "You too were dead because of the shortcomings and sins in which you once lived." Verkuyl's *New Berkeley Version,* (1945, 1959, 1969) reads very similarly: "You, too, were dead in your trespasses and sins" (cf. NIV). It is obvious that modern translators prefer to supply the copulative verb so as to make a complete sentence.

The English Revised Version (1881) followed the general lead of the KJV, only modifying it to read: "You *did he quicken,* when ye were dead through your trespasses and sins." The ASV (1901) simply changed *did he quicken* to *did he make alive.* The RSV followed rather closely, with this wording: "You he made alive, when you were dead through the trespasses and sins." But the NEB (NT, 1961) conforms more nearly to the pattern set by private translations in this century. It reads: "Time was when you were dead in your sins and wickedness."

The question is: Does the context justify the insertion found in similar terms in the three standard versions? The verb "quicken" does not occur until verse 5. It would seem that the copulative verb, as in the above recent translations, is adequate and less open to criticism.

## Trespasses and Sins (2:1)

The Greek noun *paraptōma* (trespass) has already been noted (1:7). What is the difference between "trespasses" and "sins"? Vincent makes this distinction: *"Trespasses,* special acts. *Sins,* all forms and phases of sin: more general" (3:374). Salmond says: "Etymologically, *paraptōma* points to sin as a *fall,* and *hamartia* to sin as *failure."* But he adds: "It is impossible to establish a clear distinction between the two nouns in the plural forms, as if the one expressed *acts* and the other *states* of sin, or as if the former meant single trespasses and the latter all kinds of sins" (EGT, 3:283). He takes the whole as a general declaration that it is by sin we are made dead.

But most commentators find some distinction. Eadie writes: "Perhaps while the first term refers to violations of God's law as separate and repeated acts, the last . . . may represent all kinds of sins, all forms and developments of sinful nature" (p. 118). He says more specifically: "Thus *paraptōmata,* under the image of 'falling,' may carry an allusion to the desires of the flesh, open, gross, and palpable, while *hamartiai,* under the image of 'missing the mark,' may designate more the desires of the mind, sins of thought and idea, of purpose and inclination" (p. 119). This seems to be a helpful, as well as valid, distinction. It is in agreement with what Olshausen had already declared: "The plural *hamartiai* of course denotes also workings of sins, not, however, sinful *acts,* so definitely as *paraptōmata,* but rather inward sinful movements of the soul in desires and words" (5:54).

The thought seems to be that what makes the natural

man spiritually dead is not only his violation of God's laws. This would constitute him condemned to die. But it is something deeper. He is not only subject to death or even under the sentence of death; he is actually dead, because under the control of a sinful nature.

## In or Through? (2:1)

Is it "in trespasses and sins" or "through trespasses and sins"? In the Greek no preposition occurs; it is simply the dative case, which can be rendered several ways. The "in trespasses" form would be called the locative dative; "through trespasses" would be the instrumental dative.

The older translators took it the first way. "In" is used by Wycliffe, Tyndale, the Great Bible, the Geneva Bible, and the KJV. But the RV (English and American) has "through," which is equivalent to "by means of." Weymouth agrees. *The Twentieth Century New Testament* is even more specific. It reads: "because of," as do Goodspeed and Williams. The RSV has "through," but the *NBV* and the *NEB* have "in."

What do the commentators say? Olshausen writes: "Men are of course here called *dead* through transgressions" *(ibid.)*. Salmond says emphatically: "The dative is the instrumental dative, 'by trespasses,' not *in* them" (3:283). Alford makes it "causal dative," which would be much the same. Similarly, Meyer writes: "The dative denotes the 'efficient cause' of the death" (p. 356). Ellicott prefers "by," not "in," holding that the dative here indicates the instrumental cause. Westcott adopts "through." A. T. Robertson, however, says that it is the locative here.

It is evident that the matter is not fully settled. Probably the best solution is to allow both meanings to the dative. It is certainly true that sin is the cause of our spiritual death. But it is just as correct to say that we are dead "in" our sins.

When two possible interpretations of a grammatical construction in the Greek seem equally well supported, it may be the part of wisdom to adopt both, rather than committing oneself irrevocably to either one alone. Often both applications may be made in preaching, even in the same sermon.

## Walked or Lived? (2:2)

The verb *peripateō* is used 39 times in the Gospels, always for physical walking. Seven out of the eight times it occurs in Acts it is also in the literal sense (exception—21:21). But Paul uses the term only in the metaphorical sense (32 times in his Epistles). It occurs most frequently in Ephesians (8 times).

Thayer notes that by Paul it is used "Hebraistically, *to live*"; specifically, "to regulate one's life, to conduct one's self" (p. 504). Arndt and Gingrich write: "In the New Testament this use of the word is decidedly Pauline. . . . Elsewhere it is reasonably common only in the two small Johannine letters, *live, conduct oneself, walk,* always more exactly defined" (p. 655).

Literally the verb means "walk *about,* implying *habitual* conduct" (Vincent, 3:67). Weymouth's translation brings this out: "Which were once habitual to you while you walked."

Though most English versions give the literal translation "walk," the metaphorical term "live" is used by Goodspeed, Williams, and NIV. Both renderings are equally acceptable.

## Course or Age? (2:2)

How did they formerly live? Literally the answer is: "According to the age *(aiōn)* of this world *(cosmos)*." But that does not seem to make good sense in English.

Of the 128 times *aiōn* occurs in the NT, it is translated "ever" 71 times, "world" 38 times, and "age" only twice in KJV. The basic meaning of the term is *"a space of time, as,* a lifetime, generation, period of history, an indefinitely long period; in New Testament of an indefinitely long period, *an age, eternity"* (A-S, p. 122).

But what is its meaning in this passage? Eadie and Salmond agree that "course" is the most suitable translation here. The former says: *"Aiōn* sometimes signifies in the New Testament—'this or the present time'—certain aspects underlying it . . . It is its 'course,' viewed not so much as composed of a series of superficial manifestations, but in the moving principles which give it shape and distinction" (p. 122). Salmond writes: "In such a connection as the present *aiōn* comes near what we understand by 'the spirit of the age,' but is perhaps most happily rendered *course,* as that word conveys the three ideas of *tenor, development,* and limited continuance" (EGT, 3:283).

## Aion and Cosmos (2:2)

What is the distinction between these words so often translated the same way in KJV? A. T. Robertson speaks of the "curious combination" of the two terms here and differentiates them thus: *"aiōn* (a period of time), *kosmos* (the world in that period.)" (4:524). Similarly Salmond observes: "The *kosmos* is the world as the objective system of things, and that as evil. The *aiōn* is the world as a world-period, the world as transitory" (EGT, 3:283). Goodspeed renders the whole clause clearly: "In the midst of which you once lived under the control of the present age of the world."

## Prince of the Power of the Air (2:2)

The RSV retains this translation, perhaps because it has become a fixed biblical phrase in the minds of Christians. Other versions vary considerably. Verkuyl (NBV) has "The prince of the aerial powers." Williams reads, "The mighty prince of the air." Goodspeed has "The master-spirit of the air." *The Twentieth Century New Testament* reads, "The Ruler of the Powers of the air." The NEB has "The commander of the spiritual powers of the air."

The first term, *archōn,* means "ruler," from *archō,* "I rule." The second, *exousia,* means "authority." The third, *aēr,* is obviously the origin of English "air" (cf. "aerial"). It was used by Homer and other early writers for the lower and denser atmosphere in distinction from *aither* (cf. "ether"), which referred to the higher, rarer realms. Arndt and Gingrich translate the phrase: "The ruler of the kingdom of the air" (p. 20).

Meyer agrees with most commentators in identifying this as the devil, ruling over demons, who were supposed by the Jews to have their main base of operations in the air. He writes: "The *devil* Paul here represents as *the ruler of the might of the air,* in which *exousia* is *collective,* denoting the totality of the mighty ones (the demons, Matt. xii. 24) concerned. This *exousia* has its seat in the air, which exists between heaven and earth" (p. 358).

## Sons of Disobedience (2:2)

This is a more accurate translation than "children of disobedience." The phrase is a typical Hebraism. "Sons of disobedience" (RV) suggests "belonging to disobedience as sons to a parent" (Vincent, 3:375). It is the same construction as "sons of light" (1 Thess. 5:5). Salmond comments: "The term *huios* (son) in its topical sense and followed by the genitive of a *thing,* expresses what is in intimate relation to the thing, what belongs to it and has its innate quality. 'Sons of disobedience' are those to whom disobedience is their very nature and essential character, who belong wholly to it" (EGT, 3:284). Thayer notes that in the NT *apeitheia* (disobedience) carries the connotation of "obstinate opposition to the divine will" (p. 55).

## Prince—Spirit (2:2)

These two words seem to be in apposition in this verse, both referring to the devil. But the former is in the accusative case and the latter in the genitive. So grammatically they cannot be appositives. "Spirit" has to modify "prince," as does *exousia* in the previous clause.

The correct explanation seems to be that, just as we have the Spirit of God or Christ, so we have the spirit of Satan—"that particular Spirit whose domain and work are in evil men" (EGT, 3:284). God influences men through His Holy Spirit. Satan influences them through His evil spirit. This can also be thought of as his hosts of demons who carry out his will in seeking to defeat God's will. C. S. Lewis, in his *Screwtape Letters,* has indicated something of the manner in which these demonic forces operate to tempt men and lead them astray.

## Conversation or Conduct? (2:3)

There are three different Greek words which are translated "conversation" in the KJV, and none of them means "conversation" as we use the term today.

"Had our conversation" is all one word in the Greek, *anestraphēmen.* The verb *anastrephō* occurs 11 times in the NT and is translated 8 different ways in KJV: "return" (Acts 5:22; 15:16); "have . . . conversation" (here and 2 Cor. 1:12); "live" (Heb. 13:18; 2 Pet. 2:18); "abide" (Matt. 17:22); "overthrow" (John 2:15); "behave" (1 Tim. 3:15); "be used" (Heb. 10:33); "pass" (1 Pet. 1:17).

A look at the lexicons shows that the word does suggest a variety of meanings. Thayer has "1. to turn upside down, overthrow . . . 2. to turn back . . . to return . . . 3. to turn hither and thither . . . to turn one's self about, sojourn, dwell . . . to conduct one's self, behave one's self, live" (p. 42).

The verb is compounded of *ana,* "again," and *strephō,* "turn." Hence it literally means "turn again." Arndt and Gingrich note that transitively it can mean "upset, overturn," as in John 2:15. In the passive it is used reflexively in the sense "turn back and forth." Figuratively it is used of human conduct, with the meaning "act, behave, conduct oneself, live"; that is, practice certain principles (p. 60).

Deissman, in his *Light from the Ancient East,* insists that this ethical use of *anastrephō* is not necessarily Semitic—as Thayer held—since it is found commonly in non-Semitic Greek situations. He cites an example from an inscription at Pergamum (p. 312), and several more from the same place in his *Bible Studies* (p. 194). Moulton and Milligan furnish quotations from the papyri in which the verb is used with the connotation "conduct oneself, behave" (VGT, p. 38).

For this passage Arndt and Gingrich suggest: "live in the passions of the flesh," which means "be a slave to physical passion" (p. 61). It is quite clear that the best translation of the verb here is "lived" (ASV, RSV, NEB, NASB, NIV).

## Desires or Wishes? (2:3)

The word *thelēma* occurs 64 times in the NT and is translated "will" 62 times, including 6 times in Ephesians. Here alone it is rendered "desire"; and in Rev. 4:1, "pleasure."

It comes from the verb *thelō,* which basically means "wish" or "will." It may refer primarily to desire (wish, wish to have, desire, want) or to purpose (wish, will, wish to do) (AG, p. 355).

The word "fulfilling" is literally "doing" *(poiountes).* So Arndt and Gingrich would translate this clause "doing what the flesh desires" *(ibid.).*

## Mind or Thoughts? (2:3)

The Greek word translated "mind" is not *nous,* but *dianoia* (in the plural). It means "understanding, intelligence, mind" (as the organ of thinking), but also *"mind* as a kind of thinking, disposition, thought." Here it suggests *"senses, impulses* in a bad sense" (AG, p. 186). Moffatt has "impulses."

In spite of the fact that the translation "mind" is retained in ASV and RSV, it would seem that the better rendering is "thoughts" (so Weymouth, Williams, Goodspeed, NIV).

## Sins or Trespasses? (2:5)

"Sin" in the KJV New Testament is usually the translation of *hamartia* (172 times) or the related term *hamartēma* (4 times). But here the Greek word is *paraptōma,* the most common rendering of which is "trespass" (so 9 times in KJV, 7 times "offence," and 3 times "sin"). Almost all the modern versions correctly have "trespasses" here.

## Quicken or Make Alive? (2:5)

In the time when the KJV was made, the verb "quicken" meant "to live or restore life to, to make alive" (OED, 8:54). It was only a little later (1626) that Bacon used it in its modern sense, "to hasten, accelerate" (*ibid.*, p. 55).

The Greek word is *synzōopoieō*, found only here and in Col. 2:13. It is compounded of *syn*, "together," *zōē*, "life," and *poieō*, "make." Hence the ASV gives the correct rendering for today: "Made us alive together." This brings out the proper connection and contrast with "dead."

Paul was especially fond of compounds with *syn*. He believed in a spiritual "togetherness"! That much-used term today would have been very meaningful for him. In verses 5 and 6 he has three of these compounds: make alive together, raise up together, and make to sit together. There are over 175 Greek compound words in the New Testament with the prefix *syn*, and many of these are found only in Paul's Epistles.

## Exceeding or Surpassing? (2:7)

The great apostle was also fond of compounds with *hyper*, the equivalent of the Latin *super*. He believed ardently and enthusiastically in a super religion—not just barely getting by, but an abundant life in Christ Jesus.

The word "exceeding" is a participle, *hyperballon*. The verb *ballō* means "throw" or "cast." So *hyperballō* is literally "throw beyond." But in the NT it is used only figuratively (five times) in the sense "exceed, surpass, transcend" (A-S, p. 458). The participle would therefore mean "exceeding" or "surpassing." Arndt and Gingrich translate the participle as "surpassing, extraordinary, outstanding" (p. 848). The NBV and RSV both have "immeasurable."

## Workmanship or Handiwork? (2:10)

The Greek word is *poiēma,* from *poieō,* "I make." It occurs elsewhere in the NT only in Rom. 1:20, where it is translated very literally "the things that are made." Abbott-Smith defines the word as meaning "that which is made or done, a work" (p. 369). *The Twentieth Century New Testament* (1900), Weymouth (1902), and the NEB (1961) have "handiwork." This and "workmanship" (KJV, ASV, RSV, NASB, NIV) are equally good.

## Without or Separate from? (2:12)

Paul writes that his Gentile readers were once "without Christ" (KJV), "separated from Christ" (RSV), "outside Christ" (Moffatt), "apart from Christ" (Weymouth).

The word *chōris* is properly an adverb, meaning "separately, apart." But in the NT (with the exception of John 20:7) it is used as a preposition—"separate from, apart from, without" (A-S, p. 486). The King James translators adopted the weakest rendering, "without" (35 out of 39 times). "Apart from" fits better in most passages. Probably here the strongest meaning should be chosen—"separate from" (NEB, NASB, NIV).

## Aliens or Alienated? (2:12)

The Greek has the perfect passive participle of *apallatrioō,* "being in a state of alienation from." Arndt and Gingrich would translate it: "excluded from" (p. 79). Because it is a verb form, "alienated from" (RSV) is preferable to "aliens" (KJV).

## Commonwealth or Citizenship? (2:12)

Most English translations follow the KJV in adopting

"commonwealth." The NBV has "the right of Israel's citizenship."

The Greek word *politeia* has both meanings. In the NT it occurs only one other time, in Acts 22:28, where it clearly means "citizenship." But does it have that sense here?

The word comes from *politeuō,* "to be a citizen," which is from *politēs,* "a citizen," and in turn from *polis,* "a city." This is due to the fact that "politics" was first related to the Greek city-state. One was not a citizen of a country, but of a city, such as Athens or Sparta. These were independent and autonomous.

While *politeia* can mean both "commonwealth" and "citizenship" (or the rights of a citizen), Salmond correctly observes: "The first of these is most in harmony with the theocratic term *tou Israel,* and so is understood by most" (EGT, 3:292). Eadie comments: "'The commonwealth of Israel' is that government framed by God, in which religion and polity were so conjoined, that piety and loyalty were synonymous, and to fear God and honor the king were the same obligation" (p. 164).

## Without God or Atheists? (2:12)

The Greek word is *atheoi* (only here in NT), and one is tempted to translate, or rather transliterate, it, "atheists." But this temptation must be resisted. While it does mean "atheists in the original sense of being without God and also in the sense of hostility to God from failure to worship him" (Rob., WP, 4:526), yet Eadie is probably correct in objecting: "Not 'atheists' in the modern sense of the term, for they held some belief in a superior power" (p. 167).

In classical Greek the word meant "slighting or denying the gods" (Plato), "godless, ungodly" (Pindar), or "abandoned by the gods" (Sophocles). But in the NT it means "without God, not knowing God" (A-S, p. 11).

Cremer says there are two main meanings of the term. First it was used actively in the sense "godless, forgetful of God." In the second place it was used passively—"without divine help, forsaken by God, excluded from communion with God." The latter is its meaning here (p. 281).

Salmond writes: "The adjective *atheos*, which is never found in the Septuagint or in the Apocrypha, and only this once in the NT, in classical Greek means *impious* in the sense of denying or neglecting the gods of the State; but it is also used occasionally in the sense of knowing or worshipping no god, or in that of abandoned by God." He goes on to say: "Three renderings are possible here—*ignorant* of God, *denying* God, *forsaken* of God" (EGT, 3:292). While Ellicott and Meyer prefer the third, probably the first fits best here. Arndt and Gingrich note that the term is used in this place "without censure" (p. 20).

## The Middle Wall of Partition (2:14)

The Greek is *to mesotoichon tou phragmou;* literally, "the middle wall of the fence"—"the *fact* of separation being emphasized in *wall,* and the *instrument* of separation in *fence*" (Vincent, WS, 3:378).

The first noun is a rare one, occurring only here in the NT. Moulton and Milligan cite only one example from the papyri and one from an inscription (VGT, p. 400). It is a compound of *mesos,* "middle," and *toichos,* "a wall." So it is translated literally here.

The second noun is from the verb *phrassō,* "fence in, stop, close." So it properly means "a fencing in." But in the NT it means a "fence" or "hedge." The latter is the KJV translation in the other three places where the word occurs (Matt. 21:33; Mark 12:1; Luke 14:23). Eadie says:

"*Phragmos* does not, however, signify 'partition;' it rather denotes inclosure" (p. 172). He concludes: "Any social usage, national peculiarity, or religious exclusiveness, which hedges round one race and shuts out all others from its fellowship may be called a 'middle wall of partition'; and such was the Mosaic law" (p. 173).

## Law . . . Commandments . . . Ordinances (2:15)

These three words occur together only here. The first is the most general and occurs about 200 times in NT. The second is more specific, suggesting particulars, and found some 70 times. The third, Greek *dogma,* occurs only 5 times. Three of these occurrences are in Luke's writings (Luke 2:1; Acts 16:4; 17:7), where the word is translated "decree." Paul uses it here and in Col. 2:14, in both of which places it is rendered "ordinances" (KJV, RSV). It may be translated "regulations" (NBV, NEB, NIV).

Probably Weymouth shows best the relationship of these three words: He has: "The Law with its commandments, expressed, as they were, in definite decrees."

## Access or Introduction? (2:18)

The word *prosagōgē,* literally "a bringing to," is found three times in the NT (Rom. 5:2; here; and in 3:12). Most translations have "access" (KJV, RSV, NEB, NASB, NIV). But Williams has "introduction." Eadie writes: "*Prosagōgē* . . . is 'introduction,' entrance into the Divine presence—an allusion, according to some, to approach into the presence of a king by the medium of a *prosagōgeus* (introducer); according to others, to the entrance of the priest into the presence of God . . . —not access secured but introduction enjoyed" (pp. 186-87).

## Strangers and Foreigners (2:19)

Paul indicates that his Gentile readers were formerly "strangers and foreigners," or "strangers and sojourners" (RSV). Weymouth has "mere foreigners or persons excluded from civil rights."

It is obvious that the two Greek words here mean much the same thing. The first, *xenos,* is properly an adjective. It means "foreign, alien." With the genitive case following, as in the twelfth verse of this chapter, it denotes "strange to, estranged from, ignorant of"; as a substantive it means "a foreigner, stranger" (A-S, p. 307). In the KJV it is always translated "strange" (3 times) or "stranger" (10 times), except Rom. 16:23, where it is rendered "host"; that is, one who entertains strangers. The term indicates one who is not a citizen.

The second word is also an adjective—*paroikos.* It is compounded of *para,* "beside," and *oikos,* "house." So its original connotation in classical Attic was "dwelling near, neighbouring"; and as a substantive, "a neighbour" (A-S, p. 346). But in late writers, as in the Septuagint and in Philo, it is used in the sense of "foreign, alien"; and so as a substantive, "an alien, a sojourner" *(ibid.).* Arndt and Gingrich note that it is used "figuratively, of the Christians, whose real home is heaven" (p. 634).

As in the case of the former term, the *paroikoi* are contrasted with citizens. In inscriptions of the second century B.C. the *politai* (citizens) and the *paroikoi* are noted as two segments of the population.

Moulton and Milligan say: "Hicks . . . has shown that *paroikos,* while never losing the idea of 'a sojourner,' 'a stranger' . . . is often found in the inscriptions in the sense of the classical *metoikos* to denote 'a licensed sojourner' in a town, 'whose protection and status were secured by the payment of a small tax,' as contrasted with *xenos,* a mere passing stranger (cf. Eph. 2:19)" (VGT, p. 496).

Whether Paul intended this distinction or simply used the two terms synonymously, we cannot be sure. But since he was himself a Roman citizen and had traveled widely, he was doubtless aware of this fine point, and may have had it in mind here. In that case, Bishop Wand's translation brings out the exact thrust of the passage: "You are no longer foreigners, or even licensed immigrants." Instead they were *sympolitai,* "fellow citizens" (so almost all the versions and translations). More than that, they were *oikeioi,* members of the "household" or "family" of God.

## What Foundation? (2:20)

It is often assumed that Paul here declares the "apostles and prophets" (probably NT prophets) to be the foundation on which the Church is built. But Meyer strongly objects. He says: "The apostles and prophets are *not* the foundation, but have *laid* it (I Cor. 3:10). *The foundation laid by the apostles and prophets* is the gospel of Christ, which they have proclaimed, and by which they have established the churches" (p. 393). Alford takes it as simply genitive of possession, not apposition.

## Chief Corner Stone (2:20)

This is all one word in the Greek, *akrogōniaios.* It comes from *akros,* "highest," and *gōnia,* "an angle." Found only here and in 1 Pet. 2:6, it means "the corner foundation stone" (A-S, p. 18). Arndt and Gingrich note that the term is "purely biblical." Thayer comments: "For as the cornerstone holds together two walls, so Christ joins together as Christians, into one body dedicated to God, those who were formerly Jews and Gentiles" (p. 24).

## Fitly Framed Together (2:21)

This again is one word in the Greek—*synarmologoumenē*. It is used "only in Christian writers" (AG, p. 792). In the NT it occurs only here and in Eph. 4:16.

## Builded Together (2:22)

"Ye are builded together" is one word—*synoikodomeisthe*. It is a double compound, formed of *syn*, "together," *oikos*, "house," and *demō*, "build." The word occurs only here in the NT.

## Habitation (2:22)

The word *katoikētērion*, "habitation," is likewise a rare one. It is found (in NT) only here and in Rev. 18:2.

One of the remarkable features of these four verses (19-22) is that they contain six compounds of *oikos*, "house." In verse 19 are *paroikoi*—those who are "beside" *(para)* the "house," not in it—and *oikeioi*, signifying those who "belong to the house" or family. In verse 20 occurs *epoikodomeō*, "build upon" *(epi)*. In verse 21 is *oikodomē*, from *oikos*, "house," and *demō*, "build"; originally the act of building, and then the building itself, as here. Verse 22 has *synoikodomeō*, already noticed, and *katoikētērion*.

Paul thinks of the individual Christian, of the local church congregation, and of the Church of Jesus Christ as a "habitation" where God, through His Spirit, dwells. He also calls the Church a "holy temple" (v. 21). The word for "temple" is not *hieron*, which is used for the whole Temple area, but *naos*, which means "sanctuary." The latter is the better translation, because it was in the sanctuary itself that God's presence dwelt. The Holy Spirit is the Shekinah, the glorious presence of the Lord, in our hearts and in the Church.

## Prisoner (3:1)

The word is *desmois,* from the verb *deō,* "bind." So it literally means "one who is bound." It is used regularly in the NT (16 times) in the sense of "prisoner."

Here Paul refers to himself as "the prisoner of Jesus Christ." The same expression occurs in Philemon, verses one and nine. In Eph. 4:1 and 2 Tim. 1:8 he calls himself a prisoner of the Lord.

This reflects an amazing faith. Actually Paul was a prisoner of the Roman Empire. But instead of bemoaning his fate—the lack of opportunity for preaching and traveling about in missionary work—he saw himself as the personal prisoner of Jesus Christ. He was bound in body, but free in spirit.

A very busy and widely traveled Christian worker once found himself flat on his back in bed. Tempted to feel sorry for himself and frustrated at his enforced inactivity, he turned for comfort to the twenty-third psalm. As he read the familiar words, "He maketh me to lie down," the Spirit suddenly put a period right at that point. The man went no farther. Here was the truth he needed. It was not ultimately the sickness that made him lie down, but the Lord—who wanted to talk quietly with His servant who had been too busy to listen attentively.

The great apostle was one of the busiest men of his day. Preaching, traveling, writing, organizing new churches—he had little time for meditation. Now he was "the prisoner of Jesus Christ," bound physically that he might be freed mentally and spiritually to meditate and pray. His thinking had time to settle, and in these Prison Epistles he has skimmed off the cream and given it to us.

## Dispensation or Stewardship? (3:2)

The word *oikonomia* is translated "stewardship" in

the Gospel of Luke and "dispensation" in the Epistles of Paul (KJV)—the only places where it occurs in the NT. We have met it already in 1:10, where neither meaning seemed to fit very well in that place.

However, here the correct sense, "stewardship," fits exactly. To Paul was committed the "stewardship of God's grace" (RSV), that he might administer this grace to the Gentiles.

## Ages or Generations? (3:5)

The word is not *aiōn,* "age," but *genea,* "generation." Most recent English translations have "generations" (RSV, NEB, NASB, NIV). Out of 42 occurrences in the NT, *genea* is translated "generation" 37 times in the KJV, "time" twice, "age" twice (here and v. 21), and "nation" once.

The meaning of the term is "1. literally, those descended from a common ancestor . . . 2. basically, the sum total of those born at the same time, expanded to include all those living at a given time," and so "generation." It can, however, mean "3. *age,* the time of a generation" (AG, p. 153). For this passage Arndt and Gingrich suggest "other times."

## Fellowheirs (3:6)

In this verse three related terms occur. They all begin with the same prefix, but this is obscured in most English translations.

The words are *synklēronoma, synsōma,* and *synmetocha* (as spelled in Westcott and Hort). The prefix *syn* is a preposition "expressing association, fellowship and inclusion" and means "with, together with" (A-S, p. 424).

The first of these three terms is translated "fellowheirs." Deissmann gives examples of this use in inscriptions of this period at Ephesus and Thessalonica (LAE, p. 92). The second word is rendered "of the same body" ("members of the same body," RSV). *Sōma,* "body," is used for the Church eight times in this Epistle (not counting the compound, which is found only here in NT). The third term, found only here and in 5:7, means "joint partaker." The simple form, *metochos,* means "partaker" or "partner."

The ASV (1901) helpfully represents the common prefix of these three Greek compounds by translating them "fellowheirs, fellow-members of the body, and fellow-partakers."

## Minister or Servant? (3:7)

*I Was Made a Minister* is the title of the fascinating autobiography of the late Methodist bishop, Edwin Holt Hughes. The book vividly documents the fact that God makes His own ministers.

The phrase is translated by both Moffatt and Williams, "I was called to serve." Ballantine has, "I became a servant"; and Goodspeed, "I became a worker."

The noun is *diakonos.* Occurring 30 times in the NT, it is rendered (in KJV) "minister" 20 times, "servant" 7 times, and "deacon" 3 times. It is the word from which comes the English term "deacon," and is probably correctly translated this way in Phil. 1:1 and 1 Tim. 3:8, 12.

But in the other instances is "minister" or "servant" more accurate? Thayer defines the term thus: "One who executes the commands of another, especially of a master; a servant, attendant, minister" (p. 138). Abbott-Smith lists these last three meanings.

To us today "minister" does not primarily connote "servant." But that is its earliest meaning. The *Oxford*

*English Dictionary* indicates "servant, attendant" as the first meaning, but labels this usage "obsolete" (4:473). Next it gives "one who waits upon, or ministers to the wants of another." This also it calls "archaic." The use of the term "minister" in an absolute sense for a clergyman began in Protestant circles in the 16th century, partly as a protest against the designation "priest" (4:474).

In the light of all this it is clear that in the NT "servant" is a more accurate translation of *diakonos* than "minister." The primary meaning of the Greek word is "one who serves." That is not what the English word "minister" connotes today.

There is a strange inconsistency in the translation of *diakonos* in Matt. 20:26 and 23:11 in the KJV. In both passages Jesus says that whoever would be great among the disciples should be their *diakonos*. But this is translated "minister" in the first instance, and "servant" in the second. The latter is, of course, correct. The same inconsistency occurs in Mark 9:35 ("servant") and 10:43 ("minister")—*diakonos* in both places.

The true meaning of the word is shown by its use in Matt. 22:13 for "servants" of a king and in John 2:5, 9 for the "servants" at the marriage in Cana. Commenting on these passages, Stott says: "In none of these instances is the *diakonos* working in his private capacity; he is the representative of a higher authority whose commission and command he is fulfilling" (John R. Stott, *The Preacher's Portrait,* p. 104).

## Less than the Least (3:8)

This is an interesting phrase. How can one be "less than the least"? What is less than zero?

The adjective *elachistos* means "smallest, least." It is already a superlative form. But here we have *elachistoteros*

—a comparative formed from a superlative! Thayer writes: "It is well known that this kind of double comparison is common in the poets; but in prose, it is regarded as faulty." He defines it: "less than the least, lower than the lowest" (p. 202).

What the apostle is seeking to say is that he felt himself the least worthy of God's grace and mercy. This passage is parallel to 1 Cor. 15:9—"For I am the least of the apostles, that am not meet to be called an apostle, because I persecuted the church of God."

## Unsearchable (3:8)

The adjective *anexichniastos* is found only here and in Rom. 11:33. It means "that cannot be traced out" (A-S, p. 36). It is used in the Septuagint in Job 5:9; 9:10; 34:24. Moulton and Milligan think that Paul borrowed the word from Job, "and it is re-echoed in early Fathers" (VGT, p. 41). It simply emphasizes the fact that no one can plumb the depths or fathom the greatness of God's grace. The riches of Christ cannot be comprehended. Yet we are "joint-heirs with Christ" (Rom. 8:17)! Salmond notes that the term is used here "not in the sense of *inexhaustible,* but rather in that of *unfathomable*" (EGT, 3:306).

## Fellowship or Stewardship? (3:9)

The expression "fellowship of the mystery" seems a bit odd. As Salmond notes, the reading *koinōnia* (fellowship) "has the slenderest possible authority" (EGT, 3:307). All the oldest and best Greek manuscripts have *oikonomia.* We have already noted the meaning of this word in connection with its use in 1:10 and 3:2; in both places the KJV translates it "dispensation." Here it means: "the *dispensation* or *arrangement* of the mystery, to wit the admission of the Gentiles on equal terms with the Jews; the *mysterion* here having the same application as in iii. 6" *(ibid.)*.

## From the Beginning of the World (3:9)

"Beginning of the world" is all one word in the Greek, *aiōnōn,* "ages." Salmond writes: "The formula *apo tōn aiōnōn* occurs in the NT only here and in Col. 1:26. . . . It means literally 'from the ages,' 'from the world-periods,' that is, *from the beginning,* or *since the world began" (ibid.)*. Ellicott defines the expression here as meaning: "From the commencement of the ages when intelligent beings, from whom it could be concealed, were called into existence" (p. 71).

## By or Through? (3:10)

One of the weaknesses of the KJV is its translation of Greek prepositions. "Of" is used constantly in the sense of "by," which it does not mean today. Here it is not "by the church," but "through the church." God will manifest His manifold wisdom *through* the Church of Jesus Christ. It is His placard display.

## Manifold or Many-sided? (3:10)

The Greek term is *polypoikilos,* an old, rare word (only here in NT). It literally means "much-variegated," or "having a great variety of forms." Salmond says: "The adjective is used of the rich variety of colours in cloths, flowers, paintings, etc." (EGT, 3:309).

It is difficult to represent this striking Greek term by any single word in English. Moffatt has, "the full sweep of the divine wisdom." *The New English Bible* says, "in all its varied forms"—a phrase which very correctly defines the meaning of the adjective. Perhaps the best single-word rendering is that adopted by Goodspeed and Verkuyl (NBV): "many-sided."

## Purposed or Realized? (3:11)

One might suppose that "purpose" and "purposed" are related terms in the Greek. But such is not the case. The first is *prothesin,* the second *epoiesen.*

The expression "eternal purpose," is literally "purpose of the ages"; that is, "the purpose which pertained to, existed in, was determined on in the ages" (Ellicott, p. 72).

The Greek word for "purpose" is *prothesis;* literally, a "placing before," or a "setting forth." It is used this way in the Synoptic Gospels, as also in Heb. 9:2 for the shewbread —literally, "the presentation of the loaves." But in Acts and Paul's Epistles it means "plan, purpose, resolve, will" —a sense found commonly in the classical Greek writers (AG, p. 713).

"Purposed" is something else. It is the exceedingly common (576 times in NT) verb *poieō,* which is translated "do" 357 times, "make" 114 times, and dozens of other ways in the KJV. It has two main meanings: first, "to make, produce, create, cause"; second, "to do, perform, carry out, execute" (A-S, p. 369).

Which is the dominant idea here? "Constituted" is preferred by Calvin, while others adopt "carried out, executed." After noting the latter, Alford writes: "I can hardly think that so indefinite a word as *poieō* would have been used to express so very definite an idea, now introduced for the first time. . . . The aorist seems to refer the act spoken of to the origination of the design." Then he adds: "Both senses of *poieō* are abundantly justified" (3:107).

Ellicott perhaps has a little broader perspective. He says: "The mention of the eternal purpose would seem to imply rather *'constituit'* ... than *'exsecutus est'* ... as the general reference seems more to the appointment of the decree than to its historical realization ... ; still the words *en Christō Iēsou to kyrio hēmōn* seem so clearly to point to the realization, the carrying out of the purpose in Jesus Christ—the Word made flesh ... —that the latter ... must be considered preferable" (pp. 72-73).

With this judgment the majority of recent translators agree. Goodspeed, NBV, and NASB all have "carried out." Williams has "executed." Moffatt and the RSV have "realized." That seems to be the thought of the passage. God's purpose of the ages was finally "realized" in Christ Jesus, our Lord.

## Boldness (3:12)

The Greek word is *parrēsia.* It comes from *pas,* "all," and *rhēsis,* "speech." Its earliest usage in classical Greek is for *"freedom of speech, plainness, openness, freedom* in speaking" (A-S, p. 347). In the Septuagint, Josephus, and also the NT, "from the absence of fear which accompanies freedom of speech" it means "confidence, boldness" *(ibid.).*

In the NT the word occurs a number of times in the dative case and is translated adverbially as "openly" or "plainly." In the noun sense it is rendered "boldness" eight times and "confidence" six times. Its basic idea is that of "freedom" (NIV).

## Confidence (3:12)

The term "confidence" here is quite another word—*pepoithēsis.* It comes from the perfect tense of *peithō,* "persuade," and so literally means "full persuasion." It is a late and rare word in Greek writers, but is found half a dozen times in the NT. In 2 Cor. 3:4 it is translated "trust," though the usage seems to be exactly the same as "confidence" in 2 Cor. 1:15 and elsewhere in the NT.

## Access (3:12)

We have already noted the Greek word *prosagōgē* in Rom. 5:2 and Eph. 2:18, the only other places in the NT where it occurs. Some prefer the rendering "introduction" rather than "access."

The reason for mentioning this word again is that we wish to note the significance of the combination of the three terms here. Many translators paraphrase the passage. Moffatt has: "through whom, as we have faith in him, we enjoy our confidence of free access." Goodspeed reads: "Through union with him and through faith in him, we have courage to approach God with confidence."

## All or Every? (3:15)

The Greek is *pasa patria,* translated in the KJV "the whole family." But since there is no article in the Greek, most modern translations have "every family." This is in keeping with strict grammatical usage.

## Family or Fatherhood? (3:15)

The word *patria* is from *patēr,* "father." It was used by Herodotus in the sense of "lineage, ancestry" (A-S, p. 349). But more commonly in classical Greek it signified "a family or tribe." It is used only three times in the NT and is translated three different ways in the KJV—"family" (here); "lineage" (Luke 2:4); "kindreds" (Acts 3:25).

Thayer defines it as follows: "1. lineage running back to some progenitor, ancestry. . . . 2. a race or tribe, i.e. a group of families, all those who in a given people lay claim to a common origin. . . 3. family . . . nation, people" (p. 495). He thinks that *pasa patria en ouranois* means "every order of angels" (p. 496).

Cremer gives the various usage of the term in classical Greek and in the Septuagint and then concludes:

> The explanation of Eph. 3:14, 15 . . . is difficult, *from whom all that is called after a father, that bears his name, i.e.* the name of a *patria.* For, . . . *pasa patria,* since *pater* . . . is named, can only mean those *patriai* who are to be traced to *this pater,* the *patriai of the children of God.* . . . Thus Luther's translation, *over all who bear the name of children,* recommends itself as best (pp. 473-74).

The following translations are at least worthy of consideration: "from whom all fatherhood in heaven and on earth is named" (Spencer); "from whom all fatherhood, earthly or heavenly, derives its name" (Phillips). It should be noted however, that A. T. Robertson rejects "fatherhood" here (WP, 4:532) as does Salmond (EGT, 3:312).

## Might or Power? (3:16)

The KJV (also RSV) has "strengthened with might." The Greek word for "might" is *dynamis,* which is correctly translated "power" in Acts 1:8—"But ye shall receive power, after that the Holy Ghost is come upon you." So the ASV is much superior here—"strengthened with power." It is the dynamic power of the Holy Spirit that strengthens us in the inner man.

The King James translators correctly rendered *dynamis* as "power" in verse 20—"according to the power that worketh in us"; that is, the inward operation of the Holy Spirit. It would have been much better if they had been consistent and done so in verse 16.

## Rooted and Grounded (3:17)

This combination is a favorite one with Paul—agriculture and architecture (cf. 1 Cor. 3:9). The first suggests roots going down deep into the soil. The second indicates the laying of a solid foundation.

The former participle is from the verb *rhizoō,* which means "to cause to take root," but is used metaphorically in the sense "to plant, fix firmly, establish" (A-S, p. 397). In the NT it occurs only here and in Col. 2:7. The latter is the verb *themelioō,* which means "to lay the foundation of, to found" (A-S, p. 205). Both are perfect passive participles, indicating a fixed state.

Most commentators feel that the two terms are intended to convey the same general thought, that of being firmly fixed or established. For instance, Salmond writes: "So here the two words probably express the one simple idea of being *securely settled* and *deeply founded"* (EGT, 3:314).

## Able or Fully Able? (3:18)

The word is *exischuō.* It is a compound of *ischuō,* which means "be strong, powerful . . . have power, be competent, be able" (AG, p. 384). The compound means "have full strength" or "be fully able." Salmond says: "The strong compound *exischuein* = to be *eminently able,* to *have full capacity,* occurs only this once in the New Testament and is rare in ordinary Greek" (EGT, 3:315). It should be translated "be fully able."

## Passes or Surpasses? (3:19)

The RSV brings out much better than the KJV the full force of the strong Greek term used here. Instead of "passeth" it has "surpasses." The Greek is the compound participle *hyperballousan.* The whole phrase means literally "the knowledge-surpassing love of Christ" *(ibid.).*

## Exceeding Abundantly Above (3:20)

This is all one word in the Greek—*hyperekperissou.* *Hyper* is the equivalent of the Latin *super,* "above." *Ek* means "out of." *Perissos* means "more than sufficient, over and above, abundant" (A-S, p. 357). So this double compound signifies "superabundantly, exceeding abundantly" (A-S, p. 458). Elsewhere in the NT it occurs only in 1 Thess. 3:10; 5:13. Arndt and Gingrich note that it is found nowhere else but in two Greek editions of Dan. 3:22 and in the *Testament of the Twelve* (Joseph 17:5). They give its meaning as "quite beyond all measure (highest form of comparison imaginable)" and would translate it here "infinitely more than" (p. 848). Ellicott renders it "superabundantly beyond" (p. 81).

## World Without End (3:21)

The closing words of this chapter are literally: "to all the generations of the age of the ages; amen." The suggestion is that of the age being composed of generations and at the same time of succeeding ages. It is the strongest possible way of saying "for ever and ever."

## Walk or Live? (4:1)

Five times in chapters four and five Paul instructs his readers as to how they should walk. In 4:1 he says, "Walk worthy of the vocation wherewith ye are called"; in 4:17, "Walk not as other Gentiles walk"; in 5:2, "Walk in love"; in 5:8, "Walk as children of light"; in 5:15, "Walk circumspectly." These passages make splendid texts for a series of sermons on "The Christian's Walk in a World like This."

The verb *peripateō* occurs 96 times in the NT. In the KJV it is translated "walk" in all but three places. In these it is rendered "go" (Mark 12:38), "walk about" (1 Pet. 5:8), and "be occupied" (Heb. 13:9).

The word has its literal meaning "walk" in the four Gospels, where it is found 39 times. It is the same for the first 7 occurrences in Acts. But in the eighth (Acts 21:21) it is used metaphorically, as in Ephesians. As would be expected, this is the dominant usage in the Epistles. The five occurrences in Revelation all carry the literal sense.

Abbott-Smith says that the word is used "metaphorically, of living, passing one's life, conducting oneself" (p. 356). This is clearly the meaning here.

## Vocation or Calling? (4:1)

Since "vocation" (KJV) is the same root as "called," it is better to translate the former as "calling" (ASV). This brings out the close connection between the two in Greek.

## Lowliness or Humility? (4:2)

The word *tapeinophrosynē* (seven times in NT) is defined as "lowliness of mind, humility" (A-S, p. 439). Thayer gives the following explanation of its meaning: "The having a humble opinion of one's self; a deep sense of one's (moral) littleness; modesty, humility, lowliness of mind" (p. 614).

The compound is derived from the adjective *tapeinos*. Cremer traces the development of the latter. Figuratively it meant:

> (a.) low, unimportant, trifling, small, paltry . . . (b.) humbled, cast down, oppressed . . . (c.) . . . modest, humble . . . submissive subject. . . . Further, the word is used in profane Greek (d.) very often in a

morally contemptible sense cringing, servile, low, common . . . and it is (e.) a notable peculiarity of Scripture usage that the Septuagint, Apocrypha, and New Testament know nothing of this import of the word, but rather, in connection with (c.), deepen the conception, and raise the word to be the designation of the noblest and most necessary of all virtues (pp. 539-40).

Trench agrees fully with this characterization of the use of *tapeinos* in classical Greek. He says: "The instances are few and exceptional in which *tapeinos* signifies anything for them which is not grovelling, slavish, and mean-spirited." As far as *tapeinophrosynē* is concerned, "no Greek writer employed it before the Christian era, nor, apart from the influence of Christian writers, after" (p. 148). The word is used in Josephus, but only in a bad sense.

Christianity took the pagan idea of humility as suggesting a cringing, servile attitude and made it the finest, noblest virtue of all. This is one of the glories of the Christian religion.

Jesus set the example when He said, "I am meek and lowly in heart" (Matt. 11:29). The two adjectives He used correspond exactly to the two nouns in this clause, "with all lowliness and meekness." There is no place in the life of the true follower of Christ for pride and self-assertion.

"Lowliness" is used here by most standard English versions. However the NEB and NIV have "humble." The NBV has "humility," as does also the NASB. Moffatt has "modesty." But that is inadequate. As noted in the quotation from Cremer, Greek writers used the adjective *tapeinos* in the sense of "modest." After describing its higher meaning, Trench says: "Such is the Christian *tapeinophrosynē*, no mere modesty or absence of pretension, which is all that the heathen would at the very best have found in it" (p. 150). Cremer agrees with this when he writes: "Humility with the Greeks was in fact nothing higher than *modesty, unassuming diffidence*" (p. 540).

## Meekness or Gentleness? (4:2)

The word *prautēs* is defined by Abbott-Smith as "gentleness, meekness" (p. 377). Occurring 11 times in the NT, it is always translated "meekness" in the KJV.

But the NEB and NIV have "gentle"; and "gentleness" is the rendering in Moffatt, Goodspeed, Williams, and the NASB. Certainly there is no meekness which does not manifest itself in gentleness. The Christian must make sure that his inward grace of meekness, implanted by the Holy Spirit, manifests itself in the outward graciousness of "gentleness."

Trench seems to have caught the true meaning of this term. He notes that it is not "mere natural disposition. Rather is it an inwrought grace of the soul; and the exercises of it are first chiefly towards God." He continues: "It is that temper of spirit in which we accept his dealings with us as good, and therefore without disputing or resisting; and it is closely linked with the *tapeinophrosynē,* and follows directly upon it (Ephes. iv. 2; Col. iii. 12), because it is only the humble heart which is also the meek" (p. 152). Put in simplest terms, meekness is submissiveness to the will of God.

## Endeavouring or Eager? (4:3)

The verb is *spoudazō*, which literally means "to make haste," and so "to be zealous or eager, to give diligence" (A-S, p. 414). In the KJV it is translated "endeavour" in two other places, but be "diligent," do or give "diligence" five times, and once each "was forward," "labour," and "study" (2 Tim. 2:15). "Eager" (RSV) expresses the idea of the Greek more accurately and adequately than "endeavouring."

## Union or Unity? (4:3)

The Greek word is *henotēs*, which occurs only here and in v. 13. It comes from *hen*, "one," and so very literally means "oneness."

True ecumenicity is not a union of denominations, but "the unity of the Spirit." In other words, the thing the NT teaches and that Christ desires is not organizational union but spiritual unity.

## One Body . . . One Spirit (4:4-6)

This "unity of the Spirit" (v. 3) is spelled out more specifically in vv. 4-6. The true Church of Jesus Christ is "one body," spiritually because it is maintained by "one Spirit." Here is the ecumenical emphasis of the NT. It is still God's design and desire. When we are working for this we are "workers together with him." The Middle Ages had a far greater organizational unity of the Church than obtains today. But does that mean that the one, monolithic church was more spiritual and doing a greater evangelistic work than the many evangelical denominations today? To ask the question is to answer it.

The fifth verse is of interest to those who know Greek. For it contains all three genders of the word "one"—*heis, mia, hen*—the only place like it in the New Testament. The word "one" occurs seven times in verses 4-6.

The fourth verse stresses the spiritual unity of the Church; the fifth verse, its oneness in loyalty, doctrine, and fellowship. The sixth verse points to the ultimate source of all authority in the Church—God the Father, who is "above all" (transcendent), "through all" (pervasive), and "in all" (immanent).

## Captivity Captive (4:8)

The rendering of the KJV is a literal translation, but it does not make clear sense in English. Abbott-Smith says that the abstract noun translated "captivity" is used for the concrete, "captives" (p. 15). Thayer agrees, as do Arndt and Gingrich, who render it, "prisoners of war" (p. 26). The NBV conveys this thought with its translation: "He led the captured away in captivity." The simplest and clearest rendering is: "He led a host of captives" (Goodspeed, RSV).

## Lower Parts of the Earth (4:9)

This strange expression has provoked an endless amount of discussion, especially in the older commentaries. There are two main interpretations. The first would refer it to a descent into Hades (cf. the Apostles' Creed). The second would apply it to the Incarnation. Some of the Early Church fathers, such as Irenaeus, Tertullian, Jerome, together with Erasmus, Bengel, Meyer, Alford, and others, took the former view. On the other hand, Calvin proposed the latter, and many modern commentators have followed him.

Salmond says: "Neither grammar nor textual criticism gives a decisive answer" (EGT, 3:326). If "of the earth" is taken as a genitive of apposition, it means "the lower parts which are the earth." The possessive genitive would be "the lower parts belonging to the earth"; that is, Hades. The comparative genitive would mean "the parts lower than the earth." Salmond comments: "The *katotera* may mean the parts lower than the earth itself, i.e., Hades;

but it may also mean the parts lower than heaven, i.e., the earth" (EGT, 3:327). A comparison with the great kenosis passage in Phil. 2:5-10 suggests that the latter interpretation is preferable. Salmond adopts this conclusion.

Eadie thinks the same. He says: "We agree with the majority of expositors who understand the words as simply denoting the earth" (p. 283). He further points out the fact that the comparative—"lower parts of the earth"—could very well describe Christ's lowly birth in a manger, His lowly occupation as a carpenter, His humiliating death, and His "extemporized and hasty" funeral (pp. 294-95). All this fits in with Paul's emphasis in the kenosis passage. Christ not only became a man but a servant, and humbled himself to death, "even the death of the cross." It does not seem necessary to look farther for the meaning of this obscure phrase in Ephesians.

## Apostles (4:11)

The noun *apostolos* comes from the verb *apostellō*, which properly means *"to send away, to dispatch* on service; 1. to send with a commission, or on service" (A-S, p. 54). Jesus was the first "apostle," and He chose 12 disciples to be His apostles to the world. In John 17:18 He prays: "As thou hast sent me into the world, even so have I also sent them into the world" (cf. John 20:21).

Barnabas and Paul are also called apostles (Acts 14:14). Vincent writes: "The distinguishing features of an apostle were, a commission directly from Christ: being a witness of the resurrection: special inspiration: supreme authority: accrediting by miracles;; unlimited commission to preach and to found churches" (3:389).

## Prophets (4:11)

The word is taken directly from the Greek *prophētēs*.

This comes from the verb *prophēmi,* which literally means "say before," but which can also mean "speak forth" or "speak for." Liddell and Scott note that the noun was used in classical Greek for "one who speaks for a god and interprets his will" (p. 1540). In the NT it means "inspired preacher and teacher, organ of special revelations from God" *(ibid.).* Arndt and Gingrich note that it is used "also in other senses, without excluding the actual prophets, of men who proclaim the divine message with special preparation and with a special mission" (p. 731). In the NT it seems to mean "preacher."

## Evangelists (4:11)

The word, which is a transliteration of the Greek *euangelistēs,* is found only two other places in the NT. In Acts 21:8 Philip is referred to as "the evangelist." In 2 Tim. 4:5 the young Timothy is admonished to "do the work of an evangelist."

The term comes from the verb *euangelizō* ("evangelize"), which means "proclaim glad tidings." An evangelist, then, is one who preaches the "gospel" (Greek *euangelos*), the good news that Christ has died to save men. The evangelists in the Early Church were probably itinerant preachers.

## Pastors and Teachers (4:11)

"Pastor" is the Latin term for "shepherd." The Greek word *poimēn* also means "shepherd." It is used of Christ (John 10:11, 14, 16; Heb. 13:20; 1 Pet. 2:25). Here it is used of Christian pastors. Homer, in his *Iliad,* refers to "pastors of the people" *(poimena laōn).* The pastor is to be the shepherd of his flock.

Apparently the pastors and teachers were the same.

Vincent comments: "The omission of the article from *teachers* seems to indicate that pastors and teachers are included under one class" (3:390).

## Perfecting or Equipment? (4:12)

Instead of "perfecting," some recent translations prefer "equipment" (RSV) or "to equip" (NEB).

The Greek word is *katartismos* (only here in NT). It comes from the verb *katartizō*, which means "to make *artios*"; that is, "fit" or "complete." The verb is used for mending nets (Matt. 4:21; Mark 1:19). Its basic meaning was "put in order, restore—a. restore to its former condition, put to rights . . . b. put into proper condition, complete, make complete" (AG, p. 418).

Salmond calls attention to the fact that in Polybius and Herodotus the verb carries the idea of "preparing, furnishing, equipping." So he would translate the phrase here, "with a view to the full equipment of the saints" (EGT, 3:330-31).

The comma after "saints" should be omitted. The correct meaning apparently is "for the equipping of the saints for the work of service" (NASB) or "to prepare God's people for works of service" (NIV).

## Edifying or Building Up? (4:12)

The word is *oikodomē*. It comes from *oikos*, "house," and *demō*, "build." So it refers to the act of building. In the Gospels it is used for the buildings of the Temple (Matt. 24:1; Mark 13:1-2). In the Epistles (Romans, 1 & 2 Corinthians, Ephesians) it is always used metaphorically. It is translated "building" in 1 Cor. 3:9; 2 Cor. 5:1; and Eph. 2:21. In most other pasages it is rendered "edifying" or "edification." Since these are rather outdated terms now, it is better to translate the word as "building up."

## Come or Attain? (4:13)

The verb *katantaō* properly means "come" or "arrive." But here it is used in the figurative sense of "attain." That seems to be the better translation here (NASB).

## Perfect or Mature? (4:13)

The word "perfect" is a bone of contention in ecclesiastical and theological circles. At the one extreme are those who bristle at the very mention of the term in a religious connection. At the other extreme are those who when they see the word "perfect" or "perfection" immediately assume that it refers to the crisis experience of entire sanctification. Both attitudes are mistaken.

The Greek adjective *teleios* comes from *telos*, "end." So it means "having reached its end, finished, mature, complete, perfect" (A-S, p. 442). In Heb. 5:14 it is used literally of a fully grown or mature person in contrast to a "babe," and is translated in the KJV "of full age." Here in Ephesians and in other passages in Paul's Epistles, it is employed in an ethical sense. It is translated "man" in 1 Cor. 14:20, but elsewhere in the KJV as "perfect" (17 times). The RSV renders it "mature" seven times.

The contrast with "children" (v. 14) suggests that "full-grown" is the basic connotation here, and that is the way it is given in the ASV. Salmond comments: "The state in which *unity* is lacking is the stage of immaturity; the state in which oneness in faith and knowledge is reached is the state of mature manhood in Christ." In relation to the use of "man" here in the singular, he says: "The goal to be reached is that of a new Humanity, regenerated and spiritually mature in all its members" (EGT, 3:332).

It seems evident that "mature" (RSV, NEB, NASB, NIV) is a more accurate translation here than "perfect." It should be noted that "perfecting" (v. 12) and "perfect" (v. 13) are from two entirely different Greek roots; and "perfect" is not the basic idea of either.

## Fulness of Christ (4:13)

What is meant by the *plērōma* of Christ? Salmond says: "The *Christou* is the *possessive genitive,* and the phrase means the fulness that belongs to Christ, the sum of the qualities which make Him what He is" (EGT, 3:333). Vincent carries it one point farther: "Which belongs to Christ and is imparted by Him" (3:391).

## Children or Babies? (4:14)

"Children" is the translation in all the standard English versions. But "babes" occurs in the NBV and Weymouth, while "babies" is used by Goodspeed and Williams.

The noun *nēpios* literally means an "infant." But it is used of children, and of legal minors not yet eligible to inherit the family estate. It may very well be that the idea of babyishness is intended here (cf. Heb. 5:13-14). The NIV has "infants." At any rate, the admonition is to "grow up"!

## Tossed to and Fro (4:14)

The expression "tossed to and fro" is all one word in the Greek, *klydōnizomenoi* (only here in NT). It comes from *klydōn,* which means "billow" or "wave." Hence the verb literally means "to be tossed by waves." Metaphorically it signifies "to be tossed like waves" (A-S, p. 250). Williams renders it "like sailors tossed about."

The second word, *peripheromenoi,* is literally "carried about," and is so translated in most versions. The combination of the two terms is expressed in different ways. Moffatt has "blown from our course and swayed by every passing wind of doctrine." The NEB has perhaps the most "breezy" translation: "tossed by the waves and whirled about by every fresh gust of teaching."

## Sleight or Trickery? (4:14)

The word *cubeia* (only here in NT) comes from *cubos,* "cube" or "dice." So it literally means "dice-playing." It may be rendered "cunning" (RSV, NBV) or "trickery" (Goodspeed, Williams, NASB). While the word "sleight" is still used in the phrase "sleight of hand performance," the basic idea is that of "trickery," which is probably the best translation.

## Cunning Craftiness (4:14)

This is one word in the Greek, the noun *panourgia.* It comes from the adjective *panourgos,* which literally means "ready to do anything." In the classics it means "cleverness," nearly always in the bad sense of "craftiness" (A-S, p. 336). The one word "craftiness" is perhaps an adequate rendering (RSV, NASB, NIV).

## Lie in Wait to Deceive (4:14)

The last part of v. 14, is rendered in ASV "after the wiles of error." The Greek is literally "to the method of deceit."

The word *methodeia* comes from the verb *methodeuō,*
which first meant "to treat by rule," and then "to employ
craft." So the noun means "craft, deceit." It is found here
and in 6:11, but nowhere in earlier Greek literature. It
occurs in later papyri (fifth century and following) in the
sense of "method," which has been taken over into English. Arndt and Gingrich would translate the whole
phrase here, "in deceitful scheming" (p. 500; adopted in
NASB, NIV). Vincent says that literally it should be
rendered, "tending to the system of errors," since *methodeia* means "a deliberate planning or system." He adds
that "error" includes the idea of "deceit or delusion"
(3:392).

## Speaking the Truth (4:15)

This is one word in the Greek—*alētheuontes.* The verb
*alētheuō* occurs only here and in Gal. 4:16. Thayer and
Abbott-Smith give only one meaning, "to speak the
truth." Arndt and Gingrich have "be truthful, tell the
truth."

## Joined Together (4:16)

Paul's favorite prefix for compound verbs is *syn,*
"with" or "together." Two of these occur in this verse.
They are translated "fitly joined together" and "com-
pacted" (KJV). The first, *synarmologeō,* has already been
encountered in Eph. 2:21. There it is used of a building
"framed together," that building being the Church, a
"holy temple in the Lord." Here it is employed for the
Church as the Body of Christ. The two figures are closely
related.

The second verb, *synbibazō,* means "to join or knit
together, unite" (A-S, p. 426). It is used of the physical

body, which is held together by joints and ligaments. It speaks eloquently of the unity of the spiritual Body of Christ, His Church. It is framed together as a building and joined together as a body. The first figure suggests the ancient Tabernacle in the wilderness, and also Solomon's Temple. They were both built as "the house of the Lord." In like manner the Church is "builded together for an habitation of God through the Spirit" (Col. 2:22).

The second figure is more complicated. It has to do with a vital, pulsating, moving union of parts by joints and ligaments that hold them together. Both are meaningful representations of the Church of Jesus Christ. Eadie writes: "The two participles express the idea that the body is of many parts, which have such mutual adaptation in position and function, that it is a firm and solid structure" (p. 322). The simplest translation is "joined and held together" (NIV).

## That Which Every Joint Supplieth (4:16)

"Through every joint of the supply" is the literal Greek for the KJV phrase, "by that which every joint supplieth."

The word for "joint" is *haphē,* (only here and Col. 2:19), which Arndt and Gingrich define as "ligament" (p. 124). "Supply" is *epichorēgia,* which occurs only here and in Phil. 1:19.

Salmond gives a good summary of the meaning of this verse: "The idea, therefore, appears to be that the body is fitly framed and knit together by means of the joints, every one of them in its own place and function, as the points of connection between member and member and the points of communication between the different parts and the supply which comes from the head" (EGT, 3:337). The NIV has "by every supporting ligament."

## Mind, Understanding (4:17-18)

Paul exhorts the Ephesian Christians not to walk (i.e., "live") as the Gentiles (heathen) walk, in the vanity of their "mind." The Greek word is *nous*. Arndt and Gingrich say that it "denotes the faculty of physical and intellectual perception, then also the power to arrive at moral judgments" (p. 546). Thayer defines it thus: "The mind, comprising alike the faculties of perceiving and understanding and those of feeling, judging, determining" (p. 429). For this passage he adopts the meaning: "Reason in the narrower sense, as the capacity for spiritual truth, the higher powers of the soul, the faculty of perceiving divine things, of recognizing goodness and hating evil" *(ibid.)*.

This, among the Gentiles, had become vain; that is, empty. Thayer defines the Greek word for "vanity" as meaning "what is devoid of truth and appropriateness," and for this passage he gives "perverseness, depravation" (p. 393). The key word of Ecclesiastes is "vanity." The Greek word is used there (in LXX) 40 times. The context in Ecclesiastes will suggest something of the meaning of the term. Those who adopted the heathen worship and way of life found it all to be "vanity"—sheer emptiness. When one rejects the truth, the mind is filled with unreality, and so empty of all that is eternal.

"Understanding" is the compound *dianoia*. Of this word Cremer writes: *"Dianoia,* strictly *a thinking over, meditation, reflecting,* is used in the same range, and with the same signification as the original *nous,* . . . save that the preposition *'dia'* gives emphasis to the act of reflection; and in keeping with the structure of the word, the meaning *activity of thinking* precedes the borrowed meaning *faculty of thought"* (p. 438). That is, the latter is more properly *nous,* the former *dianoia.* Cremer further notes that in the NT *"dianoia* is specially the *faculty of moral reflection, of moral understanding"* (p. 439). In this passage the two words are translated correctly in the KJV.

## Ignorance (4:18)

The word *agnoia* comes from the same root. It means *"want of knowledge, ignorance,* which leads to mistaken conduct, and forbids unconditional imputation of the guilt of the acts performed" (Cremer, p. 163). This concept seems to fit Acts 3:17; 17:30; 1 Pet. 1:14—the only other places in the NT where the word occurs.

But here it seems to be used "with sense of wilful blindness" (A-S, p. 6). Moulton and Milligan write: "The connotation of wilful blindness, as in Ephesians 4:18, is found in *The Tebtunis Papyri* I, 24.33 (B.C. 117), where an official reports the misconduct of certain persons whose plans he had frustrated, so that *legontes tēs agnoias* they left the district" (VGT, p. 5). Cremer, who wrote before the great era of papyrus discoveries, discerned this distinction in usage. He says: "This *agnoia* is with St. Paul the characteristic of heathendom, Acts xvii. 30, Ephesians iv. 18, compare verse 17, and is a state which renders repentance necessary, Acts xvii. 30, . . . and therefore eventually furnishes ground for blame, Ephesians iv. 18, as otherwise for forbearance" (p. 163).

## Blindness or Hardening? (4:18)

The former is the translation of KJV, the latter of NIV. The Greek word is *pōrōsis.* It means "a covering with a callus, hardening" (A-S, p. 395). Arndt and Gingrich define it as: "hardening, dulling, . . . dullness, insensibility, obstinacy" (p. 739). Thayer thinks that in this passage it indicates "stubbornness, obduracy" (p. 559). It is obvious that "hardness" or "hardening" is a more accurate rendering than "blindness."

## Past Feeling (4:19)

The Greek verb is *apalgeō* (only here in NT). Its basic meaning is "to cease to feel pain for," while in late Greek it signifies "to become callous, reckless" (A-S, p. 44). The RSV, following Goodspeed, reads, "They have become callous." The essential idea is that of callousness, so that it fits closely with "hardening" above.

## Lasciviousness (4:19)

*Aselgeia* is the Greek word. It means "licentiousness, wantonness, excess" (A-S, p. 63). Arndt and Gingrich define it as "licentiousness, debauchery, sensuality" and suggest for this passage, "give oneself over to debauchery" (p. 114). Thayer has a long list: "unbridled lust, excess, licentiousness, lasciviousness, wantonness, outrageousness, shamelessness, insolence" (p. 79). Moffatt, Goodspeed, and NIV have "sensuality." This seems to be the most meaningful translation for today.

## Conversation (4:22)

The word "conversation" has changed its meaning considerably since the KJV appeared in 1611. The *Oxford English Dictionary* gives as a definition of this term: "The action of living or having one's being *in* a place or *among* persons. Also figuratively of one's spiritual being" (2:940). But this meaning is labeled "obsolete."

As early as 1580 the word had come to mean, as now: "Interchange of thoughts and words; familiar discourse or talk" (3:941). This meaning finally prevailed. The correct translation here is "manner of life" (NASB) or "way of life" (NIV).

## The Old Man (4:22)

Most translations today use for this "old nature" or "old self." Weymouth, however, has a stronger rendering: "your original evil nature." This was "displayed in your former mode of life."

"The old man" (KJV) is the literal meaning of the Greek *ton palaion anthrōpon.* So the recent translations are to a certain extent interpretative. The word *palaios* means "old, ancient." It is used "of things not merely old, but worn by use" (A-S, p. 334). Thayer suggests: "We, as we were before our mode of thought, feeling, action, had been changed" (p. 494). Arndt and Gingrich say that *palaios* means "in existence for a long time, often with the connotation of being antiquated or outworn," and give the whole phrase: *"the old* (i.e., earlier, unregenerate) *man"* (p. 610).

Archbishop Trench's *Synonyms of the New Testament* is still the standard work in the field, though it very much needs to be brought up to date. It was written before the great era of the papyrus discoveries, which have shed much light on the meanings of New Testament terms. Furthermore, Trench builds largely on classical Greek, and it is universally recognized that the Koine Greek of the New Testament age was definitely different in many details from the classical language of an earlier day.

Trench indicates that *archaios* and *palaios* often appear to be used in the same sense. But when the emphasis is on "old in the sense of more or less worn out, . . . this is always *palaios"* (p. 252).

In regard to the meaning of "the old man," Eadie writes: "The words are, therefore, a bold and vivid personification of the old nature we inherit from Adam, the source and seat of original and actual transgression" (p.

339). Salmond defines it as: "the former unregenerate self in its entirety" (EGT, 3:342).

## The New Man (4:24)

The Greek is *kainon anthrōpon*. The other word for "new" is *neos*, from which the English word comes. Trench points out well the distinction between these two terms. He says: "Contemplate the new under aspects of *time,* as that which has recently come into existence, and this is *neos.*" He then adds: "But contemplate the new, not now under aspects of *time,* but of *quality,* the new, as set over against that which has seen service, the outworn, . . . and this is *kainos*" (p. 220). So "the new man" refers to the new quality of life that comes with Christ's entrance into the human heart.

Of the contrast between "the old man" and "the new man" Olshausen writes: "As in *the old* lies at the same time the idea of the obsolete, so in *the new* is that of the original, of that which corresponds with its ideal." He comments further: "But while the laying aside the old, and the putting on the new, is here referred to man, of course it is not Paul's meaning that sanctification is accomplished by our own power: Christ is our sanctification, as he is our righteousness (see on 1 Cor. 1:30); but all, that Christ through the Holy Spirit works in man, can in the form of Law be put to him as a demand, because man by his unfaithfulness can hinder the operation of the Spirit" (5:117). We do not "put off" and "put on" in our own strength, but by faith in Christ and in the power of the Holy Spirit.

As to the identity of "the new man," Ellicott writes: "It is scarcely necessary to observe that *kainon anthrōpon* is not Christ, but is in direct contrast to *ton palaion anthrōpon,* and denotes 'the holy form of human life which results from redemption'" (p. 109).

## Righteousness and True Holiness (4:24)

Paul states that the "new man" is created "in righteousness and holiness of truth" (literally). What is meant by "righteousness" *(dikaiosynē)* and "holiness" *(hosiotēs)?* Salmond notes that Plato "defines *dikaios* as the *generic* term and *hosios* as the *specific;* and he describes the former as having regard to our relations to *men,* the latter to our relations to God" (EGT, 3:344).

Olshausen writes: *"Dikaiosynē* denotes the right relation inwardly between the powers of the soul, outwardly to men and circumstances." He further states: "On the other hand, *hosiotēs* denotes . . . integrity of the spiritual life, and the piety towards God which it supposes" (5:118-19).

The word *hosiotēs* occurs in only one other passage in the NT, Luke 1:75. There it is also connected with *dikaiosynē,* only in the opposite order. The basic meaning of the word is "piety." Thayer defines it thus: "Piety towards God, fidelity in observing the obligations of piety, holiness" (p. 456). Cremer describes it as "holiness manifesting itself in the discharge of pious duties," and adds that "it denotes the spirit and conduct of one who is joined in fellowship with God" (p. 464).

## Be Angry; Sin Not (4:26)

This verse furnishes an interesting example of what one often finds in NT quotations from the OT. Paul is quoting Ps. 4:4. But in the KJV, Ps. 4:4 reads: "Stand in awe, and sin not."

The explanation of the apparent misquotation is that Paul quotes the Septuagint, which has exactly the same Greek words as here in Ephesians—*orgizesthe kai mē hamartanete.* Why, then, the common English translation of Ps. 4:4? The answer is that the Hebrew word literally means "tremble" (cf. NASB)—which may be with either awe or anger. English versions have usually chosen "awe," whereas the Septuagint translators chose "anger." *The Amplified Old Testament* (1962) has combined the ideas, with an added "but"—"Be angry, *but* stand in awe and sin not."

At first sight this seems like a strange command. Understandably there have been many attempts by interpreters to blunt its shock. Olshausen, following Chrysostom and other early writers, takes the first imperative hypothetically: "If ye are angry, as it is to be foreseen will happen, at least sin not in anger" (5:120). Beza, Grotius, and others took the first verb as interrogative: "Are ye angry?" It is doubtful if either of these explanations is valid—that is, supported by good Greek grammar.

Winer takes the first imperative as permissive. He says: "In the passage from Ephesians Paul's meaning is unquestionably this: we should not let anger lead us into sin" (p. 312). Meyer objects to Winer's position. He says: "The mere *kai* is only logically correct when both imperatives are thought of in the *same* sense, not the former as permitting and the latter as enjoining" (p. 479). His interpretation is: "In anger do not fall into transgression" (p. 478). In the seventh edition of Winer (by Lunemann) Meyer's objection is answered (it seems effectively) as follows: "For, the assertion (Mey.) that of two closely connected Imperatives the one cannot denote a permission and the other a command, is incorrect; we may say with perfect propriety: Well, then, go (I give you leave), but do not stay above an hour" (p. 312).

Eadie seems to prefer a fourth view: "The phrase is idiomatic—'Be angry'—(when occasion requires), 'but sin not;' the main force being on the second imperative with *mē*" (p. 348).

Salmond suggests a fifth interpretation: "The *kai* has

here the rhetorical sense which is found also in *atque,* adding something that seems not quite consistent with the preceding or that qualifies it, 'and yet'" (EGT, 3:345).

Alford seems to strike a mediating position. He says: "The first imperative, although jussive (expressing a command), is so in a weaker degree than the other: it is rather assumptive, than permissive" (3:125). Somewhat in line with this is the comment of Bengel: "Anger is neither commanded, nor quite prohibited; but this is commanded, not to permit sin to enter into anger: it is like poison, which is sometimes used as medicine, but must be managed with utmost caution" (4:98). He further notes that often the force of the imperative mood "falls only upon a part of what is said, Jer. x. 24" *(ibid.).*

Blass and Debrunner state that for the most part the imperative in the New Testament stays within the same limits as in classical usage. They continue: "As in the latter it is by no means confined to commands, but also expresses a request or a concession." For an illustration of this they cite Eph. 4:26 and offer the following paraphrase: "You may be angry as far as I am concerned (if you can't help it), but do not sin thereby" (p. 195).

Arndt and Gingrich approach the problem from another direction—the meaning of *kai* ("and"). They note that it can mean "but" (p. 393). The translation they offer for this passage is: "Be angry, but do not sin" (p. 583) (so also RSV). Trench says it means: "Be ye angry, yet in this anger of yours suffer no sinful element to mingle" (p. 134).

Many commentators call attention to the fact that Jesus was angry (cf. Mark 3:5). So there is an anger that is holy and just.

Moule has given a good explanation of the difference between righteous and unrighteous anger. He writes:

Anger, as the mere expression of wounded personality, is sinful; for it means that self is in command. Anger, as the pure expression of repugnance to wrong in loyalty to God, is sinless where there is true occasion for it. The Apostle practically says, let anger, when you feel it, be *never* from the former motive, always from the latter (p. 122).

## Wrath or Provocation? (4:26)

The last part of the verse reads: "Let not the sun go down upon your wrath." The last word is *parorgismos,* found only here in the NT, though occasionally in the Septuagint. Moulton and Milligan say that it "does not seem to occur outside biblical Greek" (VGT, p. 496). Salmond writes: "It differs from *orgē* in denoting not the *disposition* of anger or anger as a lasting mood, but *provocation, exasperation,* sudden, violent anger" (EGT, 3:346). Eadie explains it thus: *"Parorgismos,* a term peculiar to biblical Greek, is a fit of indignation or exasperation: *para*—referring to the cause or occasion; while the *orgē,* to be put away from Christians, is the habitual indulgence of anger" (p. 349). Armitage Robinson writes: "Here *parorgismos* is the state of feeling provocation, 'wrath'" (p. 192). But most commentators prefer "indignation" or "provocation" as the translation here. In any case, anger is not to be retained in us.

## Neither Give Place (4:27)

The KJV gives a good literal translation: "Neither give place to the devil." The word for "place" is *topos.* It means "a portion of space viewed in reference to its occupancy or as appropriated to a thing" (Thayer, p. 628). This is evidently the basis of Phillips' translation (tying it in with what precedes): "Don't give the devil that sort of foothold." That is, don't give him any place of occupancy by harboring anger in your heart. Arndt and Gingrich suggest for this passage: *"Do not give the devil a chance* to exert his influence" (p. 831). Beck follows this closely in his rendering: "Don't give the devil a chance to work." The RSV also builds on this: "And give no opportunity to the devil." Moffatt and Goodspeed use "chance." Weymouth has: "And do not leave room for the devil." Perhaps the most striking translation is that of the NEB: "Leave no loop-hole for the devil."

## Corrupt Communication (4:29)

The noun here is the common term *logos,* which means "word," and is so translated 218 out of the 330 times it occurs in the NT. But in the other places (including here), it is rendered in different ways.

The adjective is *sapros.* Thayer gives among others the following definitions: "rotten, putrid, of poor quality, bad, unfit for use, worthless" (p. 568). Arndt and Gingrich give: "decayed, rotten." They note that it is used of spoiled fish, of rotten grapes on the ground, of crumbling stones. In general it means "unusable, unfit, bad." For this passage they suggest "evil word" or "evil speech."

In the NT it is used of trees and fruit (Matt. 7:17-18; 12:33; Luke 6:43), and of fish (Matt. 13:48). Only in this place is it used metaphorically. Salmond says: "Here it does not seem to mean *filthy,* but, as the following clause suggests, bad, *profitless, of no good to any one"* (EGT, 3:347).

However, some scholars prefer the stronger meaning. Eadie renders the clause, "Let no filthy word come out of your mouth." Phillips has "foul language," and the NBV "foul speech." The standard versions read "corrupt speech" (ASV), "evil talk" (RSV), and "bad language" (NEB). Moffatt and Goodspeed have "bad word." But

Weymouth has "unwholesome words" (cf. NASB). This agrees with Salmond's conclusion, noted above. The best way to interpret the passage is to say that no bad words or even worthless words should come out of the Christian's mouth. Rather it should always be "something good" (literal Greek).

The Greek reverses the order of the words "to the use of edifying." It has "edifying of the use." The word translated "edifying" means literally "building up," from the idea of building a house. "Use" is *chreia,* "necessity" or "need." But how does this make sense in English?

Salmond suggests that *chreias* (genitive case) is either the objective genitive, "edification applied to the need," or the genitive of remote reference, "edification in reference to the need (the present need)" (EGT, 3:347). The thought seems to be that our talk should be suitable for building people up in the faith, so as to meet any needs that may be present. Eadie puts it this way:

> The precious hour should never be polluted with corrupt speech, nor should it be wasted in idle and frivolous dialogue. . . . Conversation should always exercise a salutary influence, regulated by special need. Words so spoken may fall like winged seeds upon a neglected soil, and there may be future germination and fruit (p. 353).

It should be noted that the admonition, "Grieve not the Holy Spirit of God," follows right after this. Evidently one way that we may grieve the Holy Spirit is by frivolous, worthless conversation. Actually, time is too short and valuable to be wasted. It needs to be spent in edifying words and works.

## A Cluster of Carnal Traits (4:31)

Here we find a typical Pauline list of vices a Christian should avoid. Six are mentioned.

## *Bitterness* (4:31)

Arndt and Gingrich define *pikria* as meaning figuratively: "bitterness, animosity, anger, harshness" (p. 663). Elsewhere in the NT it is found only in Acts 8:23; Rom. 3:14; and Heb. 12:15.

Eadie says that *pikria* is "a figurative term denoting that fretted and irritable state of mind that keeps a man in perpetual animosity—that inclines him to harsh and uncharitable opinions of men and things—that makes him sour, crabbed, and repulsive in his general demeanour—that brings a scowl over his face, and infuses venom into the words of his tongue" (p. 357).

## *Wrath, and Anger* (4:31)

The two Greek words are *thymos* and *orgē*. The first occurs only this one place in Ephesians. The second is found in 2:3 and 5:6, but is translated "wrath" in both places. This fact points up the confusion between the exact meanings of the two terms. *Thymos* occurs 18 times in the NT. It is translated (KJV) "wrath" 15 times, "fierceness" twice, and "indignation" once. *Orgē* is found 36 times. It is rendered "wrath" 31 times, "anger" 3 times (including here), "vengeance" and "indignation" once each. So the dominant translation for both words is "wrath." What is the difference between them?

Trench is the most helpful authority on such distinctions. He says: *"Thymos* . . . is more of the turbulent commotion, the boiling agitation of the feelings," whereas *orgē* suggests "more of an abiding and settled habit of mind" (p. 131).

## *Clamour* (4:31)

The Greek word is *kraugē*. The cognate verb means "cry out, shout." So the noun means "outcry" (cf. Acts 23:9), or "shouting." The reference seems to be to noisy arguing and quarreling. Eadie suggests that it signifies the "expression of this anger—hoarse reproach, the high language of scorn and scolding, the yelling tones, the loud and boisterous recrimination, and the fierce and impetuous invective that mark a man in a towering rage" (p. 358).

### Evil Speaking (4:31)

In the Greek this is *blasphēmia,* from which we get "blasphemy." The word literally means "railing" or "slander." When used of slandering God it is technically called "blasphemy." But here it means "slander" or "abusive speech," what is hurtful to the reputation of others.

### Malice (4:31)

The Greek word is *kakia,* from the adjective *kakos,* "bad." It is defined by Abbott-Smith as meaning "wickedness, depravity, malignity" (p. 227). Eadie says: "Kakia is a generic term, and seems to signify what we sometimes call in common speech bad-heartedness, the root of all those vices" (p. 358).

## Forgiving One Another (4:32)

In contrast to the carnal characteristics of v. 31, Paul suggests the proper spiritual attitude toward those who have wronged us. We are to be kind and tenderhearted, "forgiving" others as God has "forgiven" us.

The verb is *charizomai.* It comes from *charis,* "grace." So it means "forgive freely"—graciously, not grudgingly. That is the way God has forgiven us; so that is the way we should forgive others.

"For Christ's sake" is simply *en Christō* "in Christ." It is only in Christ that we have this gracious forgiveness from God.

## Followers or Imitators? (5:1)

"Be ye therefore followers of God." The Greek is *mimētai*, from *mimos*, "a mimic, actor." So it means "imitators." That is the rendering found in many modern translations and is grammatically correct. It is more precise than "followers."

## Dear or Beloved? (5:1)

The adjective is *agapēta*, from *agapaō*, "I love." It occurs 62 times in the NT. Forty-seven times it is rendered "beloved," 9 times "dearly beloved," 3 times "well beloved," and 3 times "dear." "Beloved" or "dearly loved" (NIV) is the correct translation. Be imitators of God because you are His children, beloved by Him. As Christians we should demonstrate daily the fact that we are children of God by acting like Him.

## Walk in Love (5:2)

As beloved children we should "keep on walking (present imperative) in love, just as Christ also loved you." The best way that we can imitate God, and thus prove that we are His beloved children, is to walk continually in love, for "God is love" (1 John 4:8, 16). Imitators of God, then, will love as He loves.

One of the worst travesties of Christianity is people who profess not only that they are children of God, but also that they are sanctified wholly, made perfect in love, and yet they are "cranky," sour, critical, unkind. We have no right to claim to be God's children unless we are seeking by the help of the Holy Spirit to be like Him in our daily lives. We disgrace the family when we fail to walk in love.

## Offering and Sacrifice (5:2)

These words may carelessly be thought of as synonymous. But they are not. The first, *prosphora*, literally means "something brought to." It aptly describes an "offering," which was "brought to" the altar. It might be composed of meal or oil, or even be a drink offering.

On the other hand, "sacrifice" is *thysia*. It comes from *thyō*, one of the meanings of which is "slay" or "kill." So it refers to animal sacrifices which were slain and offered on the altar.

Christ was both. It takes all the offerings of the OT—described in detail in the early chapters of Leviticus—to typify the many-sided work of Christ in His redemption of humanity.

## Sweetsmelling Savour (5:2)

Christ's offering for us is described as "a sweetsmelling savour." But "savour" is now used mostly for taste rather than smell. So this rendering is not the best. But worse is the awkward "an odor of a sweet smell" (ASV).

The Greek phrase means "a smell of fragrance," and so "a fragrant smell." Recent translations tend to combine this into a single adjective, giving the rendering "a fragrant offering and sacrifice to God" (Moffatt, Goodspeed, RSV, NIV).

## Filthiness, nor Foolish Talking (5:4)

The Greek word for "filthiness" is found only here in the NT. Arndt and Gingrich define its meaning as "ugliness, wickedness" (p. 24). Thayer gives "baseness, dishonor" (p. 17). The word is *aischrotēs*, from *aischos*, "shame, disgrace." Vine says that it refers to "obscenity, all that is contrary to purity" (2:98). Salmond writes: "It denotes shameless, immoral conduct in general" (EGT, 3:352).

"Foolish talking" is *mōrologia*. Trench calls attention to the fact that "fool," "foolish," and "folly" have ethical significance in the Scriptures, and gives this definition: "It is that 'talk of fools,' which is foolishness and sin together" (p. 121).

"Jesting" is *eutrapelia*. Originally this word had a good connotation—"versatility," or "keen wit," what we sometimes call "quick repartee" in conversation. But gradually it took on bad meanings, indicating "coarse jesting" or "ribaldry." The context indicates that this is the sense here.

All three of these words are *hapax legomena* (literally, "said once for all"), and are found only here in the NT. They seem to indicate Paul's acquaintance with Greek literature. The apostle says that, instead of filthiness or even foolishness in talk, the Christian should indulge in "giving of thanks." This is always in order.

## For This Ye Know (5:5)

The ASV has here "For this ye know of a surety." The RSV reads, "Be sure of this." Why add "of a surety" or change to "Be sure of this"?

The Greek literally says: "For this you know, knowing." That is an expression for "You surely know." But the Greek word for "you know" may be either indicative or imperative. In the second person plural of the present tense the form is exactly the same for both. That will explain the RSV reading here. It will also account for the change in John 5:39 from "Search the scriptures" (KJV) to "Ye search the scriptures" (ASV) and "You search the scriptures" (RSV). There are many passages in the NT where we can never be certain whether the writer intended the word to be taken as indicative or imperative.

This is one of the ambiguities of language, some of which still exist even in the rigid demands of our day for scientific exactness. Linguistic ambiguity in the Greek, often attaching also to the English, is one of the inescapable problems of NT exegesis. One can only do his best to interpret such ambiguous terms in the light of the context —which is not always definitely determinative. The NIV has: "For of this you can be sure."

## Whoremonger, Unclean (5:5)

In v. 3 there are three abstract nouns: "fornication," "uncleanness," and "covetousness." They are balanced in the fifth verse with three concrete nouns: "whoremonger," "unclean person" (one word in the Greek), and "covetous man" (one word). "Whoremonger" should be translated "fornicator," to show its connection with "fornication" (same root in the Greek). Such connections in the Greek should be preserved in English translation, if possible.

It is a black picture of heathen immorality which is suggested here, with overtones reminiscent of Rom. 1:21-32. *Pornos* ("whoremonger, fornicator") originally meant a "male prostitute." Then it came to be used in the universal meaning of "fornicator."

The modern technical distinction between adultery and fornication is not maintained in the Greek NT. While *porneia* is always translated "fornication" in the KJV (26 times), it clearly means adultery in Matt. 5:32; 19:9. There is a distinct word for "adultery," however, which occurs only 4 times in the NT (Matt. 15:19; Mark 7:21; John 8:3; Gal. 5:19)—as also "adulterer" 4 times.

## Covetousness (5:5)

The word for "covetous man," *pleonektēs,* occurs (in NT) only here and in 1 Cor. 5:10, 11; 6:10. The abstract noun *pleonexia* (v. 3), is found 10 times in the NT. It is translated "covetousness" in every place but one (Eph. 4:19—"greediness"). The word is a compound from *pleon,* "more," and *echō,* "have." So it means "greedy desire to have more" (Thayer, p. 516).

As in this passage, "covetousness" is usually found in the NT in very bad company. Arndt and Gingrich cite numerous instances of this same association in the secular Greek writers (p. 573). Trench writes: "Not merely is *pleonexia,* as signifying covetousness, joined to sins of impurity, but the word is sometimes used, as at Ephes. v. 3 . . . to designate these sins themselves" (p. 83).

Salmond thinks that in some passages in the NT (e.g., Luke 12:15; 2 Cor. 9:5; 1 Thess. 2:5) the word means simply "covetousness," but that here in v. 3 it may have "the acquired sense of *sensual* greed" (EGT, 3:352).

Eadie objects to interpreting *pleonexia* as signifying lustful desire. His explanation of the association here is: "And it is joined to these preceding words, as it springs from the same selfishness, and is but a different form of development from the same unholy root." He defines the word thus: "It is greed, avarice, unconquerable love of appropriation, morbid lust of acquisition, carrying in itself a violation of almost every precept of the decalogue" (p. 370).

Lightfoot agrees. He writes on Col. 3:5: "The attempt to give pleonexia here and in other passages the sense of 'impurity' . . . is founded on a misconception." He also observes: "Impurity and covetousness may be said to divide between them nearly the whole domain of human selfishness and vice" (p. 212).

But why is the "covetous man" called an "idolator" (and in Col. 3:5 "covetousness" called "idolatry")? Eadie suggests: "The covetous man makes a god of his possessions, and offers to them the entire homage of his heart" (p. 375). Ellicott comments: "Covetousness is truly a definite form of idolatry, it is the worship of Mammon (Matt. vi. 24) instead of God" (p. 120). Grayston writes: "Since ruthless self-assertion is the very essence of idolatry (Eph. 5:5; Col. 3:5), the word forms a bridge between sexual vice and idolatry, and may in some quarters have been a euphemism for ritual fornication" (TWBB, p. 64).

## Vain or Empty? (5:6)

The apostle warns his readers: "Let no man deceive you with vain words"—or, "empty words" (NASB, NIV). The Greek for "vain" is *kenos*, translated literally as "empty" in Mark 12:3; Luke 20:10-11. Arndt and Gingrich note that it is used figuratively as meaning "without content, without any basis, without truth, without power" (p. 429).

That is what it means here. "Vain" is not a bad translation, but "empty" brings out more forcefully the exact sense of the term.

## Spirit or Light? (5:9)

In this verse the KJV reads "the fruit of the Spirit," whereas the Revised Versions have "the fruit of the light." Why the change?

The answer is that the majority of the oldest Greek manuscripts have "light." The matter is complicated by the fact that of the two third-century papyri that contain this passage, one (P 46) has "spirit" *(pneumatos)*, while the other (P 49) has "light" *(phōtos)*. But the latter is supported by the two fourth-century manuscripts, Vaticanus and Sinaiticus.

It seems altogether likely that the phrase "the fruit of the Spirit" was borrowed from Gal. 5:22. So the internal evidence of probability combines with the external evidence of the manuscripts to suggest that "the fruit of the light" is the correct reading. This ties the ninth verse more closely to its context in the eighth verse, where "light" is the dominant word. "The fruit of the light" means what the light produces. This is "found in all that is good and right and true" (RSV); or, as Weymouth puts it, "the effect of the Light is seen in every kind of goodness, uprightness, and truth."

## Proving or Testing? (5:10)

What is meant by "proving what is acceptable unto the Lord"? The verb *dokimazō* is fairly common in the NT (23 times). It means "test, try, prove, approve." Which does it mean here? Probably "test."

The NASB has "trying to learn what is pleasing to the Lord." The NIV reads: "Find out what pleases the Lord."

The contrast between "the unfruitful works of darkness" (v. 11) and "the fruit of the light" (v. 9)—further evidence in favor of this reading—is strikingly parallel to that between "the works of the flesh" and "the fruit of the Spirit" (Gal. 5:19, 22). The plural ("works") suggests the divisiveness of sin. The singular ("fruit") symbolizes the unity and unifying quality of the good.

## Reprove or Expose? (5:11, 13)

The verb *elegchō* means "convict," or "reprove," or "rebuke." But Abbott-Smith gives for this passage "expose." He says that the verb "implies rebuke which brings conviction" (p. 144). Thayer defines the word thus: "to *convict, refute, confute,* generally with a suggestion of the shame of the person convicted" (p. 202). He also gives for this passage: "by conviction bring to light, expose" (p. 203). The first meaning given by Arndt and Gingrich is: "bring to light, expose" (p. 248). Our present passage is listed under this particular definition. So it seems that the best translation here is "expose" (RSV, NASB, NIV).

This also fits best in v. 13—"But everything exposed by the light becomes visible" (NIV). It is the light that makes a thing visible and so exposes it. The best way to combat sin is to expose it. Turn on it the light of truth, so that people can see its horrible hideousness. A. T. Robertson says that the verb *elegchō* means "convict by turning the light on the darkness" (4:543).

## He Saith or It Saith? (5:14)

The quotation in this verse has caused considerable discussion, because these exact words are found nowhere in the OT. Robertson says that they are "apparently a free adaptation of Isa. 26:19 and 60:1" *(ibid.).* The NBV changes "he saith" to "it says," and adds this footnote: "Apparently from an early Christian hymn, based on Isa. 60:1." The NEB incorporates this idea right in its translation: "And so the hymn says."

This, however, is a good example of overtranslation, involving a high degree of interpretation. Considerable restraint needs to be exercised at such points in translation work. Since the idioms of Greek and English are so different, a certain amount of interpretation is necessary to make sense. Fundamentally the demand is that we translate the words. But the ultimate obligation is always that of correctly translating the thought; for it is the spirit, not the letter, that makes alive.

The Greek verb in this introductory formula *(legei)* can with equal accuracy be rendered "he says" or "it says." The majority of recent translations treat it as neuter, "it says" or, more freely, "it is said" (NIV).

## Circumspectly or Carefully? (5:15)

Five times in the fourth and fifth chapters of Ephesians, Paul says, "Walk." First, it was, "Walk worthy of the vocation wherewith ye are called" (4:1); second, "Walk not as other Gentiles walk" (4:17); third, "Walk in love" (5:1); fourth, "Walk as children of light" (5:8). Now comes the fifth, "Walk circumspectly."

The Greek word is *akribōs*. It means "with exactness, carefully." Thayer says, "exactly, accurately, diligently" (p. 24). Vine suggests: "The word expresses that accuracy which is the outcome of carefulness" (1:25). The adverb occurs only five times in the NT. Twice it is translated "diligently" in the KJV (Matt. 2:8; Acts 18:25). The best rendering here is "carefully" (RSV, NEB, NASB).

## Fools or Unwise? (5:15)

Paul goes on to say that we are to walk "not as fools, but as wise." In the Greek there is a play on words: it says: "not as *asophoi*, but as *sophoi*." This can be brought out in English by rendering it: "not as unwise, but as wise" (RSV, NASB, NIV).

## Redeeming the Time (5:16)

The verb is *exagorazō*. The noun *agora* meant the marketplace (or forum). So the verb *agorazō* literally means "buy in the market." It came to be used in the general sense of "purchase." The prepositional prefix ex *(ek)* means "out." So *exagorazō* literally meant "buy out of the market." It was used for "redeeming" or "ransoming" slaves (cf. Gal. 3:13; 4:5). But in the middle voice, as here, it means "buy up for oneself." It is used the same way in the parallel passage in Col. 4:5. These are the only four times it occurs in the NT.

Arndt and Gingrich say that the middle form in Eph. 5:16 and Col. 4:5 "cannot be interpreted with certainty." They go on to suggest: "The best meaning is probably *make the most of the time* (which is severely limited because of the proximity of the Parousia as well as for other reasons)" (p. 271). A good translation here is "making the most of the time" (RSV), or "making the most of your time" (NASB). Since the Greek word for "time" *(kairos)* does not signify merely chronological time *(chronos)* but an opportune or appointed time, this passage may be rendered: "making the most of every opportunity" (NIV).

## Unwise or Foolish? (5:17)

The adjective translated "unwise" is a different one from that in v. 15. Here it is *aphrones*. The "a" is what is called *"alpha-*negative"; as a prefix it negates the rest of the word. English equivalents are "un" or "in," or even the same "a," as in "amoral" and "amillennial."

The *phrones* is from *phrēn*, "mind." So *aphrones* literally means "mindless." Abbott-Smith defines it as *"without reason, senseless, foolish,* expressing 'want of mental sanity and sobriety, a reckless and inconsiderate habit of mind'" (p. 72). Thayer's definition is: "Without reason, senseless, foolish, stupid; without reflection or intelligence, acting rashly" (p. 90). It is a stronger term than the one in v. 15. The best translation here is "foolish" (RSV, NASB, NIV). The only way one can avoid being foolish is by "understanding"—literally, putting together—"what the will of the Lord is."

## Excess or Dissipation? (5:18)

Paul admonishes his readers not to be "drunk with wine, wherein is excess." The last word is in the Greek *asōtia*. Here again we find the *alpha*-negative, this time with *sōtia*, which comes from the verb *sōzō*, "save." So it is the opposite of salvation. Abbott-Smith defines the word as "prodigality, wastefulness, profligacy" (p. 66). Thayer says: "an abandoned, dissolute life; profligacy, prodigality" (p. 82). Arndt and Gingrich suggest: "debauchery, dissipation, profligacy" (p. 119). The best translation is "debauchery" (RSV, NIV) or "dissipation" (NEB, NASB).

## Be Filled (5:18)

Instead of being "drunk with wine," Paul says that Christians should be "filled with the Spirit." Evidently he is suggesting that what people seek in drinking—relaxation, escape from the unendurable—one may find in being filled with the Holy Spirit. The verb is in the present imperative, which means "be continually filled with the Spirit." This is not to be a transitory experience, but an abiding one. Jesus said: "I will pray the Father, and he shall give you another Comforter, that he may abide with you for ever" (John 14:16).

## Psalms and Hymns (5:19)

This verse is closely related to v. 18. The Spirit-filled person will find a song in his soul. The Holy Spirit will be singing within, and some of this symphony of the soul ought to come out through the lips. Paul uses three terms to describe this heavenly music coming out of the human heart.

The first word is *psalmos*. It means: "1. *a striking, twitching* with the fingers (Euripides, others), hence, *a striking* of musical strings (Aeschylus, others), and hence in later writers, 2. *a sacred song* sung to musical accompaniment, *a psalm* (Septuagint)" (A-S, p. 487).

*Psalmos* occurs 70 times in the Septuagint. Most of these occurrences are in the titles of the psalms. It is obvious that the current usage of the term was for sacred songs that were to be sung to the accompaniment of musical instruments. The etymological derivation of the term suggests that these were primarily stringed instruments—which are mentioned a number of times in the psalms.

This word is used for the Book of Psalms in Luke 20:42 and Acts 1:20; for an individual psalm in Acts 13:33; for the third division of the Hebrew canon (the Writings) in Luke 24:44; and for Christian psalms in 1 Cor. 14:26, here in Ephesians, and in Col. 3:16. These are all the occurrences in the NT.

The second word is *hymnos*. Abbott-Smith describes its usage thus: "(a) in classics a festal song in praise of gods or heroes; (b) in LXX and NT a song of praise addressed to God" (p. 455). It is found elsewhere in the NT only in the parallel passage, Col. 3:16.

The third word is *ōdē*, which means "*a song, ode,* whether sad or joyful; in LXX and NT always in praise to God or Christ" (A-S, p. 490). It is found three times in Revelation (5:9; 14:3; 15:3) as well as in Col. 3:16. Since it is a general word for "songs," it is accompanied by the adjective "spiritual" *(pneumatikais)*.

These three terms are also found together in the parallel passage in Col. 3:16. So they call for a comparison. Some commentators find no difference between them, insisting that Paul was not trying to classify the various forms of Christian poetry. While admitting the truth of the latter claim, Trench asserts: "But neither, on the other hand, would he have used, where there is evidently no temptation to rhetorical amplification, three words, if one would have equally served his turn" (p. 295).

Concerning the "psalms," Trench observes: "In all probability the *psalmoi* of Ephes. v. 19, Col. iii. 16, are the inspired psalms of the Hebrew Canon" (p. 296). That is its meaning elsewhere in the NT, as we have noted, except in 1 Cor. 14:26—where it could also mean this.

The distinguishing feature of a "hymn" is that it is always addressed to God. Trench says: "Augustine in more places than one states the notes of what in his mind are the essentials of a hymn—which are three: 1. It must be sung; 2. It must be praise; 3. It must be to God" (p. 298). This is still a correct description of a hymn.

It may not be out of the way to observe here that hymns should regularly be used in the Sunday morning worship service. The minds and hearts of the people should be directed away from themselves and their own feelings, toward God in adoration and worship. Trench says: "A 'hymn' must always be more or less of a *Magnificat,* a direct address of praise and glory to God" *(ibid.).* Hymns like "Holy, Holy, Holy," "All Hail the Power of Jesus' Name," "Majestic Sweetness," or "Come, Thou Almighty King" point people toward God. That is what is needed at least one hour a week.

Lightfoot summarizes the distinction between the three words as follows: "While the leading idea of *psalmos* is a musical accompaniment and that of *hymnos* praise to God, *ōdē* is the general word for a song, whether accompanied or unaccompanied, whether of praise or on any other subject" (p. 225). Eadie comments: "The hymn was more elaborate and solemn in its structure than the ode" (p. 400).

"Speaking to yourselves" is probably better rendered "speaking to one another." This spiritual music is to be for mutual blessing and edification.

"Singing" is the Greek verb *adō*. It is used three times in Revelation (5:9; 14:3; 15:3) with the object *ōdē*. Aside from that it is found in the NT only here and in the parallel passage, Col. 3:16. It comes from the same root as *ōdē* and means "to celebrate something or someone in song" (TDNT, 1:163).

"Making melody" is one word in the Greek, *psallontes*. The verb *psallō* meant first to strike the strings of a harp or lyre. Then it meant to "strike up a tune." Finally it was used in the sense "to sing." The phrase here could be translated "singing and psalming."

This is to be "in your heart." The relation of this to "speaking to one another" is thus explained by Lightfoot: "This external manifestation must be accompanied by the inward emotion. There must be the thanksgiving of the heart, as well as of the lips" (p. 226). That is, while one is singing these songs aloud, he should be hymning them in his heart. Also, after singing together on Sunday we should carry a melody of song in our souls all the week.

The primary emphasis of all our religious singing should be "giving thanks always for all things unto God and the Father in the name of our Lord Jesus Christ" (v. 20). Probably it would be correct to say that all of us are behind in expressing our gratitude to God. The heart that is filled with praise to Him is a happy heart. One of the surest secrets of success and victory in the Christian life is forming the habit of thanking the Lord frequently throughout each day. Praise is a great dispeller of doubt and darkness.

## Submitting or Subjecting? (5:21)

"Submitting yourselves" is the present middle participle of *hypotassō,* which is thus defined by Abbott-Smith: "1. as a military term, *to place* or *rank under* (Polybius). 2. *to subject, put in subjection. . . .* Middle, "to subject oneself, obey" (p. 463). Most of the recent versions (e.g., RSV, NEB, NASB) use "subject" rather than "submit." The KJV does this in verse 24, where the verb is the same as here. The NIV has "submit" in both places.

## Husbands, Love Your Wives (5:25)

After telling the wives to be in subjection to their own husbands, Paul confronts the men with a much more difficult demand. To them he says: "Husbands, love your wives, even as Christ also loved the church."

Aside from Mark 12:38, where a word meaning "wish" is rendered by "love" (in KJV), there are two verbs that are translated "love" in the NT—*agapaō* and *phileō. Agapaō* is found 142 times. It is rendered "love" 135 times and "beloved" 7 times. On the other hand, *phileō* occurs only 25 times. It is translated "love" 22 times and "kiss" 3 times.

In classical Greek there is a third verb for love, *eraō.* Concerning this term Cremer writes: *"Eran* denotes the love of passion, of vehement, sensual desire; but so unsuitable was this word, by usage so saturated with lustful ideas, to express the moral and holy character of that love with which Scripture in particular has to do, that it does not occur in a good sense even in the O.T., save in Prov. iv. 6; . . . and . . . not at all in the N.T." (p. 10).

Trench is in essential agreement with this. Regarding the nonuse of *eros* and *eraō* in the Greek OT (LXX) he says: "It is in part no doubt to be explained from the fact that, by the corrupt use of the word, they had become so steeped in sensual passion, carried such an atmosphere of unholiness about them . . . , that the truth of God abstained from defiling contact with them; yea, devised a new word rather than betake itself to one of these" (p. 43).

The "new word" is the noun *agapē,* of which Trench says: "There is no trace of it in any heathen writer whatever" *(ibid.).* Similar is the statement of Cremer: "Not found in profane writers" (p. 13).

Today these statements may need revising. Trench wrote 100 years ago (1855, 1863), and Cremer also (Eng. trans. of 2nd ed., 1878). Arndt and Gingrich say: "Now we have an inscription that is surely pagan"—from the third century A.D. (p. 5).

But *agapē* can still be spoken of as practically unknown in pagan sources. It is used 16 times in the Septuagint, all but 5 of these in the Song of Solomon. The verb *agapaō* is used nearly 300 times in the Septuagint.

What is the difference between *agapaō* and *phileō,* the two verbs for love in the NT? It is noted above that *phileō* is three times translated "kiss"—all in connection with Judas Iscariot's betrayal of Jesus (Matt. 26:48; Mark 14:44; Luke 22:47). This gives a clue as to the distinctive meaning of the term. It describes the love of the affections. On the other hand, *agapaō* expresses the love of the will. Cremer sums it up well: *"Philein* denotes the love of natural inclination, affection,—love, so to say, originally spontaneous, involuntary *(amare); agapan,* on the other hand, love as a direction of the will *(diligere)"* (p. 11).

The most thorough recent treatment of *agapaō* is to be found in the first volume (1964) of the new English translation of a monumental work—Kittel's *Theologisches Woerterbuch zum Neuen Testament* (English: *Theological Dictionary of the New Testament).*

The greater part of this article on *agapaō* is written by
the famous German scholar, Ethelbert Stauffer. He says:
*"Eran* is passionate love which desires the other for itself"
(TDNT, 1:35). He also writes: *"Eros* seeks in others the
fulfillment of its own life's hunger. *Agapan* must often be
translated 'to show love'; it is a giving, active love on the
other's behalf" (TDNT, 1:37). Christ "loved the church,
and gave himself for it."

The verb which is used twice in Eph. 5:25 is *agapaō*.
From the above discussion it will be seen that this means
something more than affectionate love, though this is included. The emphasis is rather on an intelligent, voluntary
love. This is the kind of love that will last. Feelings fluctu-
ate. Emotions ebb and flow. Affections are often affected
by changing circumstances. But the love of commitment
can remain firm and loyal through every vicissitude of life.
This is the kind of love that a husband is commanded to
have for his wife. It is an unselfish love that seeks the best
good of its object. This kind of love will hold a marriage
together "as long as ye both shall live."

After discussing the difference between *agapaō* and
*phileō,* Abbott-Smith writes: "If this distinction holds,
*agapaō* is fitly used in NT of Christian love to God and
man, the spiritual affection which follows the direction of
the will, and which, therefore, unlike that feeling which is
instinctive and unreasoned, can be commanded as a duty"
(p. 3).

One further thought might be suggested here. While
we cannot directly control our feelings, we can control our
thoughts. The man who thinks loving thoughts about his
wife will experience loving feelings toward her.

## Sanctify and Cleanse (5:26)

In vv. 25-26 Paul moves from the love of husbands for

their wives to the love of Christ for His Church. The Greek says: "In order that He might sanctify it (or *her*), having cleansed (her) by the washing of water in (by, with) word" —"with the word" (RSV, NASB).

We speak of pardon and purity, of conversion and cleansing, as related to distinct experiences in grace. This is accurate. But there is also a purity that comes with pardon, and a cleansing that comes with conversion. When we confess our sins to God and believe in Jesus Christ, not only are our sins forgiven, but the stain of committed sins is washed away. However, there is still needed a deeper cleansing from all sin, from the carnal nature with which every human being is born.

## Word (5:26)

The meaning of this term is not entirely clear. The Greek word is *rhēma.* The most common term for "word" is *logos,* which occurs some 330 times in the NT. It is translated "word" 225 times, with dozens of other renderings for the remaining occurrences. On the other hand, *rhēma,* found 70 times, is translated "word" 56 of those times and "saying" 9 times.

The distinctive idea of *rhēma* is that it properly refers to what is said or spoken, whereas *logos* can be used for a written word. Thayer defines the term as basically meaning: "that which is or has been uttered by the living voice, thing spoken, word" (p. 562). He interprets the phrase here, *en rhēmati,* thus: "according to promise (properly *on* the ground of his *word* of promise, namely the promise of the pardon of sins)" *(ibid.).* Arndt and Gingrich say with regard to *rhēma* in this and similar passages: "Generally the singular brings together all the divine teachings as a unified whole, with some such meaning as *gospel,* or *confession*" (p. 743).

This Greek term *rhēma* is found again in 6:17—"the sword of the Spirit, which is the *word* of God." The same phrase, "word of God" (using *rhēma* rather than *logos*) occurs in Heb. 6:5 and 11:3. In 1 Pet. 1:25 reference is made to "the word of the Lord" which is preached.

It seems clear that the cleansing is to be accomplished by the power of God's word, however it may be expressed.

## Spot or Wrinkle? (5:27)

The word for "spot" *(spilon)* first meant a rock or cliff. Later it came to mean a "spot" or "stain" (NIV). Here it is used metaphorically for "a moral blemish." The Greek word for "wrinkle" is found only here in the NT. The phrase "not having spot, or wrinkle" suggests the idea of "washed and ironed." Christ wants His bride, the Church, to be neat as well as clean. When we are concerned only with being a "clean people," but do not give attention to making our personal appearance and personality attractive, so that we may attract others to Christ, we fail to be what He wants us to be.

## Without Blemish (5:27)

This is one word in the Greek—*amōmos.* It was used of sacrificial animals, which the law required should be without blemish (Num. 6:14; 19:2). So it is applied to Christ, the Lamb of God sacrificed for the sins of men (1 Pet. 1:19; Heb. 9:14). By classical Greek writers it was employed in the sense of "blameless," morally and religiously. In Jude 24 the word is translated "faultless"—"present you faltless before the presence of his glory." This forms a striking parallel to Eph. 5:27.

Verses 25-27 may be taken together as the basis for a textual sermon. Verse 25 shows us "The Provision for

Sanctification" in the death of Christ. Verse 26 gives "The Prerequisite for Sanctification" in the washing of regeneration. Verse 27 shows "The Purpose of Sanctification" in our presentation to Christ as His bride.

## So Ought Men (5:28)

"So ought men to love their wives as their own bodies." The verb translated "ought" is *opheilō*. It means "to owe, be a debtor" (A-S, p. 330). Of a similar use of the term in 1 John 2:6, Westcott says: "The obligation is represented as a debt" (*Epistles of John*, p. 50).

That is the meaning here. The husband *owes* it to his wife to love her as he loves (cares for) his own body. The one who fails to do so is not paying his honest debts.

## Nourish and Cherish (5:29)

Two terms are used to express the loving care that a man should have for his wife. The first, *ektrephō*, is found only here and in 6:4. There it is used for bringing up children. Thayer defines it thus: "1. *to nourish up to maturity;* then universally *to nourish* . . . Eph. v. 29. 2. to nurture, bring up . . . Eph. vi. 4" (p. 200). It suggests the idea of a husband caring tenderly for his wife, as a mother might care for her child.

"Cherisheth" is the verb *thalpō*. It literally means "keep warm," and so figuratively "cherish, comfort" (AG, p. 351). Thayer writes: "Like the Latin *foveo, to cherish* with tender love, *to foster* with tender care" (p. 282). The word is found only here and in 1 Thess. 2:7.

## Two Shall Be One (5:31)

This verse consists of a quotation of Gen. 2:24, an important OT passage quoted earlier by Jesus (Matt. 19:5; Mark 10:7). The verb "be joined" is literally "be glued." What many marriages need today is more of the glue of genuine, unselfish love, so that they will "stick together."

Paul is incurably and inexorably practical. He starts out by commanding husbands to love their wives (v. 25). This leads to a contemplation of Christ's love for His Church (vv. 25-27). Then he comes down to earth with a "thump" again: "So ought men to love their own wives as their own bodies" (v. 28). Once more he takes off into orbit in the heavenlies, as he speaks of Christ and the Church (vv. 29-30). In v. 31 it is human marriage again, but in v. 32 Christ and the Church. His final note, however, is on practical Christian living in the social relationship between husband and wife (v. 33).

## Obey (6:1)

The Greek word for "obey" here is *hypakouō*. It is a compound of *akouō*, which means "hear, listen." So it literally means "to listen." Thayer defines it thus: "1. properly: of one who on a knock at the door comes to listen who it is . . . Acts xii. 13. . . . 2. *to hearken to a command*, i.e. *to obey, be obedient unto, submit to* (so in Greek writers from Herodotus down)" (p. 638). Children are admonished by Paul to "listen to" their parents, which means doing what they ask.

## Live Long (6:3)

This reads literally: "In order that it may become well with thee, and thou shalt be [future tense] of long duration upon the earth." "Of long duration" is one word in the Greek, the compound adjective *makrochronois*. *Makros* means "long," *chronos* "time." So the adjective literally means "long-timed." Found only here in the NT, and rare in secular Greek, it may be translated "long-lived."

## Earth or Land? (6:3)

This is a quotation from Deut. 5:16 (cf. Exod. 20:12). In the OT passages it is a promise that if the children will honor their parents the nation will continue long in the land of promise. But Paul is now writing to Gentile Christians living in Asia Minor. So the correct rendering here is "on the earth" (KJV, RSV, NASB, NIV), not "in the land" (NEB).

## Provoke Not Your Children (6:4)

"Provoke . . . to wrath" is one word in Greek, *parorgizō*. It occurs only here and in a quotation from the Septuagint in Rom. 10:19. A good free translation of this clause is: "You fathers, again, must not goad your children to resentment" (NEB). This is the other side of the coin of parent-child relationship—"Children obey your parents."

## Nurture and Admonition (6:4)

The first of these two terms is *paideia* in the Greek. It comes from *pais*, "child." Abbott-Smith gives the following comprehensive definition of it: "1. *the rearing of a child* (Aeschylus). 2. *training, learning, instruction* (Plato, others): Eph. 6:4; II Tim. 3:16. 3. As in the Septuagint (Prov. 3:11; 15:6, others), *chastening, discipline:* Heb. 12:5, 7, 8, 11" (p. 333). These are all the occurrences in the NT.

The second word is *nouthesia*. Literally it means a "putting in mind." It is found elsewhere in the NT only in 1 Cor. 10:11 and Titus 3:10. In each instance it is rendered "admonition." Arndt and Gingrich translate the phrase here: "discipline and instruction" (p. 608). That is about as close to the Greek as one can come.

## Eyeservice (6:6)

This term closely represents the Greek compound *ophthalmodoulia*. Arndt and Gingrich say it means "service that is performed only to attract attention . . . , not for its own sake nor to please God or one's own conscience" (p. 604). The word occurs in the parallel passage in Col. 3:22, but nowhere else in Greek literature.

## Menpleasers (6:6)

This compound, *anthrōpareskos,* is likewise found in the NT only here and in Col. 3:22. Moulton and Milligan say that the word, "which starts in the Septuagint and *Psalms of Solomon,* was presumably as much a coinage as our own 'men-pleasers,' but made in a language where compounds are more at home than in ours. If this is a 'Biblical' word, it is only an instance of the fact that every Greek writer made a new compound when his meaning required one" (VGT, p. 43).

## Good Will (6:7)

The Greek word is *eunoia* (only here in NT). Arndt and Gingrich give its meaning for this passage as "zeal, enthusiasm."

## Forbearing Threatening (6:9)

The verb is *aniemi.* Originally used in the sense of "loosen, unfasten," it came to mean "give up, cease from"

(AG, p. 69). That is its meaning here. Bultmann writes: "The basic meaning of the word *aniemi* is the relaxation of tension" (TDNT, 1:367). This is the sort of thing that is needed in human relationships.

Eph. 5:21—6:9 deals with the social application of the gospel to three areas of life: the relationship of husbands and wives, parents and children, masters and slaves. The same six classes are instructed in a similar fashion in Col. 3:18—4:1. This is one of several close parallels between these two Epistles of Paul. The apostle was interested not only in theology but also in practical Christian living.

## Finally (6:10)

In Greek it is *tou loipou.* The Textus Receptus (late MSS) has *to loipon* (accusative case), which means "for the rest." The meaning of *tou loipou* (genitive case) is given in Blass and Debrunner as "from now on, henceforth"; that is, genitive of time (p. 100). But Arndt and Gingrich say: "In Eph. 6:10 the meaning is probably rather finally, bringing the matter to a conclusion" (p. 481). Phillips translates it, "In conclusion."

## Be Strong (6:10)

The verb is *endynamoō.* It comes from *dynamis* (dynamo, dynamic). One is tempted to translate it, "Be dynamic!" The whole clause is paraphrased in NEB: "Find your strength in the Lord."

## The Power of His Might (6:10)

The first noun is *kratos,* which is used in Homer for bodily strength. The second is *ischys,* which means "strength, power, might" (AG, p. 384). But neither noun is *dynamis,* which is most properly translated "power." So the best rendering here is "the strength of his might" (RSV, NASB).

## The Whole Armour (6:11)

Paul exhorted his readers: "Put on the whole armour of God." The verb is used regularly of putting on clothes. It may be translated "be clothed with." "Whole armour" is one word in Greek, *panoplia.* It comes from *pan,* which means "all," and *hopla,* "arms, weapons." The word is used metaphorically here and in v. 13. Elsewhere in the NT it occurs only in Luke 11:22, where it has the literal sense, *"full armor* of a heavily-armed soldier" (AG, p. 612). Vine writes: "Among the Greeks the *panoplia* was the complete equipment used by heavily armed infantry" (1:75). The different parts of this armor are mentioned in the verses that follow v. 13.

## Wiles of the Devil (6:11)

In the Greek, "wiles" is *methodeias,* from which comes the English word "methods" (cf. Phillips).

The cognate verb, *methodeuō* is found in the Septuagint, but not in the NT. On the other hand, the noun *methodeia* has not been discovered in any earlier writings. In the NT it occurs only in 4:14 (see comments there), here, and in verse 12 in Papyrus 46 (third century).

The treatment of this word in modern reference works furnishes a striking example of recent progress in this field. Among older scholars, Thayer declares that *methodeia* "is not found in profane authors" (p. 395); that is, secular writers. Abbott-Smith says, "not found elsewhere" (p. 282). But Moulton and Milligan give several examples of the use of this word in the papyri of the fifth and sixth centuries (VGT, p. 394), always in the sense of "method." Arndt and Gingrich include this information in their lexicon and suggest the translation, "stratagems" (military context).

The context indicates that here the word carries an evil connotation. Perhaps the best translation is "the devices of the devil" (NEB).

## We Wrestle Not (6:12)

Literally the first part of this verse reads: "Because there is not to us the wrestling against blood and flesh." The word for wrestling is *palē.* Thayer notes that beginning with Homer this word was used to describe "a contest between two in which each endeavors to throw the other, and which is decided when the victor is able *thlibein kai katechein* (to press and to hold down) his prostrate antagonist, i.e., to hold him down with his hand upon his neck" (p. 474). Paul taught that Christians should be "more than conquerors" through Christ (Rom. 8:37).

## Our Enemies (6:12)

In this verse the apostle names four things against which we wrestle (cf. 1:21). The first is "principalities." The Greek word is *archē,* which literally means "beginning" (cf. John 1:1). But here it means "sovereignty, principality, rule" (see rather full discussion on 1:21).

Delling writes: *"Archē* always signifies 'primacy,' whether in time: *'beginning'* . . . or in rank: 'power,' 'dominion,' 'office'" (TDNT, 1:479). It is used both ways in the Septuagint and the New Testament. With regard to the use here, Delling says: "They are spiritual beings (Eph. 6:12), related to angels according to Rom. 8:38" (p. 483).

The second term, "powers," is literally "authorities" *(exousias)*. This is also found in 1:21, where its sense is explained in the comments there.

The other two terms, however, differ from those in 1:21. Both are expressed in phrases. The first is "the rulers of the darkness of this world"; literally, "the world-rulers [one word] of this darkness." Arndt and Gingrich define this as meaning: "the rulers of this sinful world" (p. 446).

The last expression is "spiritual wickedness in high places"; literally, "the spirits of wickedness in the heavenlies." This underscores the truth that there are wicked spirits which may tempt men in their highest moments of spiritual fellowship.

## Stand (6:13)

Again Paul urges his readers to take up "the whole armour (panoply) of God." With this they can "withstand in the evil day"—the day when the devil makes his heaviest assaults. He adds: "and having done all, to stand." The ASV and RSV translate this exactly the same way. The NASB improves this somewhat by strengthening the second verb: "and having done everything, to stand firm."

The expression "having done" hardly seems adequate for the Greek *katergasamenoi*. This emphatic compound verb (from *ergazomai*, "work") means "to effect by labour, achieve, work out, bring about" (A-S, p. 240). Thayer defines it as "to perform, accomplish, achieve," and says that here it means: "having gone through every struggle of the fight" (p. 339).

Arndt and Gingrich suggest two interpretations. The first is that of doing everything prescribed, putting on every piece of the armor. But they also find support in Herodotus and Thucydides (Greek historians) for the meaning "overpower, subdue, conquer," and give for this passage: "after proving victorious over everything, stand your ground" (p. 423).

Many of the best commentators object to the meaning "overpower" in this passage. While admitting that *katergazō* has that sense in classical Greek, they insist that it does not in the NT. Alford writes: "To finish, or accomplish, is the invariable Pauline usage of the word when taken in a good sense" (3:146). Meyer says that the verb "retains its ordinary signification, 'to achieve, accomplish, complete,' and is not . . . to be taken in the sense of . . . *overpower,* in which sense it is . . . usual enough, but is never so employed by Paul . . . or elsewhere in the N.T." (p. 542). Eadie agrees with this. Salmond writes: "There is no reason to depart from the ordinary sense of the verb . . . *doing thoroughly, working out,* especially (the *kata* being intensive) accomplishing a difficult task" (EGT, 3:385). He adds: "The ability to withstand when the fight is on is to be sought with a view to holding one's position when the conflict is at an end,—neither dislodged nor felled, but *standing* victorious at one's post" *(ibid.).* Lenski thinks that the neuter "all" rules out "overpower," which would require the masculine. But he holds that *stēnai* means: "'to stand' as victors" (p. 663). It would seem that, while we cannot stress the idea of "having overcome all things," yet this is implied in the closing word, *stēnai*—"stand as victors."

## Girt About with Truth (6:14)

Paul writes: "Stand therefore, having your loins girt about with truth." But the latter verb is middle, not passive, and so is correctly translated: "having girded your loins with truth" (RSV, NASB). The NEB renders this clause: "Buckle on the belt of truth."

Vincent notes that the loins constituted "the point of

junction for the main pieces of the body-armor, so that the girdle formed the common bond of the whole," and adds: "Truth gives unity to the different virtues, and determinateness and consistency to character." Helpfully he defines "truth" as meaning "the agreement of our convictions with God's revelation" (3:408).

Concerning the different items mentioned here, Vincent remarks: "The principal terms in this description of the Christian armor are taken from the Septuagint of Isaiah" (p. 407). The girdle of truth is mentioned in 11:5; the breastplate of righteousness and helmet of salvation, in 59:17; the sandals of peace, in 52:7. In addition, one might find an allusion to the Sword of the Spirit in 49:2.

## Breastplate of Righteousness (6:14)

The Greek word for breastplate is *thōrax,* first meaning "breast" and then "breastplate." "Of righteousness" is the genitive of apposition. It means the breastplate which is righteousness. This refers to the righteousness of Christ, made available to us through faith. Lenski says of this: "It is the central part of all saving truth. The heart of the Word makes our heart invulnerable against Satan" (p. 667). (The function of the breastplate was to cover the vital organs of the body, particularly the heart.)

Vincent describes the breastplate in the Roman armor as being a "corselet of metal scales fastened upon leather or linen, or of flexible bands of steel folding over each other" (p. 408). The "cuirasses" were heavy breastplates of chain mail worn by the Roman spearmen.

## Sandals of Peace (6:15)

The literal wording is: "And have shod yourselves as to the feet in readiness of the gospel of peace." Lenski writes: "The general sense is: 'ready, eager courage that is due to the gospel which fills us with the peace of God'" (p. 667).

The Greek word for "preparation" is found only here in the NT. Vincent says of it: *"Hetoimasia* means *readiness;* but in Hellenistic Greek it was sometimes used in the sense of *establishment* or *firm foundation,* which would suit this passage: *firm-footing"* (3:409). The Roman soldiers wore sandals, "bound by thongs over the instep and round the ankle, and having the soles thickly studded with nails" *(ibid.).* God's peace gives us firm footing in fighting the enemy.